Eyes Wide Shut

Behind Stanley Kubrick's Masterpiece

Eyes Wide Shut

Behind Stanley Kubrick's Masterpiece

Nathan Abrams and Georgina Orgill

LIVERPOOL UNIVERSITY PRESS

Stanley Kubrick Studies

Stanley Kubrick Studies is a major international series showcasing high quality research and representing the dynamism and vibrancy of the study of Kubrick. Volumes are intended for an international readership, through their empirical research, interpretative approach and emphasis on what interaction between different types of evidence can tell us about Kubrick's films. The aim of Liverpool University Press and the series editors is to build upon and develop the community of global Kubrick scholars by publishing the constantly evolving research on Stanley Kubrick. The series is edited by Nathan Abrams (Bangor University) and Georgina Orgill (Stanley Kubrick Archive, University of the Arts London).

First published 2023 by
Liverpool University Press
4 Cambridge Street
Liverpool
L69 7ZU

British Library Cataloguing-in-Publication data
A British Library CIP record is available

ISBN 978-1-83764-515-2

Typeset by Carnegie Book Production, Lancaster
Printed and bound by CPI Group (UK) Ltd, Croydon CR0 4YY

Contents

PART THREE: RECEPTION

Acknowledgements

The editors would like to thank the team at Liverpool University Press, especially John Atkinson, not only for believing in this project from the outset and giving it the green light but also for doing the same for the whole Stanley Kubrick series. Given COVID, it has been something of a Herculean task shepherding these chapters and their authors to this point. We would also like to thank Research England, the British Association for American Studies and the US Embassy in London for supporting the conference out of which this book emerged. The editors would like to dedicate the book to their families and pets.

Introduction

Nathan Abrams and Georgina Orgill

Over 20 years since its release, Stanley Kubrick's *Eyes Wide Shut* remains a complex, visually arresting film about domesticity, sexual disturbance and dreams. This was the final enigmatic work from its equally enigmatic creator. It continues to puzzle viewers – uncertain how to respond to the film's unique tone and atmosphere, as well as to its messages. That Kubrick died before post-production could be completed has reinforced the film's status and mythos. Adding to the mix, *Eyes Wide Shut* is widely considered to be a very personal film, perhaps even his most personal, compounded by the fact that it was his last. It has left an indelible mark on our popular culture and remains as relevant as ever. Much maligned and much misunderstood when it first came out, *Eyes Wide Shut* has since been the subject of an animated debate and discussion among critics and academics in which, however, its critical reputation has slowly recuperated as the film has been reassessed. It has been explored from a wide variety of disciplines and methodological perspectives. Strangely, in those 20 years, there have been plenty of academic articles and chapters published on the film, but only two books – Michel Chion's slim BFI Classic volume and Robert P. Kolker and Nathan Abrams' *Eyes Wide Shut: Stanley Kubrick and the Making of His Final Film.*[1]

This volume builds upon that pioneering work and complements it in three crucial ways. First, it features a range of critical perspectives from a multiplicity of authors. Second, it focuses on elements that Chion ignored and to which Kolker and Abrams could only allude, for reasons of length. It almost serves as a companion to what Kolker and Abrams called their 'archaeology' of *Eyes Wide Shut*, which explored the film from its initial conception in the 1950s and its continuing reception some seven decades later and 20 years after its initial release. *Behind Eyes Wide Shut* brings together scholars from diverse disciplinary backgrounds, as well as someone who worked on the film itself, to explore *Eyes Wide Shut* now, discuss its impact and consider its position within Kubrick's *oeuvre* and the wider visual and socio-political culture.

Third, it takes advantage of newly released material in the Stanley Kubrick Archive that was not available to previous scholars (while Kolker and Abrams mined the Archive, more material has been added since their book was published). Opened in 2008, the Stanley Kubrick Archive is a vast collection of records created, collected and used by the director himself that have been conserved, protected and made available to researchers at the University of the Arts London's (UAL) Archives and Special Collections Centre (ASCC) at Elephant and Castle in London. The opening of this resource for students, academics, fans and members of the public has transformed the way Kubrick and his films are studied, shown and written about, allowing us a much greater insight into his working methods and vast array of research materials. The Stanley Kubrick Archive is clearly now central to the study of Kubrick and his films. This, of course, has had an incalculable benefit on the study of *Eyes Wide Shut* and the Archive has certainly been instrumental in facilitating this wave of Kubrick scholarship and the critical reassessment of *Eyes Wide Shut*.[2]

This volume emerged from a symposium held in December 2019 at the Archive, to mark the twentieth anniversary of the film's release. The only one of its kind to be held in the UK, the event was a collaboration between the ASCC and Bangor University. It featured a wide range of academics discussing the film from a variety of perspectives, as well as a keynote address from Yolande Snaith, who choreographed the orgy sequence (and who has a chapter in this collection about her experience), and a panel of those who worked on the film, including the masked 'mysterious woman' Abigail Good, Kira-Anne Pelican, who worked in the art department, artist Fangorn (Chris Baker), and Warner Bros. director of European technical operations Tim Everett.

Based on Viennese Jewish writer Arthur Schnitzler's 1926 novella *Traumnovelle*, *Eyes Wide Shut* can be described as an erotic psychodrama. It starred then-married couple Tom Cruise and Nicole Kidman. Released in 1999, this film was the first project Kubrick had finished for 12 years (since the release of *Full Metal Jacket* in 1987). The film follows the sexually charged adventures of a New York City doctor named Bill Harford, who embarks on a night-long odyssey of discovery after his wife reveals that she once had almost cheated on him. As Bill wanders through the city, he encounters a series of strange and mysterious individuals, including a masked woman at a secret society orgy and a high-end prostitute who offers him a glimpse into the darker side of human sexuality. Ultimately, the film explores themes of fidelity, temptation, jealousy and the nature of reality.

When Kubrick first alighted upon *Traumnovelle* is the subject of some debate. Kolker and Abrams suggest it was in the 1950s, in contrast to the 'official' story that it was in the late 1960s. He was interested in exploring the novella's main themes of sexuality, psychology, adultery and dreams. In any case, over the decades Kubrick wrestled with adapting it before hiring novelist Frederic Raphael in November 1994 to begin working on the screenplay. A press release, issued by Warners on 15 December 1995, declared that *Eyes Wide Shut* would be Kubrick's next film. Production began on 4 November 1996 and, after an arduous shoot, the longest continuous shoot in filmmaking history, it wrapped on 17 June 1998. Post-production lasted until March 1999 when a near-final copy was assembled for screening to Warner executives. Kubrick's sudden death on 7 March, which came just six days after delivering his final cut to Warner Bros, held up post-production but intensified the anticipation surrounding the film's release. A small team composed of the editors Nigel Galt and Melanie Viner-Cuneo, Kubrick's brother-in-law and executive producer Jan Harlan, his erstwhile assistant Leon Vitali and his widow Christiane Kubrick worked to create a finished film as close to the director's wishes as possible, in his absence. They handled almost everything from post-production recording, the dubbing of sound and recording additional dialogue, via the storing of film data on a computer, camera shot details, laboratory instructions, foreign prints and translations and dubbing into other languages, to the order and size of the end-credit cards, marketing and publicity, distribution of the film and video and DVD releases. The film was released in the United States on 16 July 1999, to mixed reviews. It continues to be what some might see as one of Kubrick's most misunderstood films, as explored in the December 2019 issue of the BFI's *Sight & Sound* magazine.

The chapters in this volume have been chosen to maintain a gender balance and a range of contributors from junior to senior, but also to provide a broad range of critical and theoretical approaches towards *Eyes Wide Shut*, blending textual with more contextual approaches that also draw on the latest insights from the Stanley Kubrick Archive. They offer close readings of the film, considering its position at the end of the twentieth century against shifting critical, theoretical, popular and hypothetical understandings.

We have grouped the chapters to form three clear parts within the book. In the first, the three opening chapters focus on the film's production. Filippo Ulivieri opens the collection, focusing on pre-production by tracing the origins of Kubrick's love for the story behind *Eyes Wide Shut* and also what influenced him along the way in making the film. Ulivieri illuminates Kubrick's long-standing interest in Arthur Schnitzler's novella. He shows how Kubrick had longed to make a film dealing with marriage and jealousy since his youth, how marital infidelity was a deeply felt topic and how the director engaged with the work of other filmmakers who had made films on the same subject. He concludes that, among Kubrick's movies, *Eyes Wide Shut* does stand out as a very intimate film. To write his chapter, Ulivieri employs a fascinating reverse-time structure in presenting the history of Kubrick's various attempts to bring *Traumnovelle* to the screen – much like the process of researching history itself.

Contemporary feminist choreographer Yolande Snaith worked on the production of *Eyes Wide Shut* and so provides a key interpretation and perspective – from the inside of the production – rather than the standard academic approaches to looking at her role in choreographing the famous orgy sequence. Her chapter 'A Choreographic Liaison' offers invaluable and authentic insights into Kubrick's working process through its unique lens into the experience, perceptions and observations of her role as a choreographer, and her reflections from inside the research and creative process of collaboration with Stanley Kubrick for the masked ball and orgy scenes of *Eyes Wide Shut.* Snaith recounts in detail the genesis of what was to become the apex of the film and the painstaking selection process throughout the search for the ideal male and female bodies for these controversial scenes. Snaith demystifies some assumptions about the process of choreographing and filming the masked ball, and illuminates the nature of the relationship between cast, choreographer, director and crew, offering some insight into Kubrick's complex *modus operandi* as a visionary and uncompromising film director. In tandem with her documentation, she brings to light some profound resonances with her 1996 dance film *Swinger*, made in collaboration with director Ross MacGibbon, which prompted Stanley Kubrick to invite her to choreograph *Eyes Wide Shut.* Snaith's fascination with the book was shared by Kubrick, and *Swinger* (based on texts from Roland Barthes's *A Lover's Discourse*) provided an entry point for their early discussions of the core themes of *Eyes Wide Shut*: love, lust, fantasy, obsession, jealousy, betrayal, infidelity, self-destruction. Retrospectively, Snaith identifies some striking parallels with key sections of *A Lover's Discourse*, and how Barthes's language is reflected in narrative constructs, psychological subtexts and significant images within *Eyes Wide Shut.* Snaith reflects upon her overall experience as a kind of 'choreographic liaison', an extraordinary adventure, a metaphorical love affair with the making of a film by Stanley Kubrick, filled with all the drama, seduction, intensity, tensions, agreements and disagreements that love affairs often have, and finally coming to an end with a sense of both gratitude and loss.

Manca Perko focuses on an often-overlooked aspect of Kubrick's work, namely collaboration, with a specific focus on the post-production of *Eyes Wide Shut*, which is particularly interesting given how many believe the film was left unfinished. By focusing on *Eyes Wide Shut*'s post-production, Perko considers the input of other, external collaborators including graders, editors and the laboratory that processed the film, to reassess and problematize the authorship of the film. Her essay raises important questions regarding the question of authorship which are especially salient given how Kubrick has such a reputation for total control, unlike other filmmakers who routinely receive the 'auteur treatment'.

The four central chapters primarily concentrate on thematic readings of *Eyes Wide Shut*. Catriona McAvoy and Karen A. Ritzenhoff explore gender and sexuality in the film, as well as in Kubrick's career, through a feminist lens. They show how Kubrick struggled to explore female sexuality but argue that he ultimately failed. By focusing on the film's female characters, *Eyes Wide Shut* may appear to be about male sexuality but it tells us more about male vulnerability and the male fear of female sexual power.

They conclude by exploring the film's disturbing legacy and how *Eyes Wide Shut* continues to speak to our own troubled times. In the currently popular re-evaluations of Kubrick's work, the observation is often made that his films were uncannily prescient. *2001: A Space Odyssey* (1968) is frequently lauded as demonstrating future technologies, and *Dr. Strangelove* (1964) is cited as showing a political landscape horrifyingly like the presidency of Donald Trump. *Eyes Wide Shut*, however, speaks most urgently to our times when considering the #MeToo movement against sexual abuse, sexual harassment and rape culture, in which people publicize their experiences of sexual abuse or sexual harassment; the rise of INCELS – so-called 'involuntary celibates' or members of an online subculture of people who define themselves as unable to get a romantic or sexual partner despite desiring one – whose discussions are characterized by resentment and hatred, misogyny, misanthropy, self-pity and self-loathing, racism, a sense of entitlement to sex, and the endorsement of violence against women and sexually active people; and contemporary discussions around toxic masculinity and privilege.

By contrast, Joy McEntee investigates fatherhood, parenting and daughters in the film but also situates it within Kubrick's career and *oeuvre*. McEntee compares Kubrick's status as a devoted father to the ambivalent representation of the daughters in the film, unpacking their significance and placing these daughters, as well as their parents, in the wider context of parenthood and childhood that Kubrick depicted throughout his career.

Ohad Landesman, meanwhile, is focused on the mechanization of the sexualized individual in *Eyes Wide Shut*. The film, he argues, is saturated with statuesque and death-like performances, oscillating between reality and dream to depict a critical account of social rituals in a modernized civilization by the end of the twentieth century. High society's empty manners, socially constructed behaviours and treatment of sex as a mechanized and passionless ritual that becomes a consumerist commodity, are all aestheticized through a continuous effort to inanimate the animate, to emphasize corpse-like and defunct human behaviours, and to exhibit emotionally devoid facial expressions and dispositions traditionally associated with inanimate machinery. In Kubrick's last film, Landesman concludes, the ending of the millennium is evoked in apocalyptic terms as a moment when individuals lose their souls and become shadowy ghosts victimized by a mechanizing society.

Finally in this section, Marie Bennett revisits Kubrick's use of music in the movie. As with his previous films, Kubrick incorporated existing classical music into *Eyes Wide Shut*'s soundtrack including Wolfgang Amadeus Mozart, Franz Lizst, Dmitri Shostakovich and György Ligeti. Here, Bennett focuses on analysing the music of Mozart and Ligeti used in the film to consider how Kubrick weaves music and narrative predictively, thematically and illuminatively.

The final three chapters focus on the reception of the film. Eddie Falvey offers an uncommon and welcome approach to Kubrick, as he situates *Eyes Wide Shut* in the context of film-industry trends of the 1990s, including the blockbuster and the 'quality film'. Rather than treating the film as a rarefied artistic form, he considers the film as a commodity during a crucial period of transition for Hollywood that was under way at the time Kubrick's final feature was produced – the major studios were responding to various industrial forces, renegotiating their staple product in light of shifting cultural and commercial imperatives – to place *Eyes Wide Shut* within the cycle of 1990s blockbusters.

Jeremi Szaniawski, to an extent, is in dialogue with Falvey in seeking to address the film's critical misunderstanding, to redress it in terms of the film's genre ambiguity, as well as arguing for the tangible and intangible ways in which the film operates with tempo and rhythm, akin to a body parading and moving forward under a cloak of dread and grimacing mask of frozen laughter.

Advancing arguments first posed by David Church and I.Q. Hunter among others, by grounding the film in the late 1990s alongside others that came out around the same time, Matt Melia also explores the film's reception to argue that *Eyes Wide Shut* is not only a cult film but the last cult film of the twentieth century.

Finally, to wrap up the chapters and the book overall, noted film scholar Robert P. Kolker provides an Afterword on a more personal note. He supplies a fitting end to the collection, providing both a personal reflection and a critical reassessment.

Taken together, we hope that these new essays encourage further reflection on a film that is still yielding new insights after nearly quarter of a century.

Notes

1 Michel Chion, *Eyes Wide* Shut (London: BFI, 2002); Robert P. Kolker and Nathan Abrams, *Eyes Wide Shut: Stanley Kubrick and the Making of His Final Film* (New York: Oxford University Press, 2019).

2 For more on the Stanley Kubrick Archive, please read Georgina Orgill and Richard Daniels, 'Kubrick and the Archive', in Nathan Abrams and I.Q. Hunter, *The Bloomsbury Companion to Stanley Kubrick* (London: Bloomsbury Academic, 2021), pp. 305–315.

PART ONE: PRODUCTION

1

The Jealousy Movie: Stanley Kubrick and the Root of *Eyes Wide Shut*

Filippo Ulivieri

Eyes Wide Shut polarized the opinions of both critics and its audiences. The commentators who didn't particularly like the film nevertheless conceded that it gave the impression of being a very personal work. Jack Kroll wrote in *Newsweek* that '[t]he film clearly meant a great deal to Kubrick'. 'What's most fascinating', echoed Amy Taubin in *Film Comment*, 'is how openly personal it is'. 'Kubrick had a strong personal commitment' to the film's theme, Philip French corroborated in *The Observer*. 'You can sense an intimate connection between director and subject', added Michael Wilmington in the *Chicago Tribune*. 'This is personal filmmaking' (Jonathan Rosenbaum, *Chicago Reader*), 'imbued with Kubrick's uncomfortable personal vision' (Angie Errigo, *Empire*). Everybody agreed that *Eyes Wide Shut* is the director's 'most heartfelt film' (Bob Graham, *San Francisco Chronicle*).[1] None of these critics explained their claims.

The same opinion was held by members of Kubrick's family. 'It's a very personal film,' said Jan Harlan, Kubrick's executive producer and brother-in-law. 'It's Stanley's film and every word in it is his.'[2] Kubrick 'felt very strongly about this subject and theme', emphasized his daughter Anya: *Eyes Wide Shut* is 'a very personal statement from my father'.[3] A few anecdotes from the production seem to support this view; Kubrick's wife Christiane once revealed that the Harfords' apartment in the film is a replica of the Central Park West property in which the Kubricks lived in the early 1960s.[4]

The universal assumption is that *Eyes Wide Shut* is Kubrick's 'most personal' film.[5] But what does this mean, exactly? Is *Eyes Wide Shut* more revealing of Kubrick's personality, or perhaps of his artistry? And why is this so? Why should this particular film be held special among Kubrick's works?

I would like to express my gratitude to Peter Krämer, Michele Pavan Deana, Ian Roscow and Michelle G. Turner for their invaluable feedback.

Maybe, as Philip French wrote, 'because *Eyes Wide Shut* completes the Kubrick cycle, it has a special importance'. Or perhaps, if we follow Jack Kroll, it is because the film 'deals with the most personal of subjects, sex'.[6] Coming after a series of films that investigate past, present and future states of existence, with *Eyes Wide Shut* Kubrick told a contemporary, intimist story: 'In what is truly the riskiest film of his career,' Janet Maslin wrote, 'the man who could create a whole new universe with each undertaking chose the bedroom as the last frontier.'[7]

Critics sometimes share an often-misguided tendency to consider the last work as the culmination of an artist's career, that which reveals his or her preoccupations more clearly. I believe that all works of art are the product of the artist's sensibility, personality and experiences, regardless of which point in the artist's life span they were produced in. In other words, all works are personal to serious artists.

Likewise, it is easy, obvious even, to say that a marital story must draw from an artist's personal background. This may even be truer for a film that shows a psychoanalytical subtext, derived from a literary work that is in itself imbued with the burgeoning analysis of the unconscious mind. Yet it is equally obvious to note that 'everybody is an expert on the topic', as Harlan said when presenting the film: 'there's nobody who doesn't relate to what's going on'.[8] James B. Harris, Kubrick's producing partner in the 1950s and 1960s, explained the point further:

> Stanley has always reminded me that relationships are probably the most well-received subject by audiences because everyone is interested in relationships. Of course, anything that has to do with adultery and betrayals and violations of promises and vows in relationships is always interesting. That's what makes interesting stories and interesting movies, I think.[9]

There is hardly anything original in Kubrick's selection of this subject matter, which has been treated widely, in all arts, throughout human history. Frederic Raphael, co-screenwriter of *Eyes Wide Shut*, concurs:

> Whether or not adultery was a particularly interesting topic to him is really not very interesting, or surprising. It's been a topic of western fiction since … forever. I don't believe that Kubrick was much more, or less, obsessed with infidelity than a host of writers who have dwelt on the theme. See Tony Tanner's *Adultery in the Novel*.[10]

Yes and no. I do see something special in Kubrick's selection of Arthur Schnitzler's *Traumnovelle* as material for a film. This particular story occupied Kubrick's imagination for the longest time, developing an obsessional quality that was unprecedented even by Kubrick's standards.

Thanks to documents from the Stanley Kubrick Archive, original interviews with key collaborators and an analysis of the film's visual language, this chapter will assess the personal quality of *Eyes Wide Shut* by showing how much Kubrick longed to make a film about marital infidelity, and how engaged he was with the work of other filmmakers who had explored the subject before him. An investigation into Kubrick's early, formative years will also question assumptions usually made in Kubrick scholarship, specifically about the role of Ruth Sobotka. The result will hopefully contribute to a deeper understanding of Kubrick's thirty-plus-year obsession with *Traumnovelle* and what he really expressed in *Eyes Wide Shut.*

Production history: what lies beneath

Eyes Wide Shut is the outcome of a long process that involved several radically different attempts at adapting the novella.

The film's laborious gestation affected its materialization, too. Distributed in July 1999, *Eyes Wide Shut* entered pre-production five years before, in the summer of 1994. Shooting the film took a notoriously long time (by consulting documents in the Stanley Kubrick Archive, I calculate 294 days, spread over 579 calendar days, including 19 for re-shooting with actress Marie Richardson – slightly over 1 year and 7 months) with post-production lasting for 9 months, brought to a halt only by Kubrick's death. Nor was the adaptation a straightforward job: Raphael was the writer whose input convinced Kubrick *Traumnovelle* could indeed become a film, and the two worked on the screenplay from November 1994 to June 1996; this did not stop the director from considering other options, which he did with Sara Maitland at the end of 1995 and Michael Herr in mid-1996, both unsuccessfully. Before hiring Raphael, Kubrick had also worked on *Traumnovelle* with Candia McWilliam for a few weeks in July 1994.[11]

What I find most fascinating is discovering how *Traumnovelle* pervaded Kubrick's career: it is the one story to which Kubrick immediately returned every time he finished another film. Looking back in time, we can see how *Traumnovelle* was always there, on his mind.

In the early 1990s, Kubrick was developing a Second World War espionage film based on Robert Marshall's *All the King's Men*, expanding

Brian Aldiss's 'Supertoys Last All Summer Long' into the sci-fi epic *A.I. Artificial Intelligence*, and preparing *Aryan Papers*, a Holocaust-themed drama adapted from Louis Begley's *Wartime Lies* (1991). When these projects collapsed, for various reasons, Kubrick turned to *Traumnovelle* and made it as *Eyes Wide Shut*.[12]

A decade earlier, when actor and consultant Lee Ermey had a car accident thereby causing a hiatus in the shooting of *Full Metal Jacket*, interest in *Traumnovelle* had promptly risen again. In April 1986, Kubrick contacted *A Clockwork Orange* author Anthony Burgess to help him crack the mysteries of Schnitzler's ending, but the writer did not reply.[13] Undaunted, when *Full Metal Jacket* was completed, Kubrick solicited opinions on *Traumnovelle* from several readers he had hired to write reports on books that seemed promising source material. This survey didn't produce any idea that unblocked Kubrick. He also tried to include a political, conspiratorial subtext in the adaptation, again in vain.[14]

During and after the making of *The Shining*, between 1977 and 1983, he had discussed *Traumnovelle* with writers Diane Johnson and Michael Herr, thought about comedy playwright Neil Simon as a possible writing partner, questioned John le Carré about how to approach the story, written to Arthur Schnitzler's grandson Peter, asked his assistant Tony Frewin to draft a scene, and had satirical writer Terry Southern send a few tentative dialogue sequences.[15] In these years Kubrick oscillated between a comic take on the story and an erotic thriller,[16] but neither approach seemed to work.

In 1976, following the release of *Barry Lyndon* (1975), Kubrick asked Gaby Blau, his lawyer's daughter, to write a concept for the story; despite appreciating her effort, Kubrick didn't use it.[17] He then sent the book to Anthony Burgess and started a written conversation, only to interrupt it without getting the needed closure.[18] Kubrick also briefly contemplated an art-house approach to the story, with Woody Allen playing the lead.[19]

After *A Clockwork Orange*, he had committed to the project for the first time, with an announcement from Warner Bros. in April 1971.[20] This attempt failed because Kubrick had problems with the last third of the narrative.[21]

In May 1968, a month after the release of *2001: A Space Odyssey*, Kubrick had enquired about buying the rights to the story, with the help of journalist and future screenwriter Jay Cocks. This marks the first documented evidence of the material being selected for a film.[22]

Although this recurrence is shared by other unrealized projects – most notably *Napoleon* which was set in motion in July 1967 and still thought about in 1987, and a film about Nazi Germany which occupied Kubrick repeatedly from the early 1970s – *Traumnovelle* is indeed special in the sense that it is the longest-running, constantly active project in Kubrick's career. Despite all his uncertainties about tone, subtexts and structure, *Traumnovelle* was the single literary property for which Kubrick never ceased to renew his option and which he proposed to virtually every writer he got in touch with.[23]

Kubrick's obsession with *Traumnovelle* even predates 1968. We do not know when Kubrick first read it, but an inventory in the Stanley Kubrick Archive reveals that the book was amongst his belongings in 1963.[24] Kirk Douglas claimed that his psychiatrist suggested it to Kubrick in 1959.[25] Even if a third-party account is less factual than a document, especially when coming from someone who has been proven to indulge in self-aggrandizement,[26] Kubrick's interest in Austrian literature and specifically in Schnitzler around the late 1950s is confirmed by three facts: Harris told me they considered adapting Schnitzler's short story 'The Death of a Bachelor' in 1956, around the time they developed an adaptation of Stefan Zweig's *Burning Secret*;[27] in January 1959, Kubrick contacted cartoonist Jules Feiffer and asked him to develop 'a modern love story … much in the same mood and feeling as some of Arthur Schnitzler's works';[28] a few months later, Peter Schnitzler visited the set of *Spartacus* to discuss his grandfather's works with Kubrick.[29]

The lasting impact of *Traumnovelle*

While studying Kubrick's unmade films, I noticed another intriguing thing. As implied by Harris, several projects that Kubrick developed throughout his career are about relationships.[30] However, once the director decided on *Traumnovelle* in 1968, he stopped considering new source material on this subject, as if *Traumnovelle* were for him the quintessential story about romantic or sexual relationships, or at least his favourite.[31]

Traumnovelle must have been crucial to Kubrick's understanding of male–female dynamics, for he used it as a blueprint during the script-writing phase in different projects. A certain Schnitzlerian air was breathed into the *Napoleon* script, when Kubrick had Napoleon watch an orgy from a distance, without feeling brave enough to participate; also, it can be argued that the romantic relationships between Napoleon and Josephine, and between Josephine and Barras, had a certain *Reigen* flavour to them.[32] Kubrick also stated in an interview that Napoleon's 'sex life was worthy of Arthur Schnitzler'[33] and he marked a passage in J. Christopher Harold's *The Mind of Napoleon*, deeming an encounter between Napoleon and an unknown woman to be 'very Schnitzler'.[34]

Kubrick discussed *Traumnovelle* with Diane Johnson, to shape the marital relationship between Jack and Wendy Torrance in *The Shining*.[35] The script that Johnson originally wrote showed Wendy as a more rounded character, 'so that the kind of deteriorating relationship between the married couple was pretty much explicit and acted out'. Johnson said to me that *Traumnovelle* was a source of inspiration for such deterioration: 'It was all happening kind of at the same time: the script [of *The Shining*] was being written, *Traumnovelle* was being read, and we talked about aspects of it too. [Schnitzler's story was used] as a kind of subtext.'[36] At a certain point, the script even featured an orgy in the Overlook Hotel ballroom, blending *Traumnovelle* and 'The Masque of the Red Death' by Edgar Allan Poe, a source that is quoted in Stephen King's novel.[37]

It does seem that there is something special about *Traumnovelle*. But why? Or, to put it in Kubrick's own terms, what was the obsessional element about this particular story that sustained such a long interest?

It is not easy to answer. The writers Kubrick approached wondered why, too. To begin with, they didn't really like *Traumnovelle* themselves. Frederic Raphael said it was 'kinda maddening … good but not that good [and] very dated'.[38] John le Carré thought it was 'an incomplete erotic novel' that worked as a mysterious piece on paper but 'did not withstand the naturalistic treatment' of cinema. Sara Maitland told Kubrick she found it 'really boring' and Diane Johnson expressed a similar opinion: the story didn't grab her; she 'thought it was clumsily Freudian' and, when she talked about it with Michael Herr, she remembers that both 'did not get it, [they] both wondered what the appeal of this story was for Kubrick'.[39]

The exception is Candia McWilliam, who had no problem with Kubrick's choice of material and understood its potential immediately: 'it was all about the unknowability of those we love, [which is what] he wanted that film to be about'. During our conversation, Candia admitted that she too felt there was something special about the project:

> A very great deal about that film was personal, and I never wanted to be ... impertinent as to ask why. [But she sensed that] the story at that point was very clearly about the mutual manipulation of jealousy. Which is torture, it's what we can do to one another, in the most intimately painful way. Who hasn't felt atrocious jealousy, and atrocious remorse, and who hasn't in the end felt that fidelity is absolutely crucial, especially after it's too late and one's broken it? And it's heartbreaking.[40]

A clue to understanding why *Traumnovelle* resonated so much with Kubrick comes from the press release of the film: it is a single sentence and the only thing that Tom Cruise and Nicole Kidman were allowed to say during the entire production phase. *Eyes Wide Shut* was marketed as 'a story of jealousy and sexual obsession'. Following McWilliam's insight, the keyword is jealousy. One of the reasons why *Traumnovelle* was such a long-cherished project is because it gave Kubrick the chance to finally make a 'jealousy movie'.

The 'jealousy movies': come to grips with it

Kubrick's interest in this type of film is revealed by film director Albert Brooks, who received a call from Kubrick out of the blue, after the release of *Modern Romance* (1981). 'How did you make this movie?' Kubrick asked Brooks. 'This is a brilliant movie, the movie I've always wanted to make about jealousy.'[41] *Modern Romance,* a wordy, neurotic comedy of self-deprecating humour, alerted Kubrick during a period when he was considering a comic adaptation of *Traumnovelle.* Brooks's film touches exactly on jealousy and sexual obsession, and it features moments that chime with bits of *Eyes Wide Shut,* such as the protagonist's inner soliloquy inside a car or the fact that he sees couples in love while wandering at night.

Albert Brooks was not the only fellow director on whom Kubrick kept his eye. *Eyes Wide Shut* is filled with references to films by several filmmakers who had beaten Kubrick at solving the 'jealousy movie' problem. A blatant example is *Love in the Afternoon* by Eric Rohmer (1972), which tells the same story as *Eyes Wide Shut*: a man is tempted with infidelity but in the end returns to his wife. Kubrick drew several scenes from it. The film opens with the main character picking up his personal effects and switching the lights off before leaving his apartment – a sequence that is closely replicated in *Eyes Wide Shut,* and which is absent from the scripts by Raphael. Moreover, both opening scenes include casual views of bathroom intimacy in married couples; later both husbands are seen lost in their thoughts inside taxi cabs. More significantly, *Love in the Afternoon* ends with a reconciliation of sorts, in which the wife explicitly asks her husband to make love to her, a scene very close to the *dénouement* of *Eyes Wide Shut* – which again was not written by Raphael. It could be worth mentioning that the couples in both films were played by actors married to each other in real life.

Several films referenced in *Eyes Wide Shut* were directed by people whom Kubrick knew personally. It has been noted by Kubrick fans online

Figure 1.1 First frame: looking for something before going out.

Figure 1.2 Watching his daughter in her bedroom.

Figure 1.3 Lost in thoughts in a taxi cab.

that the scene with the old charmer features two lines of dialogue that are seemingly lifted from James Cameron's *True Lies* (1994): 'Do you like the period?' asks Juno (Tia Carrere); 'I adore it' replies Harry (Arnold Schwarzenegger). A receipt in possession of Kubrick's assistant Emilio D'Alessandro shows that Kubrick rented a 35mm copy of *True Lies* on

Figure 1.4 *Who is she, really?*

Figure 1.5 Last frame: reconciliation takes place in the bedroom.

5 August 1994, a date which matches the beginning of pre-production of *Eyes Wide Shut*. D'Alessandro remembers Kubrick summoning Cameron to discuss the film and keeping a copy of the screenplay of *True Lies* in his office.[42] If the influence on the film's title is speculation – *True Lies* is an oxymoron as is *Eyes Wide Shut* – documents in the Stanley Kubrick Archive prove that Kubrick changed that dialogue during rehearsal to include the exchange.[43] The film is, after all, James Cameron's take on the 'jealousy movie'.

Figure 1.6 Seduction through art.

Another scene that Kubrick deliberately changed, to wink at one of his friends, is Alice's phone call to Bill. Initially, it was set in the bedroom but it was reshot and moved to the kitchen so that Alice is seen watching Paul Mazursky's *Blume in Love* (1973) on TV.[44] Like *Modern Romance*, *Blume in Love* is a variation on the on-again-off-again type of relationships and an exploration of the theme of jealousy – all its subplots revolve around jealousy. Ultimately it is, like *Eyes Wide Shut*, a statement on true love, something that both Mazursky and Kubrick seem to say can only be achieved within the boundaries of marriage.

Of course, Mazursky was not a random choice. He was one of Kubrick's friends during his youth in Greenwich Village and acted in *Fear and Desire* (1953). Indeed, another film by Mazursky proved to be an even more direct source for *Eyes Wide Shut* – *Next Stop, Greenwich Village* (1976), an autobiographical work in which Mazursky gave dramatic form to his experiences as an aspiring actor in the 1950s. Essential to its narrative is the protagonist's love story with a girl and her betrayal with one of his friends. This was inspired by Mazursky's then-girlfriend cuckolding him with Howard Sackler, the writer of *Fear and Desire* and *Killer's Kiss* (1955).[45] The scene in *Eyes Wide Shut* in which the Harfords embrace each other after Alice's dream is closely modelled on a scene in Mazursky's film. The visual allusion is particularly fitting given that it connects two couples dealing with betrayal – real or imaginary – and trying to make peace.

The number of visual quotations of other jealousy movies in *Eyes Wide Shut* is an indication of both the theme's importance for Kubrick and his awareness of its universality.

Figure 1.7 Heartbroken embraces.

Naturally, Kubrick's best friend and former business partner holds the place of honour with *Some Call it Loving*, a film Harris wrote, directed and produced in 1973. 'You don't often get a chance, in a lifetime, to make a film that personal', he once commented.[46] An exploration of sexual fantasies and erotic role-playing, the film tells the story of a man who awakens an enchanted princess but cannot find happiness. When Harris adapted John Collier's short story 'Sleeping Beauty', he deliberately discarded everything but the core idea. In the original story, the awakened girl turns out to be very unpleasant and selfish, while Harris made her the quintessential dream girl. The film's main character Robert Troy (Zalman King), troubled by his masochistic fantasies, would like to start afresh and 'get back to normal relationships', as Harris said, 'really romantic',[47] thanks to a 'totally innocent girl' who would help him 'get away from his sexual games'.[48] His idealized version of love is destined to fail because he cannot help but include her in his fantasies and games. What originally was a satirical take on a romantic view of love – Collier wrote '[i]t is the fate of those who kiss sleeping beauties to be awakened themselves'[49] – becomes in Harris's hands a study about the impossibility of reconciling sexual dreams with real life in the absence of a clear understanding and acceptance of one's own inclinations.

Kubrick directly quoted *Some Call it Loving* in the Sonata Café scene in *Eyes Wide Shut*. The staging, blocking and camera movements are identical to the jazz club scene in Harris's film. Earlier in *Eyes Wide Shut*, during the Christmas party, the music band leader had said '[t]he band's gonna take a short break now, and we'll be back in ten minutes'. This line, again added by Kubrick during rehearsals,[50] is lifted from *Some Call it Loving*: the closing line uttered by Robert Troy at the end of his gig is '[w]e're going to take a short break; we'll be right back'. One could also argue that the film's warm, glowing cinematography, or the dream castle in which Harris's story unfolds, suggested the look and feel of *Eyes Wide Shut*, complete with some Klimt imagery and costume choices.

Figure 1.8 Jazz sessions.

What I find more relevant, though, is the scene in which the awakened girl tells Robert the nature of her potion-induced sleep.

> I don't remember when I fell asleep, [she says in the film] but it couldn't have been too long after when I had a dream. It was more like a nightmare: a man, someone I've never seen before, was kissing me … and I couldn't seem to do anything to stop him. Then he would stop and go away … Then it would start again … lots of strange men would kiss me and touch me, and I couldn't stop them.

The resemblance to Alice Harford's monologue about her dream is striking:

> Then I was lying in a beautiful garden … and a man walked out of the woods … He – he was kissing me, and then we were making love. Then there were all these other people around us … Everyone was fucking. And then I – I was fucking other men, so many, I don't know how many I was with.

Figure 1.9 Some Call it Eyes Wide Shut.

Harris told me that he hadn't read *Traumnovelle* at the time, so he couldn't have drawn from Schnitzler to write these lines. But he said that he and Kubrick 'had plenty of discussions about sex and women', so I wonder whether this dream sequence stemmed from the conversations the two friends had about 'the likes and desires of people'[51] or, to put it in other words, male fantasies and fears. It is a very Schnitzlerian scene, in any case; another question would then be whether Kubrick saw relationships through an Austrian intellectual lens. If Kubrick educated Harris on what is inside a male psyche, it may have been Schnitzler and Freud who educated Kubrick on the matter.

Kubrick did not discussed these themes in relation to the film because he died before the release of *Eyes Wide Shut*. It also remains debatable whether he would have engaged in a discussion about the meaning of his film, like Harris has, given that he always preferred the audience to come up with their own interpretations. However, in the years previously Kubrick had spoken a few times about his admiration for Schnitzler, and about *Traumnovelle* in particular, a work that he thought 'tries to equate the importance of sexual dreams and might-have-beens with reality'.[52] The same can be said about *Some Call it Loving*. In this regard, the films are sibling works.

The recurring presence of jealousy

Jealousy is the subject of *Eyes Wide Shut*. But the topic of jealousy is an undercurrent that reoccurs throughout Kubrick's career and of which Bill Harford is only the most evident manifestation. In *Barry Lyndon*, Redmond Barry (Ryan O'Neal) is jealous of his cousin Nora (Gay Hamilton) when she flirts with Captain Quinn (Leonard Rossiter), and later Lady Lyndon (Marisa Berenson) is jealous of Barry, who betrays her several times. In *Lolita* (1962), Charlotte Haze (Shelley Winters) is jealous of Humbert Humbert (James Mason), who is in turn madly jealous of Lolita (Sue Lyon). The same is true of George Peatty (Elisha Cook), who is jealous of his wife Sherry (Marie Windsor) in *The Killing*. Finally, in *Killer's Kiss* Vincent Rapallo (Frank Silvera) is perhaps the most jealous character in all of Kubrick's filmography, to the point of becoming a violent criminal. We can also spot traces of jealousy in several unrealized projects: for example, Napoleon and Josephine are mutually jealous in the *Napoleon* script. But jealousy can be found in less obvious places, too, like in *A.I. Artificial Intelligence* where the little robot boy David (Haley Joel Osment) is jealous of Monica's (Frances O'Connor) love for her true son.

It is also significant that Kubrick told his wife Christiane that, during his studies in anthropology for *2001: A Space Odyssey*, he learned that

> primitive man's greatest fear was to discover he hadn't actually generated his offspring. In the animal kingdom, a female secretly leaves her pack to mate with external males to renew the gene pool. Males in her pack must not know, or they would kill her. This is the origin of jealousy.[53]

Jealousy was also on Kubrick's mind when he was writing *The Shining*: early in the adaptation he considered planting 'an innocent admission by Wendy that she has thoughts but never has and never would be unfaithful. What kind of thoughts. Sexy dreams.' Kubrick proposed Jack should have 'a jealous fantasy of Wendy in bed with others ... Could a scene start like this and turn into something horrible?'[54]

The closer we get to Kubrick's early projects, the more jealousy becomes prominent and connected with marital infidelity. Infidelity is central to the plot of both *Burning Secret* and especially 'The Death of a Bachelor', a psychological study of three husbands reacting to the news that their wives had cheated on them with the same man. Several plot sketches that Kubrick jotted down around this time deal precisely with dysfunctional marriage, jealousy and adultery. One, titled *Jealousy*, tells the story of a wealthy New York business manager who suspects his wife is having an affair. With a growing sense of paranoia, he begins to have visions of his wife's infidelity and decides to take revenge by sleeping with a stranger, something he ultimately cannot bring himself to do. *Married Man* is about a husband who cannot stand his wife any longer; since he cannot leave her, he accuses her of betrayal with one of his friends; the plot works and he is free to marry his friend's mistress. Another archived document, titled *The Perfect Marriage*, contains a series of philosophical reflections on the 'marriage story', as Kubrick termed it, which is inevitably connected to cheating and shows clear links to Schnitzler's insights into the psychology of men and women.[55] It is possible that these story ideas were the basis of an unrealized project, written in collaboration with Calder Willingham, and announced in 1956 as *The Unfaithful Wife*.[56] It is revealing that various recurring narrative and visual motifs in these writings – a wife's confession, sexy dreams, haunting fantasies of betrayal, etc. – are closely reminiscent of Schnitzler's own plot devices and imagery.

Married Man helps us bring into focus another aspect of jealousy. An excerpt shows it as something that the husband would like his wife to feel about him: marriage is 'like drowning in a sea of feathers', the young Kubrick had him say, 'Sinking deeper and deeper into the soft, suffocating depths of habit and familiarity. If she'd only fight back. Get mad or jealous, even just once.'[57] Fifty years later, Kubrick would have this very feeling uttered by a female character: '[a]nd why haven't you ever been jealous about me?' Alice cries out in front of her husband in *Eyes Wide Shut*.

Stability vs. adventures

In another revealing quote about *Traumnovelle*, Kubrick gave us a key to understanding his connection to Schnitzler's stories. 'The theme of the story,' Kubrick explained, 'is that people have a desire for stability, security, habit and order in their lives, and at the same time they would like to escape, to seek adventures, to be destructive.'[58]

This is precisely what he was trying to express in these early writings. All the protagonists live the unending conflict between stability and adventure. A few incomplete stories are about Greenwich Village male characters who indulge in numerous affairs but dream of a more stable future. For example, in an untitled fragment a boy, tired of casual encounters, builds a family with a girl, in the suburbs, with two kids: '[d]reary', wrote Kubrick, 'end with irony – and they lived happily ever after'.[59] Kubrick would come back to it in an iteration of *Traumnovelle* he sketched in 1979: the main character falls in love with a porn actress, excited by her unconventionality; the twist comes when she expresses a desire to marry him, have a family and become a good wife.[60]

It is no surprise that Schnitzler's stories, which often revolve around this very duality, struck a powerful chord in Kubrick. In a sense, it is not even important to understand why he selected *Traumnovelle.* We could say it encapsulated these themes better than other stories, or that it added a dreamlike quality that surely appealed to Kubrick, but that would be, as he said, 'a bit like trying to explain why you fell in love with your wife: she's intelligent, has brown eyes, a good figure. Have you really said anything?'[61] *Traumnovelle* was simply the story Kubrick wanted to live the rest of his life with.

Questioning Ruth Sobotka's influence

By looking at the chronology of Kubrick's projects we see how, though elements of dysfunctional male–female relationships are present from the beginning, stories about jealousy and marital strife cluster around 1956. It is the year in which Kubrick's marriage with Ruth Sobotka began to unravel.

Sobotka was a Vienna-born ballerina whom Kubrick met in late 1946. They began to live together in 1952 or 1953 and married in January 1955.[62] Sobotka was very erudite, spoke many languages, was passionate about the performing arts and was part of the New York avant garde. She contributed to Kubrick's education in many ways, and some scholars conjecture it was she who introduced him to Austrian literature, and perhaps to *Traumnovelle* itself.[63] Their marriage suffered from conflicting views about their respective careers and, according to some sources, Kubrick's jealousy of his wife.[64] The breaking point came in the summer of 1956 when Kubrick received a letter from an anonymous person who claimed that Sobotka was being unfaithful while she was touring Europe with the New York City Ballet.[65]

Kubrick's jealousy of Sobotka has been widely (and wildly) commented on, to the point it has become a cliché. It was first hinted at in John Baxter's biography,[66] and discussed in a 1999 *Mail on Sunday* article titled 'Did Kubrick drive his second wife to suicide and is that why he made this haunting film of sexual obsession?'[67] Using hearsay and Baxter's opinions to connect the dots, the article drew a direct line between Sobotka's death in 1967 and Kubrick's obsession with *Traumnovelle,* as if it were fuelled by remorse over and regret for their failed marriage and possibly her tragic demise. For the record, Sobotka did not commit suicide and her death had nothing to do with Kubrick.[68] Yet psychoanalyzing an artist is always tempting, and the 'Sobotka connection' has subsequently become unavoidable in Kubrick studies even though,[69] as with the critics' opinion about *Eyes Wide Shut* being a personal film, there is little evidence. Accordingly, I interviewed Gerald Fried, who, in addition to composing the music for Kubrick's early films, was one of his closest friends during his formative years in Greenwich Village. I am aware that what follows could be taken as a highbrow version of the tabloid story just mentioned, but if it is acceptable to draw parallels between Arthur Schnitzler's sexual life and his stories of jealousy and promiscuity, I think what happened in Kubrick's life can at least shed some light on his attachment to such stories.

On the topic of human relationships, according to Fried, Kubrick was 'appalled and [at the same time] fascinated by the length people would go to, perhaps especially men, to achieve some sexual advantage at the risk of truth and honesty, and even decency'. Kubrick 'was troubled by the facility with which people can betray one another, or betray a marriage, for the sake of a little ... biological aggrandizement. It's a little scary,' Fried said, 'to know that people we see every day, and trust, and love, are capable of this kind of psychological bifurcation.'[70]

Interestingly, this is precisely what Tom Cruise said in an interview: 'Stanley had understood and was very clear on this: people often have a split personality, just as they passed from darkness to light, and vice versa, permanently'.[71] This ties in with what Candia McWilliam said, that the film she was writing for Kubrick had to be about the unknowability of those we love. Fried elaborated: '[i]t was as if Stanley was appalled by the concept of someone looking at you right in the eye, without blinking, and lying about a sexual affair. That, to him, was a horror story.'

'It troubled him deeply, infidelity. And it happened to him, too,' Fried said, referring to that fateful letter Kubrick received in 1956. Sobotka disputed its veracity, as did many of their mutual friends; Fried even tried to reconcile the two, but Kubrick didn't want to listen and ended the marriage. According to Fried, Kubrick had been very apprehensive about Sobotka travelling for months at a time, and the possibility of her betrayal had haunted him. 'I think Stanley found out all about infidelity and the difficulties and the requirements of marriage, and then, when he understood that he too was subject to those kinds of feelings, I think he was very troubled and didn't like it.'

Figure 1.10 A Kubrickian horror story.

> There was a dread of the female in him, was there not? [Raphael wondered after seeing *Eyes Wide Shut*.] I don't think it has to do with his resentment of his supposedly adulterous second wife, or his wish for it. I think that the fear of women runs through the entirety of his work. I think that Kubrick's horror of what women might mean, or might do, or might be doing, is what is expressed in *Traumnovelle* and what he made of it.[72]

Kubrick's youth: a Schnitzlerian story

During our conversations, Gerald Fried made some remarks that, to me, confirm how central the dichotomy between stability and adventure, which is at the core of Schnitzler's philosophy, was for Kubrick, too. The person who most succeeded in fulfilling the desire to lead an exciting life in the Greenwich Village circle was Howard Sackler. According to Fried, Sackler seemed concerned only with 'getting kicks' out of life, even

> to take pleasure in destroying marriages … I think there was a kind of admiration for Sackler's masculine power. I remember we were talking about it and I got this feeling that it was not 100% disapproval of Sackler's behaviour. It was disgusting and we felt like punching him out, but there may have been an element of, My gosh, this fellow has a power that we don't have.

Anya Kubrick explained that *Eyes Wide Shut* reflects the moral philosophy of her father. The central idea in the film, she said, was that 'we are all both good and evil, and if you think you have no evil in you, you're not looking hard enough'.[73] In other words, in his last film Kubrick explored the male psyche with the honesty and knowledge of someone who does not consider himself exempt from the issue he is analysing. This chimes with the anecdotes about Kubrick's admiration for Kirk Douglas's purported sexual competence and voracity during the shooting of *Paths of Glory* and *Spartacus*, when Douglas apparently had an assistant who pimped women for him, two or three times a day.[74] Frederic Raphael wrote very perceptively how, '[l]ike Schnitzler's hero, Kubrick was fascinated and appalled by things he witnessed but could not quite bring himself to do'.[75]

These are all eminently Schnitzlerian situations, testing the friction between dreaming a life filled with adventures and the lack of audacity to live them; between being repelled by the ruthless behaviour of those who cheat on their partners, and at the same time fascinated by that freedom and power.

Conclusion: character and experience expressed as filmmaking

James Harris gave shape to his own tendencies and fears in *Some Call it Loving*. The film was a way to acknowledge his inability to have a solid relationship because he indulged in his sexual fantasies: 'I wanted to make the point that if the girl is everything you wanted to be and you still have a problem, the problem must rest within yourself. You can't blame the girl for that, which John Collier did.'[76] Even though *Some Call it Loving* is not an autobiographical film, the film's hero can be seen as an oblique persona for Harris: 'if you have multiple relationships in your life, you keep moving on from one girl to another, as I had … Could there be something wrong with all the girls? It had to be something within myself that was causing these abortive relationships.'[77]

Perhaps, then, what 'a personal film' means is a connection, a reflection between the artist and the hero of the story s/he chooses to tell. Like Harris with Robert Troy, perhaps Kubrick saw something of himself in Fridolin, the husband in Schnitzler's novella. 'I suppose so', Raphael told me, 'I mean, he would have to, to some extent, otherwise it just wouldn't be interesting, would it?'[78] Even without stressing the connection between Bill Harford and Kubrick much, *Eyes Wide Shut* is the film in which the director expressed his personal views of love and marriage. If Harris let the hunger for 'adventures' loose – Robert Troy's story ends without

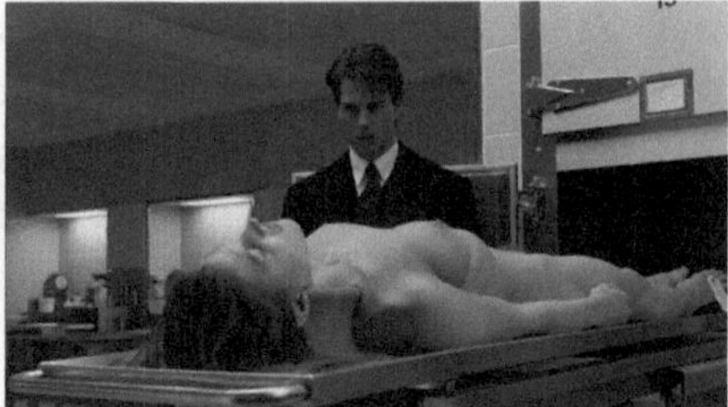

Figure 1.11 The two heroes in the face of temptation.

reconciliation – Kubrick focused on the 'stability' side of the equation – Bill returns to his wife and they both want their marriage to work. 'The fact that he's been married three times, I'd say pretty much says he's marriage material', Harris told me with a laugh; 'Stanley was a man who believed in the sanctity of marriage'.[79]

Collier's 'Sleeping Beauty' is a parable about the risks of following our sexual fantasies, which Harris purified from its moralizing undertones and used as a springboard for an honest and unrepressed film. *Traumnovelle* is the story of a marriage that holds despite internal and external forces, which Kubrick followed very closely. Fridolin – and Bill Harford – is a character caught between dreams and reality, who lingers amid the opposite forces of order and disorder for a long time, until he ultimately chooses to return to his wife, remain faithful to her and restore stability, habit, security. Robert, in Harris's film, is equally caught between dreams and reality but, in contrast to Kubrick's hero, he chooses to bring the girl home and indulge his fantasies, paving the way for more adventures. The choice of source material and how it is adapted reflects Harris's and Kubrick's respective personalities and life experiences.

Marital infidelity was a deeply felt subject for Kubrick, one that he tried to bring to the screen throughout his entire life. The fear of what might lie beneath the surface of marriage is yet another taboo subject that he explored in his films, each tackling an unspeakable, suppressed issue – the Jungian 'Shadow' and the excitement of war in *Full Metal Jacket* (1987), the vanity and ephemeral nature of all human deeds in *Barry Lyndon*, and so on. As with any artist, what he observed and experienced during his youth forged his sensibility. When he encountered Arthur Schnitzler's stories of inner conflict, Kubrick immediately acknowledged the author's calibre: '[i]t's difficult to find any writer who understood the human soul more truly and who had a more profound insight into the way people think, act, and really are',[80] Kubrick said in an interview. Perhaps he even recognized himself in those stories. As Diane Johnson said, '[d]efinitely

I think that Fridolin spoke to Stanley in a powerful way, in a way that caused Stanley to stick with him for all those decades'. Jay Cocks was the most perceptive when he said 'I think Stanley found a soulmate there, in Schnitzler's approach'.[81]

Notes

1 Jack Kroll, 'Dreaming with *Eyes Wide Shut*', *Newsweek*, 18 July 1999, https://www.newsweek.com/dreaming-eyes-wide-shut-168680; Amy Taubin, 'Imperfect Love', *Film Comment* 35.5, Sept./Oct. 1999, p. 33; Philip French, 'Keep your shirt on …', *The Observer Review*, 12 July 1999, p. 7, https://www.theguardian.com/film/1999/sep/12/philipfrench; Michael Wilmington, 'The Sexy, Scary, Stylish *Eyes Wide Shut* is Stanley Kubrick's Final Masterpiece', *Chicago Tribune*, 16 July 1999, https://www.chicagotribune.com/news/ct-xpm-1999-07-16-9907170013-story.html; Jonathan Rosenbaum, 'In Dreams Begin Responsibilities', *Chicago Reader*, 23 July 1999, https://www.jonathan-rosenbaum.net/2020/02/in-dreams-begin-responsibilities/; Angie Errigo, 'New Films: *Eyes Wide Shut*', *Empire* 123, Sept. 1999, p. 13; Bob Graham, 'An Eyeful: Kubrick's *Eyes Wide Shut* is an Absorbing Tale of Jealousy and Obsessiveness in a Marriage', *San Francisco Chronicle*, 16 July 1999, https://www.sfgate.com/movies/article/An-Eyeful-Kubrick-s-Eyes-Wide-Shut-is-an-2919599.php. Websites all accessed on 8 June 2023.

2 In Josh Young, 'An Eye-opener for Everyone Concerned', *The Sunday Telegraph*, 10 July 1999.

3 In Richard Schickel, 'All Eyes on Them', *Time* 154.1, 5 July 1999, pp. 65–70, https://scrapsfromtheloft.com/movies/eyes-wide-shut-all-eyes-on-them-review-by-richard-schickel/. Accessed on 8 June 2023.

4 In Andrew Biswell, 'No Longer *Eyes Wide Shut*', *The Scotsman*, 5 October 2002, p. 3.

5 Kroll, 'Dreaming with *Eyes Wide Shut*'.

6 French, 'Keep your shirt on'; Kroll, 'Dreaming with *Eyes Wide Shut*'.

7 Janet Maslin, '*Eyes Wide Shut*: Danger and Desire in a Haunting Bedroom Odyssey', *The New York Times*, 16 July 1999, https://archive.nytimes.com/www.nytimes.com/library/film/071699eyes-film-review.html.

8 Anon., '*EYES WIDE SHUT* 1999 press conference w. Tom Cruise & Nicole Kidman COMPLETE', *DVDVision* YouTube channel, https://youtu.be/3X7-4UA5xIc.

9 Author's interview with James B. Harris, 23 June 2010.

10 Author's interviews with Frederic Raphael, 4–13 May 2020.

11 Frederic Raphael, *Eyes Wide Open: A Memoir of Stanley Kubrick* (New York: Ballantine Books, 1999); author's interview with Sara Maitland, 23 August 2008; Michael Herr, *Kubrick* (New York: Grove Press, 2000), pp. 17–18; author's interview with Candia McWilliam, 21 November 2007.

12 Filippo Ulivieri, 'Waiting for a Miracle: a Survey of Stanley Kubrick's Unrealized Projects', *Cinergie: Il Cinema e le altre Arti* 12 [online], December 2017, pp. 95–115, https://cinergie.unibo.it/article/view/7349/.
13 Stanley Kubrick, 'Letter to Anthony Burgess', 23 April 1986, uncatalogued material, Stanley Kubrick Archive, LCC, UAL (hereafter 'SKA').
14 James Fenwick, *Stanley Kubrick Produces* (New Brunswick: Rutgers University Press, 2020), p. 195.
15 Author's interview with Diane Johnson, 12 May 2017; Kubrick, '*Shining* SK Editing Notes to Jack + Lloyd Book 1', 17 July 1979, SK/15/4/1, SKA; author's interview with John le Carré, 3 September 2008; Anthony Frewin, 'Letter to Stanley Kubrick', 29 October 1981, SKA; Terry Southern, 'Letter to Stanley [Kubrick]', 1 July 1983, SK/17/6/7, SKA.
16 Fenwick, *Stanley Kubrick Produces*, pp. 194–5.
17 Fenwick, *Stanley Kubrick Produces*, p. 194.
18 Stanley Kubrick, 'Letter to Anthony Burgess', 15 October 1976, Anthony Burgess Papers 1956–1997, MS-0601, 83.1, Harry Ransom Center, The University of Texas at Austin.
19 Author's interview with Jan Harlan, 16 September 2016.
20 Anon., 'Kubrick Will Make WB's *Traumnovelle*', *Daily Variety*, 20 April 1971, p. 1.
21 Michel Ciment, *Kubrick: The Definitive Edition* (London: Faber and Faber, 2001), p. 269.
22 Stanley Kubrick, 'Filing card', in Alison Castle, *The Stanley Kubrick Archives* (Cologne: Taschen, 2005), p. 482.
23 Ulivieri, 'Waiting for a Miracle'.
24 Anon., 'Inventory of SK possession in his London apartment (books etc)', SK/11/9/77, SKA.
25 Kirk Douglas, *I am Spartacus: Making a Film, Breaking the Blacklist* (New York: Open Road, 2012), p. 195.
26 Tom Benedek, 'Kirk Douglas' revisionist history', *Salon* [online], 9 November 2012, https://www.salon.com/test/2012/11/08/kirk_douglas_revisionist_history/.
27 Author's interview with James Harris, 4 May 2010.
28 Stanley Kubrick, 'Letter to Jules Feiffer', 2 January 1959, Jules Feiffer Papers, General Correspondence, 1951–1993, Library of Congress Manuscript Division.
29 Peter A. Schnitzler, 'Letter to Stanley Kubrick', 27 May 1959, SK/9/4/1/2, SKA.
30 Ulivieri, 'Waiting for a Miracle'.
31 Filippo Ulivieri, 'Kubrick Unknown: the Unmade Films of Stanley Kubrick – Cracking the Kube Episode 2, part 1', 15 November 2022, https://www.youtube.com/watch?v=I7dDyKsxmi0.
32 Stanley Kubrick, '*Napoleon* screenplay', in Alison Castle (ed.), *Stanley Kubrick's 'Napoleon' – The Greatest Movie (N)ever Made* (Cologne: Taschen, 2011).

33 Joseph Gelmis, *The Film Director as Superstar* (New York: Doubleday & Co., 1970), p. 387.
34 Castle, *Napoleon*, p. 54.
35 Catriona McAvoy, 'Creating *The Shining*: Looking Beyond the Myths', in Tatjana Ljujić, Peter Krämer and Richard Daniels (eds), *Stanley Kubrick New Perspectives* (London: Black Dog Publishing, 2015), p. 285.
36 Author's interview with Johnson.
37 Catriona McAvoy, 'The Uncanny, The Gothic and The Loner: Intertextuality in the Adaptation Process of *The Shining*', *Adaptation* 8.3, Dec. 2015.
38 Raphael, *Eyes Wide Open*, pp. 24–25.
39 Author's interviews with le Carrè, Maitland, Johnson.
40 Author's interview with McWilliam; Paul Joyce, *The Last Movie: Stanley Kubrick and Eyes Wide Shut* (Lucida Productions, 1999).
41 Mitchell Fink, 'Battling Leroys Look to Reheat the Romance', *Daily News*, 12 August 1999, p. 17.
42 Author's interview with Emilio D'Alessandro, 21 November 2006; anon., 'Receipt for *True Lies*', United International Pictures, 5 August 1994, in the possession of Emilio D'Alessandro.
43 'Script 1996', SK/17/1/8, SKA; the original lines were 'Do you like Bonnard?', 'Yes, I do'.
44 'Slate by Slate Frame Clips', SK/17/4/3/4, SKA.
45 Paul Mazursky, *Show Me the Magic* (New York: Simon and Schuster, 1999), p. 19.
46 Anon., 'Cable Column: a conversation with James B. Harris', *Galaxy*, March 1982, p. 43.
47 Nick Pinkerton, 'Interview: James B. Harris', *Film Comment* [online], 2 April 2015, http://www.filmcomment.com/interview-james-b-harris-part-one/.
48 Author's interview with James Harris, 26 November 2010.
49 John Collier, *The John Collier Reader* (New York: Alfred A. Knopf, 1972), p. 439.
50 'Script 1996', SK/17/1/8, SKA.
51 Author's interview with James Harris, 27 June 2014.
52 Ciment, *Kubrick*, p. 156.
53 Yann Tobin and Laurent Vachaud, 'Brève rencontre: Christiane Kubrick et Jan Harlan', *Positif* 464 (October 1999), p. 43, author's translation.
54 McAvoy, 'The Uncanny, The Gothic and The Loner'; Catriona McAvoy, 'An Interview with Diane Johnson', in Daniel Olson (ed.), *Studies in the Horror Film: Stanley Kubrick's The Shining* (Lakewood, CO: Centipede Press, 2015), p. 548.
55 Fenwick, *Stanley Kubrick Produces*, pp. 75–76. Being unable to consult the material first-hand, I rely on Fenwick's review. These texts are undated; their chronology may vary as more analyses are conducted. For example, Peter Krämer suggests they may belong to an early phase of Kubrick's career.
56 Ulivieri, 'Waiting for a Miracle'.

57 Dalya Alberge, 'Newly Found Stanley Kubrick Script Ideas Focus on Marital Strife', *The Guardian* [online], 12 July 2019, https://www.theguardian.com/film/2019/jul/12/newly-found-stanley-kubrick-script-ideas-focus-marital-strife.
58 Michel Ciment, 'Entretien avec Stanley Kubrick (sur *A Clockwork Orange*)', *Positif* 139 (June 1972), p. 29, author's translation.
59 Fenwick, *Stanley Kubrick Produces*, p. 75; Mick Broderick, James Fenwick and Joy McEntee, 'Missing Links: Exploring Traces of Kubrick's "Unknown" Early Works', *Senses of Cinema* [online], October 2020, http://www.sensesofcinema.com/2020/feature-articles/missing-links-exploring-traces-of-kubricks-unknown-early-works/.
60 Fenwick, *Stanley Kubrick Produces*, p. 194.
61 Ciment, *Kubrick*, p. 167.
62 Philippe Mather, *Stanley Kubrick at Look Magazine* (Bristol: Intellect, 2013), p. 184; Vincent LoBrutto, *Stanley Kubrick* (London: Faber and Faber, 1998), p. 101.
63 The first mention is in Kent Lambert, 'Sobotka, Ruth (1925–1967)', in Gene D. Phillips and Rodney Hill, *The Encyclopedia of Stanley Kubrick* (New York: Facts on File, 2002), pp. 338, 371; Lambert does not provide a reference for his claim. The information is repeated in Rodney Hill, '*Eyes Wide Shut*', in Castle (ed.), *Kubrick Archives*, p. 482. Nathan Abrams is more cautious and includes Sobotka among a few possible sources, in his *Stanley Kubrick: New York Jewish Intellectual* (New Brunswick: Rutgers University Press, 2018), pp. 240–241; the question is again repeated in Robert P. Kolker and Nathan Abrams, *Eyes Wide Shut: Stanley Kubrick and the Making of His Final Film* (New York: Oxford University Press, 2019). I find it telling that scholars debate when and how Kubrick first read *Traumnovelle* when little attention is given to the equally uncertain circumstances in which he discovered Vladimir Nabokov's *Lolita* – further proof of the perceived special quality of *Eyes Wide Shut*.
64 Christiane Kubrick in Dalia Karpel, 'The Real Stanley Kubrick', *Haaretz*, 3 November 2015, https://www.haaretz.com/1.4880226; David Vaughan in Sharon Churcher and Peter Sheridan, 'Did Kubrick Drive his Second Wife to Suicide and is that Why He Made this Haunting Film of Sexual Obsession?', *The Mail on Sunday*, 18 July 1999.
65 Vaughan in John Baxter, *Stanley Kubrick: A Biography* (New York: Carroll & Graf, 1997) p. 91, and in Churcher and Sheridan, 'Did Kubrick Drive his Second Wife to Suicide?' A more precise account is from this author's interview of Gerald Fried, 19 November 2018, 26 September 2019, and email correspondence.
66 Baxter, *Stanley Kubrick*, p. 91.
67 Churcher and Sheridan, 'Did Kubrick Drive his Second Wife to Suicide?'
68 Sobotka died on 17 June 1967 while in hospital after a brief illness. Author's interview with Michelle G. Turner, 6 March 2006.

69 For example, Abrams wrote that Kubrick's renewed interest in *Traumnovelle* after *2001* 'may have [been] prompted by [Sobotka's] sudden and tragic death'; see his *Stanley Kubrick*, p. 241. Sobotka plays a major role in David Mikics's *Stanley Kubrick: American Filmmaker* (New Haven, CT: Yale University Press, 2020); however, his characterization of her marriage with Kubrick bears no resemblance to the accounts of people familiar with the events. Though only vaguely connecting Sobotka with *Traumnovelle*, Mikics speculates that Kubrick's marriage to her was used by the director as a blueprint for the male–female relationships depicted in *Killer's Kiss*, *Lolita* and *The Shining*, and in some of his early plot sketches, as if Kubrick had written those female characters to 'fantasize about walking away from the clingy Ruth Sobotka', 'Ruth the suction cup, the wife who fastened herself to him relentlessly in her effort to become essential to her husband's work'. See his *Stanley Kubrick*, pp. 67, 152, 154. Presenting a different view, Vaughan told Churcher and Sheridan ('Did Kubrick Drive his Second Wife to Suicide?') that 'Ruth was a liberated woman and refused to be confined to the sidelines of Stanley's life'. Michelle G. Turner adds that '[Sobotka] was prodigiously talented ... not only a dancer ... but a costume designer and an art director ... a painter and an actress ... [Kubrick and Sobotka] both had intense career ambitions; there is considerable evidence that Sobotka tried to accommodate her professional life to Kubrick's career'; in 'Letters to the Editor: The Maligned Second Wife', *Haaretz*, 11 November 2005, https://www.haaretz.com/1.4881416.

70 All quotes by Gerald Fried are from author's interviews, 19 November 2018, 26 September 2019, and email correspondence.

71 Jean-Paul Chaillet, 'Entrevue avec Tom Cruise', *Ciné Live* 27, September 1999, author's translation.

72 Author's interview with Raphael.

73 Schickel, 'All Eyes On Them'.

74 Raphael, *Eyes Wide Open*, p. 48.

75 Raphael, *Eyes Wide Open*, p. 111.

76 Author's interview with Harris, 27 June 2014.

77 Pinkerton, 'Interview with Harris'.

78 Author's interview with Raphael.

79 Author's interview with Harris, 27 June 2014.

80 Robert Emmett Ginna, 'The Odyssey Begins', *Entertainment Weekly*, 9 April 1999, pp. 16–22.

81 Author's interview with Johnson; author's interview with Jay Cocks, 29 March 2017.

2

A Choreographic Liaison: Collaborating with Stanley Kubrick

Yolande Snaith

Meeting Stanley Kubrick

One day in the spring of 1997, my manager rang. She told me that Stanley Kubrick wanted to meet me, to talk about the possibility of choreographing his new film. I remember being silent for some time, not quite believing what I was hearing. I had seen *2001: Space Odyssey* and *A Clockwork Orange*, and *The Shining* was one of my all-time favourite movies, but I couldn't grasp the how and why of Stanley Kubrick wanting to meet with me! A day or two later, the phone rang. It was Stanley. At that time I was immersed in the development of my own dance theatre work with my company Yolande Snaith Theatredance, an Arts Council-funded touring company based in London. I was not actively seeking choreographic commissions within the commercial feature film industry; I had created several short dance films in collaboration with film directors, composers and designers funded by the Arts Council of England, independent film companies and the BBC, and I had always been passionate about creating my own work, in my own way, and as much as possible on my own terms, to be in control of my own unique creative processes, my artistic vision (something that Stanley strongly empathized with).

Stanley had requested some showreels of my work from my manager. It was one of the short dance films titled *Swinger*, made in collaboration with director Ross MacGibbon, that caught his attention: a 30-minute adaptation of a full-length stage piece my company had created and toured in 1995; *Swinger* was not specifically about swingers and was a deliberate play on the taboo around the word. It was created a year before the release of the movie *Swingers* – which I knew nothing about – and what with the timing my chosen title became rather controversial in the dance world, which was unfortunate. Stanley Kubrick loved it. For many years I had been fascinated by Roland Barthes's book, *A Lover's Discourse.* I loved the language, and the repeated reference to the term 'the other' as an object of projection, desire, obsession and fantasy. I loved the encyclopedic structure of the book and the categorizations of amorous feelings, internal utterances and outbursts of language racing through the mind of the lover. I was intrigued by the poetic titles of what he defined as 'figures' and fragments, such as 'I am Engulfed', 'I Succumb', 'To Love Love', 'The Unknowable', 'How Blue the Sky Was', 'When My Finger Accidentally' and 'The World Thunderstruck'. *A Lover's Discourse* applies the tools of structuralism to examine the vast territory of love. Compiled of 'fragments' and 'figures', the series of many short chapters leads the reader through a labyrinth of the states of mind of the lover. These writings dissect the anatomy of desire into detailed, philosophical and emotional explorations both of languages, and of the internal dialogue navigating the landscape of love.

Swinger was a dance theatre adaptation of the book, with an actor embodying the mind of the writer, and speaking a montage of monologues constructed from Barthes's texts. Passionate dances between strangers accompanied fragments of a lover's thoughts. The players oscillated between transitory states of being, from ecstasy to melancholy, lust to longing, and embrace to solitude. The dancers physically negotiated various seductive couplings, trios and quartets, sometimes slow and sensuous, sometimes tense and combative, sometimes playful, flirtatious, and at times verging on the edge of eroticism. A huge pendulum dominated the centre of the stage, swinging ominously through their world of instability and change, governing their fate.

Manipulated by the performers, the pendulum circled or sliced through space, skimming over the surfaces of stage furniture, built at acute angles in line with the trajectory of the swing; a wooden bed, a table and a chair. The dancers often dodged, ducked, lurched, fell and rolled to get out of its path, in rigorously choreographed sequences. The language of the scenic action, visual imagery and dance created a metaphorical playground for the themes running through the text, a landscape of desire; the dancers embodied states of mind, emotions, fantasies, projections and relationships; their interactions with the scenic elements played with danger, tested their limits and tempted fate. The concept for this psychological forcefield of danger, instability and drama was largely inspired by one passage in *A Lover's Discourse* in the fragment 'This Can't Go On':

Figure 2.1 Photo: Tony Nandy. Dancer Jane Howie. Scenic design: Robert Innes-Hopkins.

> I am a Daruma doll, a legless toy endlessly poked and pushed, but finally regaining its balance, assured by an inner balancing pin (But what is my balancing pin? The force of love?). This is what we are told by a folk poem which accompanies these Japanese dolls:
>
> Such is Life
> Falling over seven times
> And getting up eight.[1]

During my first meeting with Stanley, much of our conversation focused on *Swinger*, and *A Lover's Discourse*. This seemed to provide an entry point

Figure 2.2 Photo: Tony Nandy. Actor: Hassani Shapi, dancers: Desiree Kongeroed, Stephen Hughes. Scenic design: Robert Innes-Hopkins.

for Stanley to connect with me and explore some core themes that were central to *Eyes Wide Shut*: love, lust, fantasy, obsession, jealousy, betrayal, infidelity and self-destruction. He asked many questions about my creative process for *Swinger*: how and why did I select sections of text for the actor's monologue? What was it that drew me to *A Lover's Discourse*? What was my process of directing the actor to speak whilst moving? How did I work with the dancers to achieve the flowing, sensual movement qualities? What was the nature of my collaborative relationship with the scenic designer, composers and the film director?

Stanley had a very paternal presence and listened attentively and patiently. In many ways he reminded me of my own father, his physicality and the way he dressed, pockets everywhere, heavy boots, the way that he sat with such surrender to gravity in his chair, focusing all his attention on me with the steady stare of his wide-open eyes, peering over his spectacles. My dad was just like this too, so I felt strangely at home. He was highly appreciative and complimentary about many aspects of the film. I remember telling him how frustrated I was that the producers of my film insisted that the text be colloquialized, to make the language more accessible to a television audience, which seemed totally ridiculous to me because it was the distinct specificities of Barthes's language that inspired the piece.

We also talked about how divisive the stage version was in terms of audience response. Dance fans just wanted to watch the dance without the actor, theatre people wanted the actor's monologue without dance and some people found the synthesis between text and choreography refreshing and enthralling. In response to this Stanley said to me 'well, you are ahead of your time'. I felt incredibly honoured, and strangely, simultaneously overwhelmed and at ease. In retrospect, I feel there was greater significance in Stanley choosing me because of my appreciation and interest in this subject matter than if I had been a well-known choreographer within the feature film industry. This deeper connection was clearly more important to him.

Reflection and re-examination of my own, and Stanley's, fascination with Roland Barthes's *A Lover's Discourse*, and my film *Swinger*, illuminates how this key connection between us is embedded in the counterpoint themes of *Eyes Wide Shut*: the self-destructive, revengeful path upon which a disturbed and jealous husband embarks, and the inner thoughts, images and psychological drama playing out in the main protagonist's mind. I am drawn immediately to the fragment entitled 'We are our own demons':

> Demons: It occasionally seems to the amorous subject that he is possessed by a demon of language which impels him to injure himself and to expel himself – according to Goethe's expression – from the paradise which at other moments the amorous relation constitutes for him.
>
> A specific force impels my language toward the harm I may do myself: the motor system of my discourse is the wheel *out of gear*: language snowballs, without any tactical thought of reality. I seek to harm myself, I expel myself from my paradise, busily provoking within myself the images (of jealousy, abandonment, humiliation) which can injure me; and I keep the wound open, I feed it with other images, until another wound appears and produces a diversion.
>
> The demon is plural ('My name is Legion', Mark 5:9). When a demon is repulsed, when I have at last imposed silence upon him (by accident or effort), another raises his head close by and begins speaking. The demonic life of a lover is like the surface of

> a *solfatara*; huge bubbles (muddy and scorching) burst, one after the other; when one falls back and dies out, returning to the mass, another forms and swells further on. The bubbles 'Despair', 'Jealousy', 'Exclusion', 'Desire', Uncertainty of Behavior', 'Fear of Losing Face' (the nastiest of all the demons) explode in an indeterminate order, one after the next: the very disorder of Nature.[2]

These excerpts of language resonate as I consider Bill's state of mind after hearing his wife's erotic fantasy; an internal emotional whirlwind, masked by the detached persona of a well-practised doctor. As Bill journeys through the ensuing narrative, every seductive encounter, and every temptation to infidelity, turns sour, or is jettisoned at a crucial moment, and ultimately leads him into a decadent, dangerous underworld, at odds with his own sense of morality, decency and basic humanity. When I read *A Lover's Discourse* now, much of it strikes a chord with the internal mechanisms at play that steer Bill Harford's adventure.

Following our introductory discussion, Stanley described to me, in fairly abstract terms, the scene that he wanted me to consider choreographing: a surreal, sensuous, seductive, suggestive but not explicit dance by beautiful, semi-naked, masked women, and possibly men too. This 'performance or entertainment' was set in a secretive, exclusive men's society in the lavish home of a very wealthy, important man, such as a politician. He was adamant that the women have a specific body type and showed me a selection of photographs by Helmut Newton of naked models wearing high stiletto heels: sleek, long-legged, stylish, elegant. The men should have the classic, muscular, perfectly proportioned bodies, as depicted in the famous image of the Vitruvian Man by Leonardo da Vinci. He showed me an image of the ideal woman's body type on his computer screen, and pointed out to me what was so essential: the line of the shoulders, the shape, size and proportion of the breasts, the length of the legs, the leanness of limbs, the relationship between the size of the hips and the bust. We spent considerable time discussing the details of these women, and he asked me whetther I could find dancers who would meet this essential image.

Initially, I experienced some discomfort in scrutinizing every detail of a woman's body in this way, being a feminist and habitually non-conformist to these kinds of cultural stereotypes and ideals of beauty and body type. By contrast, in Schnitzler's novel *Dream Story,* the women at the masked ball are described as 'sensuous to slender figures, and from budding figures to figures in glorious full bloom', suggesting a more diverse range of body types and ages, so this selectivity was clearly a development of

Stanley's choice.[3] In retrospect, once I had become more familiar with the script and the core themes of *Eyes Wide Shut*, there was something about the language of that conversation with Stanley, the obsession with these exclusive images of women, the descriptive details of body parts, as well as core themes and moments in the film, that harked back to the language of *A Lover's Discourse*. Alice reveals her naked body in the opening of the film, distinctly establishing this very particular beautiful body, and all the women Bill is tempted by have a similar body type to Alice. In Schnitzler's novel, when Fridolin visits the corpse of the mysterious Baroness D, he can only recognize her by details of her body, the body and not her masked face that had intoxicated him with desire: '[t]hat wonderful, blooming body that yesterday had tortured him with longing?'[4] Then he goes on to describe details of the dead body, illuminating qualities that speak to the absence of what had so enthralled him in life:

> He looked at the yellowish, wrinkled neck, noticed the two small girlish, yet slightly sagging breasts, between which the breastbone stood out under the pale skin with gruesome clarity, as if the process of decay already had set in; followed the contours of her lower body, noticing the way the well-formed thighs spread out impassively from shadowy regions that had lost their mystery and meaning; and observed the slight outward curve of the knees, the sharp outline of the shin bones and the slender feet with toes turned in.[5]

The language of Alice's fantasy monologue and Bill's reaction to her fantasized infidelity also resonates with the language of *A Lover's Discourse*; the writing in which I had been so immersed throughout the research and creation of *Swinger*. For example, in the fragment titled 'Ravishment':

> Ravishment: the supposedly initial episode (though it may be reconstructed after the fact) during which the amorous subject is 'ravished' (captured and enchanted) by the image of the loved object (popular name: love at first sight; scholarly name enamoration).[6]
>
> What suddenly manages to touch me, ravish me, in the other is the voice, the line of the shoulders, the slenderness of the silhouette, the warmth of the hand, the curve of a smile, etc. Whereupon, what does the aesthetic of the image matter? Something accommodates itself exactly to my desire (about which I know nothing); I shall

> therefore make no concessions to style. Sometimes it is the other's conformity to a great cultural model which enthralls me.[7]

Reflecting on some key images and scenes in the film, I am drawn to Roland Barthes's words: firstly, the opening scene of Alice casually dropping her black dress to reveal her slender, white, elegant naked body, framed by two tall Grecian pillars, establishing in an instant an iconic image of classical beauty, resonant with contemporary cultural ideals of femininity. Secondly, in Alice's fantasy monologue, she reveals how she was immediately ravished by the image of the naval officer, and her overwhelming feeling that she would be willing to sacrifice everything to be with him. Thirdly, when Bill enters the masked ball and witnesses the disrobing ritual, he is suddenly exposed to the extraordinary, ritualistic disrobing of a group of exquisitely beautiful naked women, a scene that is powerfully immersive and darkly seductive. In the fragment 'Ravishment', Roland Barthes writes:

> the first thing we love is a scene. For love at first sight requires the very sign of its suddenness (what makes me irresponsible, subject to fatality, swept away, ravished): and of all the arrangements of objects, it is the scene which seems to be seen best for the first time: a curtain parts: what had not yet ever been seen is discovered in its entirety, and then devoured by the eyes: what is immediate stands for what is fulfilled: I am initiated: the scene consecrates the object I am going to love.[8]

In one short scene in *Swinger*, a beautiful blonde dancer, dressed in a skimpy, white, silk undergarment, stands motionless in glowing lighting, as the pendulum swings from one side of the frame to the other, suggesting the passing of time, suspense, eternity. Her body is slender and classically feminine; the camera slowly zooms in on her angelic face whilst we hear the central actor's voice speaking from the fragment 'Waiting':

> A mandarin fell in love with a courtesan. 'I shall be yours', she told him, 'when you have spent a hundred nights waiting for me, sitting on a stool, in my garden, beneath my window'. But on the ninety-ninth night, the mandarin stood up, put his stool under his arm, and went away.[9]

This scene calls up the image of the mysterious woman standing on the balcony and redeeming herself, as well as Bill's repeated encounters with desire that are suddenly abandoned at the last moment. These images of the courtesan and the mysterious woman are loaded with a notion of unattainability, unknowability and the sense of Bill's emasculation.

At the end of the film, when we see Bill's mask on the pillow of the marital bed, and Bill breaks into sobs, I am reminded of the words from the fragment 'Catastrophe':

> Violent crisis during which the subject, experiencing the amorous situation as a definitive *impasse*, a trap from which he can never escape, sees himself doomed to total destruction.
>
> Two systems of despair: gentle despair, active resignation ('I love you as one must love, in despair'), and violent despair: one day after some incident, I shut myself in my room and burst into sobs: I am carried away by a powerful tide, asphyxiated with pain; my whole body stiffens and convulses: I see, in a sharp, cold flash, the destruction to which I am doomed.[10]

Having briefed me on the details of the scene in question, Stanley led me into a room to sit and read the script, but only up to the end of the masked ball and orgy scenes; he forbade me to read any further. He gave me a copy of Schnitzler's *Dream Story* to take home and read. I was already intrigued by the mystery and secrecy, and excited by this unique opportunity.

The creative process

Having accepted the proposition, negotiated the contract and postponed an upcoming company production, the search for performers for the 'orgy scene' began. Stanley asked me about some of the dancers in *Swinger* who might fit the bill. Several auditions for dancers were held in London. I led groups of applicants through various sensual movement processes, and videoed individuals dancing, but most importantly, all were photographed topless and wearing only panties or briefs, from every angle. But these auditions produced no dancers with the ideal body shape for Stanley's vision. We moved on to auditioning models, striptease artists and pinup girls, coachloads of them from all over the country. It soon became clear to me that Stanley was more concerned with body type than finding bodies with any movement skill or artistic quality. Auditions became merely a cold, impersonal, uncreative matter of photographing models from every angle, many whose breasts were too large, contours too curvaceous, skin the wrong colour, too short, or proportioned differently to the Helmut Newton ideal. I was frustrated, but at the same time strangely fascinated by this level of obsession and perfectionism, to select only the ideal bodies, even though the process did not align with my own values around body politics and attitudes towards women; when we found them, how was I going to work with them if they had no dance training or movement abilities? Selecting the men was much easier, however; it seemed that many trained male dancers' bodies naturally achieved the desired Vitruvian Man ideal.

When I watch the film now, with so much distance from the process, I can see his vision more objectively; when women of one particular body type, skin colour and age range are assembled *en masse*, stripped naked and masked with fantasy identities, they somehow become totally depersonalized, even dehumanized, they suggest some kind of select rare breed, or some other species altogether. They appear like a surreal menagerie of exotic creatures, an immaculately groomed collection of handpicked clones. As we journey through the orgy scene, I see a lavish mansion filled with anonymous, obedient, high-fashion, feline, fetish pets, being initiated and used ritualistically, but with no apparent sense of passion or sensuality. It is like a surreal, erotic vision from a dream, and taken to a far greater extreme than in Schnitzler's *Dream Story*.

Eventually, Stanley selected a group of beautiful women, and some perfectly proportioned male dancers, a mixture of young white people with movement skills ranging from merely striking still poses for a camera, to contemporary dance and ballet. I remember working initially with the women only for long hours in the studio, beginning with stretching and movement training. We tried various approaches to moving with surreal and seductive qualities. Abigail Good was one of my group of models, and she came with an abundance of enthusiasm and willingness to try absolutely anything. She was a naturally beautiful mover, with an elegant fluidity and suppleness. Abigail was an absolute joy to work with. Some of the models were more resistant and less motivated, unused to so much physical work, their muscles ached and they were worried about getting injured, and how that might impact their ability to work as models. One very young woman was rude and disrespectful, refusing to do things and repeatedly yelling 'fuck off, I ain't doin' that!' It was a challenging struggle at times. The male dancers joined us a few weeks later. I requested various pieces of prototype furniture to work with in the studio, items that might exist in the rooms of the mansion where this scene would take place: sofas, armchairs, a table and a bed. Over several weeks we created many short vignettes on and around the furniture, with all the models wearing only G-strings, half-masks and high heels, likewise the men wearing half-masks and jockstraps.

During rehearsals, I played a range of background music to set alternate moods, dynamics and atmospheres: short choreographies in various combinations of men and women in duets, trios, quartets and larger groups, where their bodies rolled, slid, curled, lifted, hugged, caressed, teased, wrapped and wriggled around each other seductively and suggestively, but never explicitly. Nothing ever became pornographic. As a choreographer of contemporary dance theatre, I was intent on being true to my own creative and aesthetic sense of engaging, skilful, choreography, whilst being committed to the task I had been given, and what I believed Stanley wanted me to produce. In my own creative processes, I am well-practised at exploring ideas collaboratively with performers, experimenting with different approaches, generating a range of possibilities through short sketches, and building up a varied palette of starting points for further development. Stanley's personal assistant Leon Vitali visited rehearsals regularly and videoed the fruits of our work to show him. Feedback from Stanley was appreciative; he made suggestions of various things to try and he was happy for us to continue working in this way. We kept playing and creating for days and weeks on end, creating new sequences, videoing and waiting for further instructions.

Twenty-one years later it is hard to remember the exact order of events, but one day I was called in to meet with Stanley, and we talked about how things were going. He presented a new task for me to work on, shifting away from the seductive dances: the masked ballroom scene and the disrobing ceremony. I was to explore ceremonial formations and sequences of movement, gestures and actions to create a ritualistic disrobing of the women. This was an exciting proposition for me, as I have always been fascinated by religious ceremonies and rituals, and the striking costumes and head-dresses worn by religious or spiritual figures, nuns, priests, gods, deities and so forth. Indeed, versions of these images had been featured in my dance theatre work going back to the mid-1980s. So, with the models fashioned in long black hooded robes, and one of my company dancers, Russell Trigg, playing the master of ceremonies, we began to create rituals in a range of formations: processions, lines, circles, perambulations, bows, choreographing various ways to ceremonially disrobe, revealing the almost naked beautiful bodies of the women. I played music to set the scene; religious choral music, Gregorian chants, church organ and music by various contemporary composers that I liked, including Jocelyn Pook.

I particularly loved *Backward Priests,* an incredible piece by Jocelyn that seemed to create a surreal, haunting and otherworldly atmosphere. When Stanley watched the rehearsal videos a light went on in his eyes. He asked 'what is that music?' It was not long before Stanley called Jocelyn to discuss composing the music for the masked ball.

During this time Stanley also invited me to visit locations for the mansion, including Elveden Hall, where the scene was eventually shot. He called me in to look at a selection of Venetian masks that had arrived from Italy. He led me into a large studio where many Italian masks were displayed on long tables. He asked me to help him choose the most striking selection. They were incredible! So many beautiful, handcrafted carnival masks of commedia dell'arte characters such as Il Capitano, Pantalone, Harlequin and Scaramouche, as well as more unusual Picasso-esque versions. It was important to see them and helped me to visualize Stanley's vision of this scene, with its large crowd of extras surrounding the ritual dance, wearing black robes and these dramatic masks. With all of this in mind, I created some frame-by-frame drawings of how I imagined the choreography might play out, as if seeing the drama evolve within the screen, with additional written descriptions underneath. When I presented these to Stanley during a meeting, he brushed them aside and seemed irritated, saying 'these don't make any sense to me'. I felt somewhat humiliated and realized that it was not a good way to share my choreographic vision with him. In 2020, I watched *Filmworker,* a documentary about Leon Vitali by director Tony Zierra. I was astounded

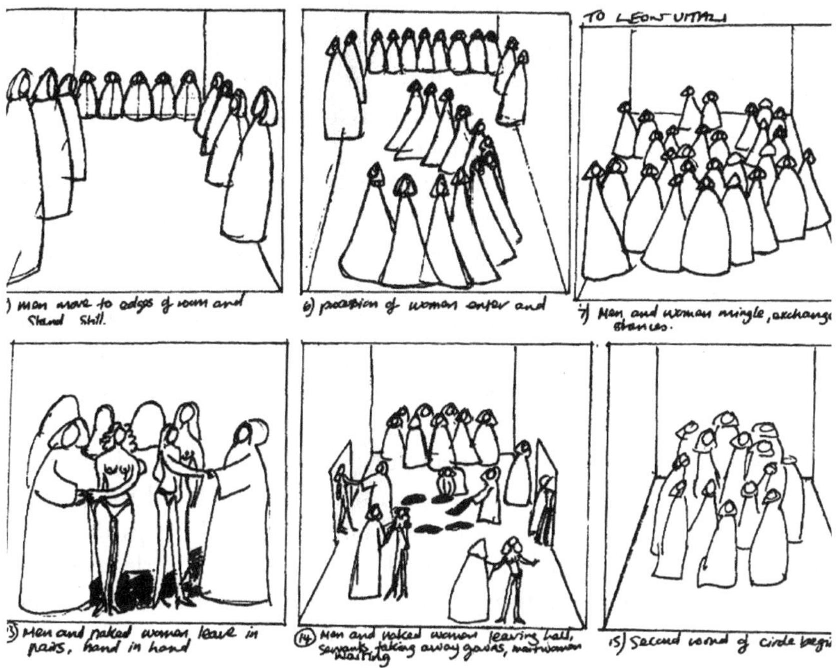

Figures 2.3 and 2.4 Yolande Snaith's frame-by-frame drawings with captions imagining the orgy scene choreography.

to see my drawings appear briefly amongst research materials for *Eyes Wide Shut*. I was not aware that Stanley had kept them and wondered whether perhaps he had studied them after all!

After about three months of rehearsals over the summer of 1997, with various sketches of disrobing rituals added to the repertoire of possible choreography for the orgy, there were still no dates set for the shoot. Everyone was on hold. Possible dates were mentioned, then retracted. Stanley then called me in and handed me a folder of photocopied lithographs of what looked like seventeenth- or eighteenth-century pornographic orgy scenes, often involving three or more people, including monks, cooks, maids, lords and ladies, in domestic, religious and secluded settings, four-poster beds, parlours, kitchens, a garden swing, the scullery, a banqueting hall and even in front of a church organ. These illustrations depicted characters engaged in sexual acts, where all manner of bizarre and complicated physical entanglements were performed. Stanley talked to me about developing the seductive dances more in this direction. Alarm bells went off inside me, as this was clearly very explicit, pornographic. I asked him whether he wanted the movement to go in the direction of simulated sex and he said he did. It was an uncomfortable conversation, partly because this was not what I had agreed to choreograph, and I wasn't interested in choreographing pornography.

I knew that the cast of models was not contracted to simulate sex as this would require a higher rate of pay. Most of the models were very clear that there would be no 'humping'. Furthermore, their agents were adamant that they were not contracted to perform anything explicitly sexual. I explained all this to Stanley who responded 'well, we will have to look for models who will agree to do humping'. I was exasperated! After three months of training models to move and choreographing sketches, now Stanley wanted the orgy to be a full, out-and-out, simulated sex orgy. The possibility of psychological manipulation crossed my mind; perhaps all this time I was being buttered up in the hope that I and the models might be willing to venture out of our comfort zones. Perhaps the work so far was just a warm-up in his mind, also providing a little seductive entertainment in the meantime. I will never know! Ironically, aside from the film, the only material 'souvenir' I have of my experience of working with Stanley Kubrick is that folder of pornographic prints, directly from his hand.

The shoot

The orgy scene was put on hold whilst investigations into models willing to simulate sex were conducted, and the focus shifted entirely onto the masked ball scene. In the autumn of 1997, the shoot was finally scheduled. We arrived on location at Elveden Hall. A huge red carpet was laid out in the centre of the ballroom and the large crowd of extras costumed in black robes and Venetian masks inhabited the surrounding cloisters. Stanley had decided on a circular formation for the ritual choreography, and there were long hours of rehearsals where the choreography was developed in relation to music and the mapping of the camera movements, angles, wide shots and close-ups. The choreography of the ritual is highly distilled from all the ideas explored in the studio and seems very simple, it looks easy and not something that would necessarily have needed a choreographer of contemporary dance to create. But in reality, hours of rehearsal were spent with the models to achieve the perfection of body position, smooth timing and control, to kneel, fold forward, unfold, stand and raise arms to disrobe, all in perfect unison. The movement was not set to any recognizable beat, fixed speed or countable timing other than a few key initiators when the master of ceremonies pounded his staff on the ground. The timing had to be embodied and felt in real time by the women. I was grateful to have Russell Trigg working with me in that role; having collaborated with me as a dancer for several years, Russell often read my mind; his quiet, dedicated presence was very supportive. As I watch the ritual scene now, his even-paced, perfectly timed, elegant revolutions, whilst controlling the swing of the incense burner, clearly provide a securely anchored centre for the timing, the hub of the wheel.

Whilst on location at the Hall, I spoke with Tom Cruise during a break between shoots. We discussed *Swinger*, choreography and dance. I learned for the first time that Stanley had given my film to him to watch and that perhaps it had informed the development of Tom's character. I sat thinking about that for quite some time during the shooting, and also later whilst sitting at the monitor with Stanley and Tom watching the playback of each take, listening in on their discussions. In retrospect, and once I had seen *Eyes Wide Shut*, the interconnecting threads of themes related to the concept of a psychological forcefield of love fell into place.

The most interesting and demanding developments of the choreography took place on set, in collaboration with Stanley and the crew. We had arrived with a basic structure and sequence of movements mapped out, but I was to discover that the extent of the essential choreography was far more complex than the movements of the performers alone, and involved intricately detailed timings where many elements needed to be perfectly synchronized at specific moments in relation to the tracking speed and trajectory of the camera, and the walking pace of the cameraman; these included the revolutions of the master of ceremonies, the swing of his incense burner, the amount and direction of the smoke wafting out of it, and also the position of the blindfolded organist at the far end of the hall in relation to the circle of women. Getting the unpredictable movement of the smoke perfect seemed to take forever. This complexity of multiple elements coinciding in split-second moments is reminiscent of the choreographic process in *Swinger*, where fast-moving bodies and the swing of the pendulum almost colliding with dancers and objects were the core elements. Perhaps Stanley had foreseen this, and only here did I understand what the role of choreography played in his filmmaking. Indeed, filmmaking has its own, internal, choreographic mechanisms: the timing, speed, focus and direction of the camera movement and physical action of the cameraman, in relation to the movement of performers, objects and unpredictable elements such as smoke, fire, weather. This was fascinating to me, and Stanley's uncompromising perfectionism was something I have never experienced either before or since; we shot take after take after take until all elements were synchronized, in each and every moment exactly as he wanted, however long it took.

During these shoots I would be sitting with Stanley off set in the hallway, or a cloister of the ballroom, watching the monitor. We would replay the shoot and scrutinize it. Stanley would ask my opinion, point out details that still were not perfect, make suggestions and give me directions to instruct the performers to alter their timing, movement or spatial position. During this process, Stanley proposed to add a new section before the women stood up, passing a kiss around the circle, an element of the choreography that was created entirely on set. This passing kiss added a mysterious, secretive and strangely poetic detail within the decadently seductive world of the film. I sensed that Stanley could only fully realize what he wanted to see, what the film needed within the grand scheme of things, once he was on a shoot and able to give all his creative energy and attention, in collaboration with his crew, to the scene at hand and its relationship to the film's overall form and content. This was where the magic happened. This made complete sense to me and I felt honoured to assist him to achieve his vision.

It was during these few weeks that I truly understood what my role was, as a 'Choreographer' in Stanley's world, and how I perceived the essential nature of my collaborative relationship with him. Up until this point I had experienced doubts and confusion; I soon realized that this film was not an opportunity for me to contribute choreography that really displayed my own choreographic vision and artistry. I began to understand that I was contributing towards the research for the orgy and the masked ball, and that through these months of work Stanley had been evolving a clearer vision of what the film needed, which had moved away from the initial proposition, and in some way, I was an essential player in that evolution. I had been instrumental in sourcing music and introducing him to Jocelyn Pook. I had asked myself, what does Stanley really want from me? How can I best serve his creative process and the realization of his vision? I developed a relationship with the models and became familiar with their capabilities, resistances, needs and boundaries, and I think that they understood and respected me, to varying degrees. I had also become a vital spokesperson for them, passing on what they would and would not, could not, do.

As we worked on set, I realized how necessary this was for Stanley, as so much development of the finer details of the choreography evolved then and there, with Stanley's feedback, requests and suggestions that were always communicated to the performers through me. I became a vital liaison throughout lengthy and repeated shoots, and several problems presented themselves that I had to communicate to Stanley – the models spent so many hours kneeling, semi-naked on a hard, cold floor, that their knees became swollen and painful; we had to order bags of frozen peas to relieve the swelling. They were experiencing pain bending their knees and walking. There were enormous tension and claustrophobia on set at times; the crowds of extras were suffocating under the masks and robes, standing still, packed closely together for hours on end. On one occasion one of them fainted and was taken away on a stretcher. I remember that, on one very late night after many hours of shooting the same sequence over and over again, I insisted that we stop. The women needed to rest, or else their knees would be too injured to work the next day. I recall that one of the models became sick, or injured, and might not have been able to perform the next day, and Stanley and Leon teased me by suggesting that I should replace her, knowing full well my discomfort with the obsession with the perfect body type and that I didn't fit the bill at all, being 5ft 1 inch, short-legged, compact and muscular! I laughed and replied 'not on your life'. Stanley laughed and had a mischievous twinkle in his eyes. It was a moment filled with an unspoken subtext that resonated between the three of us.

It was an honour to collaborate with Stanley Kubrick, to learn from him, to be a fly on the wall sometimes in his visionary world, and to get a glimpse into the genius of his *modus operandi* as a film director. It was a once-in-a-lifetime opportunity that I will never forget and always be thankful for. Essentially, my experience of working on *Eyes Wide Shut* was a kind of choreographic liaison. It was an extraordinary adventure, a metaphorical love affair with the making of a film by Stanley Kubrick, filled with all the drama, seduction, intensity, tensions, agreements and disagreements that love affairs often have, and finally coming to an end with a sense of both gratitude and loss. So, to end, a short quote from the fragment titled 'The Ghost Ship' from *A Lover's Discourse* that defined the ending of *Swinger,* and that resonates with my own experience of ending my liaison with *Eyes Wide Shut*:

> How does a love end? – Then it does end? To tell the truth no one – except for the others ever know anything about it; a kind of innocence conceals the end of this thing conceived, asserted, lived according to eternity. Whatever the loved being becomes, whether he vanishes or moves into the realm of friendship, in any case I never see him disappear: the love which is over and done with passes into another world, like a ship into outer space, lights no longer winking.[11]

Notes

1 Roland Barthes, *A Lover's Discourse*. Trans. Richard Howard (New York: Hill & Wang, 2010), p. 141.
2 Barthes, *A Lover's Discourse*, pp. 80–81.
3 Arthur Schnitzler, *Dream Story*. Trans. J.M.Q. Davies (London: Penguin, 1999), p. 46.
4 Schnitzler, *Dream Story*.
5 Schnitzler, *Dream Story*, p. 94.
6 Barthes, *A Lover's Discourse*, p. 188.
7 Barthes, *A Lover's Discourse*, p. 191.
8 Barthes, *A Lover's Discourse*, p. 192.
9 Barthes, *A Lover's Discourse*, p. 40.
10 Barthes, *A Lover's Discourse*, p. 48.
11 Barthes, *A Lover's Discourse*, p. 101.

3

Stanley Kubrick's Final Film and the Question of Control

Manca Perko

Stanley Kubrick's reputation as an auteur filmmaker is typically expressed in terms of his unusual control over all aspects of the filmmaking process. In this respect, however, *Eyes Wide Shut* (1999) is particularly problematic for the discussions sparked due to the director dying before finishing the film. The fact that Kubrick passed away before *Eyes Wide Shut* was completed has prompted fans and scholars to question whether the film that we saw was the same film that Stanley Kubrick wanted us to see. At the time of his demise, *Eyes Wide Shut* was still in post-production. The editing had supposedly been finalized apart from a few minor glitches. Michael Herr recalled a telephone conversation with Kubrick who told him '[h]e couldn't possibly show me the movie in time for my deadline, because there was looping to be done and the music wasn't finished, lots of small technical fixes on colour and sound'.[1] Amy Taubin reported Warner executive Terry Semel as saying '[t]he film is totally finished except for a few colour corrections and some technical things'.[2] All these fixes on sound, colour correction and other 'technical things' were carried out by several collaborators after Kubrick's death who, although they claimed they attempted to 'stay true' to Kubrick's vision of the film, were outside his control.[3]

Those collaborators who actively supervised the post-production after Kubrick's death included his long-time assistant Leon Vitali, his co-producer and brother-in-law Jan Harlan, his wife Christiane and the editing team of Nigel Galt and Melanie Viner-Cuneo. In their presentation of the events using the post-production documentation in the Stanley Kubrick Archive, Robert P. Kolker and Nathan Abrams conclude that

> Vitali was busy handling almost everything. This included postproduction recording on the film, including the dubbing of sound

and additional dialogue recording, the storing of film data on computer, camera shot details, laboratory instructions, foreign prints and translations and dubbing into other languages, the order and size of the end credit cards, marketing and publicity, distribution of the film, as well as video and DVD releases.[4]

Vitali's key role in post-production has been belatedly acknowledged in *Filmworker* (Tony Zierra, 2017), a film documenting Leon Vitali's life story and work for Kubrick, which can be seen as a crucial corrective to the official narrative that had belittled Vitali's role hitherto.

However, this has led to questions about the film's status given Kubrick's absence. Director Christopher Nolan expressed his doubts, stating

> [Kubrick] died before the scoring sessions were complete. So, even though I think the studio appropriately put out the film as his version, knowing where that happens in my own process … it's a little bit early … It is a little bit hampered by very, very small and superficial, almost technical flaws that I'm pretty sure he would have ironed out.[5]

'Would Kubrick have approved that his labour of love was compromised in this way, that his authorial vision was unfaithfully translated on American screens?' Mattias Frey asked.[6] The latter comment suggests that, had Kubrick lived, *Eyes Wide Shut* would have been a different film. The case of *Eyes Wide Shut* problematizes the typical view of Kubrick as an auteur given the changes that were made without his direct consent. By reassessing the collaborative process behind *Eyes Wide Shut*'s post-production, this chapter aims to shed light on the ongoing debate over the finality of *Eyes Wide Shut* and hence Kubrick's authorial control. It will argue that the collaborative relationships Kubrick built played a decisive role in the successful finalizing stages of his filmmaking, especially in his absence, but also in the early stages, such as his collaboration with the laboratories in developing the negative stock, which is the first stage after production ends. In so doing, it brings into focus the role of other collaborators, analyses their work and acknowledges their creative input in a collaborative exercise such as filmmaking.

The complexity of post-production

Post-production is a complex collaborative process, involving a great number of people in finalizing the film before it was released to the audience. This complex process involves moments of collective and collaborative creativity of many individuals. Therefore, if one is to analyse the collective creativity and the collaborative process in which it occurs, the individual creative input must also be identified. As it is valid for the director to have a distinguishing style, so can his co-workers' imprint be expressed and regarded as their 'voice', displayed through various contributions, ideas as solutions to challenges, filmmaking techniques and audio-visual elements that are detectable/not detectable in the final product. These are expressions of the workers' creativity and reflect in 'behaviours, performances, ideas, things and other kinds of outputs'.[7] Identifying these can justify the idea that, in the words of C. Paul Sellors, '[i]n a collaborative medium, we should expect to find not only authored components but also varying degrees of joint authorship in the finished work'.[8] In this way, the themes of individual authorship and authorship occurring in collaborations should not be studied separately, but considered at the same time, which is the essence of this chapter.

A colour grader, for example, stylizes the colour scheme of the footage, emphasizing the visual tone and atmosphere of a film, and making it look more cinematic by 'ensuring that the film's carefully curated colour palette conveys a specific atmosphere, style, or emotion'.[9] Film colour theory presumes that certain colours in film elicit emotional responses from the audience. Manipulation of these colours can be used to guide the audience toward the intent of the author, juxtaposed against one another to send a message, or subverted to create dramatic irony. From this angle, instilling meaning leads to a questioning of the authorship of the input and the missing recognition of its impact. *Eyes Wide Shut* is a complex case study that raises the question of total control in a collaborative exercise.

Editing

Post-production collaborations are different from the collaborations at the previous stages of filmmaking, and the study of the post-production process in Kubrick's productions demonstrates how his usual control varied in its application. Kubrick's technical knowledge at the editing stage of the production was strong, which enabled him to exercise his control over the editing process. 'Writing, shooting, and editing are what you have to do to make a film', Kubrick claimed.[10] He also once said '[n]othing is cut without me. I'm there every second, and for all practical purposes I cut my own film; I mark every frame, select each segment, and have everything done exactly the way I want it.'[11] According to the director himself and specific collaborators in the editing room, Kubrick was present and did the traditional slicing and gluing of the negative together with his editor (and assistants). But Kubrick's presence in the editing room and overview of the editing process overshadows the specific input of his editors whose creative input may not have always been recognized. Tony Lawson, the editor of *Barry Lyndon* (1975), explained that he would often challenge Kubrick regarding editing decisions: 'I did take part, I did have some sort of influence and who's to say if it had been somebody else it might have been, still a Stanley Kubrick film. But it probably would have been different.'[12]

The process of editing, however, was different during the post-production of *Eyes Wide Shut*. The first change was attributable to the advances in the film industry of the time. The onset of digital technology in the 1990s brought new knowledge and experimental techniques in editing tools – non-linear editing tools such as the Avid editing program – which gave flexibility to not only the physical editing process but also the mental process of editing.[13] As Roy Perkins and Martin Stollery explain, the onset of digital editing has led to editing rooms becoming more accessible not only to editors, their assistants and the director but also to many other individuals, such as the producers.[14] George Larkin observes: 'Digital technology not only changed the process, but also the product of the filmmaking process', pointing out that the new ease of editing has 'led to a variety of people attempting to influence an edit'.[15]

The arrival of digital technology in post-production, therefore, challenged Kubrick's usual practice of control. The use of Avid in particular really tested the limits of his knowledge and proficiency, forcing him to rely on various collaborators, resulting in control shifting. On *Eyes Wide Shut*, the editor was Nigel Galt assisted by Melanie Viner-Cuneo and Claus Wehlisch, who was specifically assigned to the Avid. As Robert P. Kolker and Nathan Abrams described, '[t]hey worked on the editing nonstop throughout the day and often into the night to reach the deadline of the beginning of March 1999 for delivery of a preliminary copy of the film, which Kubrick had promised Warner Bros. They worked in a room in Childwickbury dubbed the Avid Room.'[16]

Developing the material: laboratories

Eyes Wide Shut depended to a great extent on the laboratory's competence and input in developing the film stock because of the unique look Kubrick wanted to give the movie, which is discussed in further detail below. When the film stock has been shot, whether in test shots, dailies or the finished film, the film is transferred to a laboratory, where it is developed, the quality of the print checked and sent to the film director. Laboratories are essential technical institutions that develop the filmed material from a negative. They are involved in the pre-production, production and post-production processes when it comes to grading, special effects and other corrections to the film negative, before the film's release and the creation of deliverables and copies, and creating 'screens' (the prints for cinematic release), archiving material and restoration. Because of the crucial role of laboratories in bringing the film through its final stages, the quality of the produced material represented a decisive factor for Kubrick.

Kubrick was very meticulous about his choice of laboratories. Before he started collaborating with Rank Laboratories (later renamed Deluxe Laboratories), Kubrick typically opted for a new one with each new film project.[17] The reason for this was, perhaps, the director's perfectionistic striving to raise the quality of the developed material, or because he liked to spread his business around, but it resulted in extra work when searching for the right laboratory. Kubrick's assistant Emilio D'Alessandro explained that Kubrick had a habit of developing the test shots, before the shooting had started, at several different laboratories. He recalled being instructed to deliver reels to Humphries, Technicolor and Rank.[18] The cross-checking would then determine which of the laboratories Kubrick would choose.

However, the reason for cross-checking the laboratories might not have been just because of his perfectionism, but the severity of the incidents that occurred in the laboratory process. D'Alessandro recalled Kubrick 'not being happy' with Humphries' development of the dailies.[19] Warner Bros. promotion coordinator Mike Kaplan detailed one incident during the production of *Barry Lyndon* where a negative was scratched, causing Kubrick's displeasure with Humphries Laboratories which, until that point, had been 'effectively processing the material for over a year'.[20] Commenting that 'the laboratory is quite capable of making dreadful mistakes',[21] he stopped collaborating with Humphries and, as Kaplan recalled, '[t]he technicians were devastated as Stanley removed the negative to Rank via a convoy of vehicles, followed by Humphries' managing director on foot, trying to rescue the transfer. There was no sanctioning an error of this magnitude.'[22] Kubrick's demand for excellence in technical processes from his collaborators, leading to his decision to change laboratories, serves to extend the myth of the controlling director. However, he knew when and how to take back control of his product.

Colin Flight, the operations and engineering manager at Rank Laboratories, firmly believes that it was because Kubrick possessed extreme technical proficiency himself. 'Stan was a master. He knew film', Flight said.[23] Kubrick often demonstrated his ability when describing the technical issues that could occur in the laboratory and affect a negative, specifying that 'printing machines can make the print too dark, too light or the wrong colours'.[24] Blue flashes, scratches and dirt on the negative stock, and exposure and focus issues, were the most common reasons for Kubrick rejecting the developed material. 'Question: to live with under-exposed rushes or not?' he once wrote.[25]

When it came to technical processes in which he was less proficient, Kubrick's reliance on the knowledge of his collaborators grew considerably in the later stages of making *Eyes Wide Shut*. At Rank, Kubrick collaborated closely with Colin Flight and Chester Eyre, who was the director of operations and Kubrick's contact with the laboratory. Having worked with Chester Eyre before, Kubrick had developed his trust in Eyre's supervision of the 'push in' process used on the *Eyes Wide Shut* negative. The conclusion is clear: contrary to the belief that Kubrick always got his way, he would compromise when it was explained to him what the risks were. After seeing the developed film, instead of criticizing the colours that were brought out, Kubrick understood what the laboratory people were telling him when advising him 'not to push it too far', and he took their advice.[26]

Another area in which Kubrick relied on others was in his decision to force-develop the negative of *Eyes Wide Shut*. Force-developing, or 'pushing in', is achieved when the negative is left in the developer for a more extended period than normal, and it is used to compensate for low lighting, which Kubrick used while shooting *Eyes Wide Shut*. The process creates exaggerated highlights, which Kubrick desired and, as Larry Smith, director of photography on *Eyes Wide Shut*, explained, Kubrick 'eventually decided to force-develop everything, even the day exteriors, to keep the look consistent'.[27] Because of the high risk of too much grain, it was a challenging experiment for the laboratory. As Smith recalled, '[l]ab people always worry when things are done in a non-standard manner, and at first, we were all surprised that he wanted to do it'.[28] But Rank Laboratories took on the challenge with enthusiasm, because it also brought economic benefits. Colin Flight recalled 'for us [this] was good because we charged a fortune for it, because it affected the overall processes'.[29] Smith's recognition of Rank's effort justifies their fee: 'I think Deluxe did an incredibly consistent job day in and day out. They put aside a bath just for us, and they always put our stuff through first – that was a special privilege they extended to Stanley. It was a seven-day-a-week job to make sure that what we were getting was consistent, and I give all the credit to the guys who handled that.'[30] The success of the push-in technique can therefore be attributed to the laboratory. It was in the laboratory processing of the film that Kubrick had little control owing to the highly technical process, in which he was not proficient. He was, therefore, compelled to develop trusting collaborative relationships, which, after a few changes in the laboratory facilities, he did with individual employees in Rank Laboratories.

Special and visual effects, grading and corrections

Before he died, certain written instructions, which can be found in his editing books, demonstrate that Kubrick had planned particular visual effects for *Eyes Wide Shut*. These include the example, 'flashbacks should have some form of visual fx to separate from reality'[31] for the 'naval officer' scene. After his death, at the end of March 1999, Melanie Viner-Cuneo communicated with Chester Eyre regarding the black and white and colour stock for the 'naval officer' shot, pointing out that 'colour is better'.[32] This scene ended up in 'silvery blue monochrome'[33] in the released version of the film. Whether this is down to the laboratory's suggestions, or the choices of the editors Galt and Viner-Cuneo, or such collaborators as Leon Vitali and Jan Harlan, or someone else's input, is hard to determine.

The input of another group of external collaborators, however, can be demonstrated in the process of application of special/visual effects and corrections to the film to deliver an R-rated version of *Eyes Wide Shut* and satisfy the Motion Picture Association of America's conditions. Scene 52, the 'masked ball', required many additions and corrections, as did the 'naval officer' scene. This required CGI (computer-generated imagery) leading to the forging of a close collaboration with The Computer Film Company (CFC). 'CFC had always been Kubrick's digital effects house of choice for *Eyes Wide Shut*', it was reported.[34] At the end of March 1999 Paddy Eason, the supervising digital compositor at CFC, came with Rachel Penfold to view the shots to be obscured, and in particular the naval officer shots/effects. As Paddy Eason explained:

> They [the Motion Picture Association of America] had a huge problem. When Kubrick died, the cut was known to be locked. And he was a very hands-on editor. But the agreement between Kubrick and Warner Bros. was that he was contracted to deliver an R-rated film. Nobody had had the conversation with Stanley before he died about how he was going to square that circle, because the orgy scene, as it stood, wasn't an R-rated scene.[35]

'CFC worked on 22 shots in total, adding up to 8,000 frames of material, all processed at Kubrick's specified 4,000 lines of resolution. This included converting 5 "mind's eye" shots, which feature Nicole Kidman's character and a naval officer[,] from colour to a silvery black and white, as well as two largish scratch repairs and some jump cuts.' The best example of this is the most notorious and controversial scene in the movie – the 'masked ball' scene. Colin Flight added '[t]he editorial department offered to do only minimal dissolves and fades in order to save the empty spaces, because the main intention was to do the last corrections as "he would have done them"'.[36]

Two versions of the film were made: the R-rated version and a non-rated version. To avoid an NC-17 rating, the cut that met the requirements of the Motion Picture Association of America was finished on 15 March 1999 and has six deletions and four insertions, including changes to censor some nudity shots. The added CGI can be observed in several shots by comparing the R-rated version with the non-rated version of *Eyes Wide Shut*:

1. The cloaked man in front of the couch on the right-hand side of the frame has been added.
2. A naked woman and a cloaked man have been added to the bench to conceal a graphic sex scene.
3. Two naked women have been added in front to conceal the couple on the cupboard in the background.
4. A woman and a cloaked man have been added in front of the couple at the entrance.
5. Cloaked men have been added in front of the girls on the table.
6. A cloaked man has been moved slightly to the left in one shot to conceal a couple engaging in intercourse.

The digital work done demonstrates that several shots have been altered to receive the R-rating. Eason explained that CGI work for *Eyes Wide Shut* was complex: 'From my point of view, there were a number of factors which made it tricky. The length of shots – some were over 600 frames long – with extensive Steadicam moves, and the CG figures in view throughout, required very exacting 3D motion tracking.'[37] According to documents in the Stanley Kubrick Archive, many further optical changes followed Kubrick's death: on 15 March 1999, a New York exterior shot was added to the naval officer scene; Telecine Colour (PIC) corrections were done in May; making and blacking out 'naval officer' shots, as well as a cut in/jump out shot on Alice were among these. The opticals and prints in Deluxe Laboratories were checked for updates regularly. Editor Nigel Galt commented on the success of the collaboration, acknowledging CFC's creative and technical input: 'I'm unreservedly pleased with their contribution. It provides a new benchmark for this sort of work.'[38]

The inclusion of a number of collaborators brings up the question of control again. The processes of grading, the audio-visual corrections and the additions identified at the post-production stage of *Eyes Wide Shut* need to be considered in the debate. According to Paisley Livingston, the author is anybody who intentionally expresses or communicates in the process of film production.[39] Taking this into account, CFC's report statement that '[t]he results of all CFC team's labours are astonishing, the digital figures blending seamlessly with Kubrick's human cast',[40] clearly features the individuals of the CFC team intentionally expressing or communicating in the process of post-production. Daniel Reynolds, for example, urges the development of a definition and positioning of the cinematic author in digital work, based on the fact that 'technological change likewise affects the parameters for cinematic authorship'.[41] Berys Gaut believes that authorship can be equated with the attribution of artistic expression (contribution) to an individual:

> Of course, the director, if he has authority over the other contributors, is likely to be the most important contributor of expressive and artistic properties to a film. But that is entirely compatible with the multiple authorship view: the view is not that the contribution of all authors must be of equal importance. Just because the director's is the most important 'voice' in the film does not mean that others' contributions do not entitle them to count as authors too.[42]

While Gaut's conclusion might seem too simple, it in fact relates to what some of the older advocates for collaborative authorship have argued for. While Victor Perkins saw 'noise' as an indicator of collaboration,[43] Peter Wollen saw film as 'the result of a multiplicity of factors, the sum total of a number of different contributions'.[44] Nicholas Kmet even appeals to 'researchers – and enthusiasts' to 'adjust their expectations to meet this new collaborative reality'[45] when it comes to the contribution of film composers. This leads me to the next case study that demonstrates Kubrick's collaborative practice in the post-production in *Eyes Wide Shut*'s music and sound department, and sheds light on the debate among fans and critics that stems from the film's music not being finished in time for Kubrick to have signed off on its eventual use.

Music

Kubrick was thinking about the music for the film as early as November 1998 when Claus Wehlisch set up a record player in the Avid room. But the director did not finish the sound mix before his death. One critic, Amy Taubin, argues that '[t]he sound mix would be unacceptable even in a student film, and the score, here, and in the entire second half of the movie, is shockingly heavy-handed. Since sound influences picture as much as picture does sound, no film is finished until the sound work is done.'[46]

Jocelyn Pook, the film's composer, explained that Kubrick was unsure of his choice at the beginning. 'He said, "Yeah, I really don't know what the music should be here, but try something – sexy music." That was my brief!'[47] Giving creative freedom to Pook as well as his other composers, music editors and mixers demonstrates that Kubrick was very open to ideas. As Jan Harlan disclosed, 'Kubrick was kind of musical, but he wasn't really a musician. But he did have that understanding that music was a very powerful and direct art form, more direct than film even, which is why he always gave music such priority.'[48] Harlan often provided Kubrick with ideas for the films' music. He believes that '[m]usic choices are for a filmmaker what the choice of colour is for a painter'.[49]

The choice of sound 'colours' for the film included musicians/composers like Victor Silvester, Tommy Sanderson and the Sandmen, Chris Isaak, György Ligeti and Franz Liszt, as well as many musical pieces performed by Harlan's nephew Dominic. There are numerous combinations of musical colours, tints and shades, which may or may not have resulted in a completely different 'painting' to the one that Kubrick intended. And there is evidence of this; Kolker and Abrams listed some of the instructions for music editing from the editing diary:

> Reel 5 Fix music in orgy … There are two scenes that require new scored pieces of music … Two alternative pieces of music need to be found to replace the background Frank Sinatra used in the temp mix, depending on the cost of rights for use … An alternative

> piece to the Shostakovich may need to be found for the montage sequence.[50]

Other sound processes were also planned: sound effects, Foley artists, revoicing through automatic dialogue replacement (the party scene), with the anticipation of finalizing the sound mix in June 1999, three months after Kubrick's death.

The music mix is as important as the post-production changes/corrections/additions that were applied before the film was released on 16 July 1999 – more than four months after Kubrick's death. As with the corrections, changes and additions identified in other post-production stages of *Eyes Wide Shut*, the question of authorship of the creative input is legitimately raised at this stage too. All the contributions took place in a collaborative environment on which all Kubrick's productions were heavily reliant. Although it is impossible to find an objective point of view on the working atmosphere in Kubrick's productions, the discourses that arise form a collection of perceptions of authorship, attribution of creative inputs and recognition of their impact. Immersion in these debates complicates the understanding of these concepts and consequently challenges Kubrick's reputation as an auteur and a non-collaborator, but also stresses the importance of the creative input and authorship being recognized in a collaborative medium. Jack Stillinger even argues that, in film as an industry, the 'dispersal of authorship might be deemed appropriate'.[51]

Collaboration thus represents the method of filmmaking and complicates the attribution of authorship. The answer is in researching the circumstances and the discourses that surround them. The circumstances can be detected by employing a method of historical discourse research. Thus, observing the relationships between the systems involves observing the relationships between the creators themselves. Instead of focusing on the auteur, namely the director as the carrier of authorship of the representation codes and, consequently, the sole creator of the representation systems, this approach includes other individuals in the equation. Authorship in filmmaking needs to be studied from a predisposition that, as a process, filmmaking is based on the collective actions of a group of people creating, and a collaboration between individuals in the process of creativity. Kubrick studies represents an example of how the various authorship theories and approaches have been applied in the traditional analyses and how the practice has shifted to modern approaches to collaborative authorship. My main concern is not to find a 'correct' definition of authorship, but to problematize the attribution of it to one person only. By studying 'the inter-connected creative relationships'[52] in Kubrick's crews, these issues can be brought to light. It is, in fact, opposite to Peter Wollen's view that 'these separate texts – those of the cameraman or the actors – may force themselves into prominence so that the film becomes an indecipherable palimpsest'.[53] The noises should be subject to criticism and analysis because they are, in fact, also voices.

Conclusion

The primary issue lies in the widespread belief that Kubrick was in control of the entire process of filmmaking. This is simply not true, as the results also depended on the laboratory and other external collaborators, such as the special/visual effects people, and the production company. The context of collaboration has, in many ways, become central to an understanding of Kubrick's filmmaking practice. It is, therefore, plausible to refer to the studies as modern approaches. While they are by no means new, they contain new parts in focusing on the discourse of authorship, paving the way for the theories on collaborative/collective/multiple authorship to be seriously considered and widely discussed. In answer, such theories duly emerged. They focus on the idea of the intentionalism of a group: John R. Searle's collective intentionality and 'we-intentions',[54] Paisley Livingston's creating of an utterance,[55] and the theory of joint commitment proposed by Margaret Gilbert.[56]

The debate on multiple/collaborative authorship originated from historical discussions on authorship always focusing on the individual element: '[b]y building theories of film authorship on theories of literature and literary authorship, film theorists and critics have questionably characterised film authorship as an act of individual expression, despite the collective nature of production'.[57] But a film crew is a unique and complex case. It is a group of film workers who, according to Gilbert's plural subject theory, form a 'holism'[58] – which is, however, not a sum of individual personal commitments, but individuals who subject themselves to a joint commitment. This is because, in filmmaking, there are two central processes – creativity and functionality.

Gilbert and Searle both believe that collective behaviour is not just a sum of individual intentions or commitments. It is true that film workers take on a joint commitment and engage in a collective creative process which leads to a common goal, namely production of a film – a process that involves functionality. The other process, which differentiates creative industry social groups from other types of social group, is the creative process in filmmaking. Workers in the film industry have double aspirations: they wish to contribute and, at the same time, express their creativity. They engage not only with a joint commitment, but also with an expectation to be able to express their creativity. This leads to the observation that, in filmmaking, there are two types of creative processes: joint and individual. Not only do these coexist, but the individual creative processes are crucial for the joint creative process to function; for example, it can be said that, without individual musicians, the orchestra cannot play a unified piece.

Searle continues to elaborate on the functionality of the joint creative process by presenting the individual and collective concepts of intentionality. Individual intentionality is expressed without connection to other members of the group, but at the same time, 'each player must make a specific contribution to the overall goal'.[59] This can be achieved by employing the individual's knowledge: '[t]he manifestation of any particular form of collective intentionality will require particular background skills'.[60] Even more, it is this demand for an exacting level of skill, as well as the contribution that such skills make to a collaborative process, that makes post-production exhilarating for film practitioners.[61]

As this research into post-production changes, additions and corrections has demonstrated, Kubrick's collaborators made crucial contributions to the success of the creative process (or at least the successful finalization and distribution of the film after the director's death) with their specialist knowledge of specific post-production processes. It is therefore too simplistic to regard these individual and collective contributions solely as 'noise'[62] – a perspective which Perkins and Stollery believe originates from a disjunction between film theory and professional film practice.[63] In order to get a more objective perspective on what the noises are and how to recognize the individual voices amongst them, one must join the strengths of the academic and practitioner production studies. Although Paul Wells admits that '[i]nevitably, no definitive account of authorship in cinematic practice is possible, and the discussion of the nature of authorship remains problematic',[64] he stresses how important it is to recover the debates about authorship and apply them to various fields. Joining the components of collective work and opportunities to observe 'the distinctive voices among prevailing babble of discourses during a film's production',[65] or to observe, in Perkins' words, the 'interaction between the various personalities and talents engaged in making a film'[66] resulting in 'separate texts'[67] that need to be decoded, will offer a new interpretation of creative collaboration and an alternative perspective on authorship and creative autonomy in the film industry. Trevor Ponech, for example, focuses on the factor of sufficient control, and defines the author as 'an agent' who is responsible for executing the 'A-plan', which is 'a global, synthetic blueprint or recipe regarding the finished movie's content, structure, properties, and effects, along with some of the means to achieving these ends'.[68]

It follows, then, that the input of Kubrick's close (internal) collaborators Jan Harlan, Christiane Kubrick and Leon Vitali could be considered as forming part of the collective authorship of the finished film. The case study of *Eyes Wide Shut* is complicated owing to the technological transitions to digital at the time, which Daniel Reynolds believes 'not only re-renders long-standing ontological and epistemological anxieties about the cinematic image, as scholars including Mark Williams have argued, but also intensifies anxieties surrounding industrial practices of authorship and accreditation in media production'.[69] The analysis of the post-production stages and collaboration occurring in work on *Eyes Wide Shut* demonstrates that several internal collaborators were closely involved in the work process, but more importantly, several external collaborators also entered the picture. Their technical expertise, knowledge and collaborations with Kubrick before his demise, had essentially influenced the post-production process. Whether the film would have been a different one if Kubrick had been in control of the entire post-production process will remain unanswered, but it raises the importance of recognizing other collaborators' input and brings focus to the discussion of authorship in post-production. A concretely defined, explicit model for attribution of collaborative authorship in the film industry has not been attempted in this chapter, as it is clear that every film production is an individual case with its own specifics. This study has demonstrated that there is much more research to be done into collaboration in filmmaking. This applies to the field of Kubrick studies, which is still mostly subject to the auteur approach but, with more insight into collaborative relationships, it can further develop the idea of authorship as a discourse and practice.

Notes

1 Michael Herr, 'Kubrick', *Vanity Fair*, 21 April 2010, http://www.vanityfair.com/hollywood/2010/04/kubrick-199908. Accessed 1 February 2021.

2 Amy Taubin, 'Stanley Kubrick's Last Film', in *Scraps from the Loft* (2017), http://www.scrapsfromtheloft.com/2017/12/31/stanley-kubricks-last-film-by-amy-taubin-film-comment/. Accessed 21 March 2021.

3 Author's interview with Colin C. Flight, 2018.

4 Robert P. Kolker and Nathan Abrams, *Eyes Wide Shut: Stanley Kubrick and the Making of His Final Film* (New York: Oxford University Press, 2019), p. 117.
5 Zack Sharf, 'Christopher Nolan Reveals the One Question He'd Want to Ask Stanley Kubrick – Listen', *Indiewire* (2017), https://www.indiewire.com/2017/11/christopher-nolan-stanley-kubrick-question-eyes-white-shut-1201901304/. Accessed 3 January 2021.
6 Mattias Frey, 'Fidelio: Love, Adaptation, and *Eyes Wide Shut*', *Literature/Film Quarterly* 34.1, 2006, p. 39.
7 Calvin W. Taylor, 'Various Approaches to and Definitions of Creativity', in Robert J. Sternberg (ed.), *The Nature of Creativity: Contemporary psychological perspectives* (New York: Cambridge University Press, 1988), p. 104.
8 C. Paul Sellors, 'Collective Authorship in Film', *Journal of Aesthetics and Art Criticism* 65.3, 2007, p. 270.
9 MasterClass staff, 'Color Correcting vs. Color Grading: Understanding Film Coloring', *MasterClass* (2021), https://www.masterclass.com/articles/color-correcting-vs-color-grading#what-is-color-correcting. Accessed 5 December 2020.
10 Joseph Gelmis, 'The Film Director as Superstar: Stanley Kubrick', reprinted in G.D. Phillips (ed.), *Stanley Kubrick: Interviews* (Jackson, MS: University Press of Mississippi, 2001), p. 99.
11 Gelmis, 'The Film Director as Superstar', p. 99.
12 Roy Perkins and Martin Stollery, *British Film Editors* (London: British Film Institute, 2004), pp. 102–103.
13 George Larkin, *Post-Production and the Invisible Revolution of Filmmaking: From the Silent Era to Synchronized Sound* (London: Routledge, 2019).
14 Perkins and Stollery, *British Film Editors*, p. 169.
15 Larkin, *Post-Production and the Invisible Revolution*, p. 16.
16 Kolker and Abrams, *Eyes Wide Shut*, p. 115.
17 Emilio D'Alessandro with Filippo Ulivieri, *Stanley Kubrick and Me: Thirty Years at his Side*, trans. Simon Marsh (New York: Arcade Publishing, 2016).
18 Ulivieri, *Stanley Kubrick and Me*.
19 Ulivieri, *Stanley Kubrick and Me*, p. 218.
20 Mike Kaplan, 'How Stanley Kubrick Kept his Eye on the Budget, down to the Orange Juice', *Huffington Post*, 20 February 2012, https://www.huffpost.com/entry/how-stanley-kubrick-budget_b_1287552. Accessed 19 October 2021.
21 Bernard Weintraub, 'Kubrick Tells what Makes *A Clockwork Orange* Tick', *The New York Times*, 4 January 1972, p. 26.
22 Kaplan, 'How Stanley Kubrick Kept his Eye on the Budget'.
23 Author's interview with Flight.
24 Weintraub, 'What Makes *A Clockwork Orange* Tick', p. 26.

25 Leon Vitali's file, various documentation on post-production and distribution, SK/17/5/13, The Stanley Kubrick Archive, University of the Arts London (hereafter 'SKA').
26 Author's interview with Flight.
27 In Stephen Pizzello, 'A Sword in the Bed', *American Cinematographer*, October 1999, https://ascmag.com/articles/a-sword-in-the-bed-eyes-wide-shut. Accessed 19 October 2021.
28 Pizzello, 'A Sword in the Bed'.
29 Author's interview with Flight.
30 Pizzello, 'A Sword in the Bed'.
31 Proposed digital work, CFC, Leon Vitali's file. SK/SK/17/5/13, SKA.
32 Proposed digital work, CFC, Leon Vitali's file. SK/SK/17/5/13, SKA.
33 Kolker and Abrams, *Eyes Wide Shut*, p. 119.
34 CFC, 'CFC Help *Eyes* Open in US', report in Leon Vitali's file. SK/SK/17/5/13, SKA.
35 Paddy Eason, interviewed by Jamey DuVall, The Kubrick Series (2012), http://www.thekubrickseries.com/. Accessed 10 November 2020.
36 Author's interview with Flight.
37 Eason, interviewed by DuVall.
38 'CFC Help *Eyes* Open in US'.
39 Paisley Livingston, 'Cinematic Authorship', in R. Allen and M. Smith (eds), *Film Theory and Philosophy* (Oxford: Oxford University Press, 1999), pp. 132–148.
40 'CFC Help *Eyes* Open in US'.
41 Daniel Reynolds, 'Platform Anxiety: Locating Authorship in *Tron*, *Hugo*, and *The Lego Movie*', *Journal of Cinema and Media Studies* 60.2, 2021, http://www.muse.jhu.edu/article/781344/pdf. Accessed 10 May 2021.
42 Berys Gaut, *A Philosophy of Cinematic Art* (Cambridge: Cambridge University Press, 2010), p. 122.
43 Victor Perkins, 'Direction and Authorship' (1972), reprinted in B.K. Grant (ed.), *Auteurs and Authorship: A Film Reader* (Oxford: Blackwell Publishing, 2008), p. 70.
44 Peter Wollen, *Signs and Meaning in the Cinema*, 3rd edn (Bloomington, IN: Indiana University Press, 1972), p. 104.
45 Nicholas Kmet, 'Remote Control: Collaborative Scoring and the Question of Authorship', *Revue musicale OICRM* 5.2, 2018, p. 12.
46 Taubin, 'Stanley Kubrick's Last Film'.
47 Thomas Hobbs, 'How *Eyes Wide Shut*'s Uniquely Unsettling Score was Made', *Dazed* (2018), http://www.dazeddigital.com/music/article/41996/1/eyes-wide-shut-stanley-kubrick-soundtrack-jocelyn-pook-interview. Accessed 24 January 2021.
48 Jan Harlan, quoted in Robb Peter, 'Chamberfest: For Stanley Kubrick Music Was Central to his Vision for Film', *Artsfile* (2017), https://artsfile.ca/chamberfest-stanley-kubrick-made-music-part-of-his-vision-for-film/. Accessed 24 January 2021.

49 Peter, 'Chamberfest'.
50 Kolker and Abrams, *Eyes Wide Shut*, p. 118.
51 Jack Stillinger, *Multiple Authorship and the Myth of Solitary Genius* (Oxford: Oxford University Press, 1991), p. 175.
52 Peter Cowan, 'Persistence of Vision: Film Authorship and the Role of the Cinematographer (with a case study of Gregg Toland)', unpublished PhD thesis, Manchester Metropolitan University, 2016, p. 65.
53 Wollen, *Signs and Meaning in the Cinema*, p. 105.
54 John R. Searle, 'Collective Intentions and Actions', in P. Cohen, J. Morgan and M. Pollack (eds), *Intentions in Communication* (Cambridge, MA: Bradford Books/MIT Press, 1990), pp. 401–415.
55 Livingston, 'Cinematic Authorship', pp. 132–148.
56 Margaret Gilbert, *Sociality and Responsibility* (Lanham, MD: Rowman & Littlefield, 2000).
57 C. Paul Sellors, *Film Authorship* (London: Wallflower, 2010), p. 111.
58 Gilbert, *Sociality and Responsibility*, p. 3.
59 Searle, 'Collective Intentions and Actions', p. 403.
60 Searle, 'Collective Intentions and Actions', p. 413.
61 Perkins and Stollery, *British Film Editors*, pp. 171–172.
62 Wollen, *Signs and Meaning in the Cinema*, p. 105.
63 Perkins and Stollery, *British Film Editors*, p. 7.
64 Paul Wells, *Animation: Genre and Authorship* (London: Wallflower Press, 2002), pp. 73–74.
65 James Chapman, Mark Glancy and Sue Harper (eds), *The New Film History: Sources, Methods, Approaches* (New York and Basingstoke: Palgrave Macmillan, 2007), p. 70.
66 Perkins, 'Direction and Authorship', p. 70.
67 Wollen, *Signs and Meaning in the Cinema*, p. 105.
68 Trevor Ponech, 'Authorship and Authorial Autonomy: The Personal Factor in the Cinematic Work of Art', *Canadian Aesthetics Journal* 4, 1999, https://www.uqtr.ca/AE/vol_4/trevor(frame).htm. Accessed 12 November 2020.
69 Reynolds, 'Platform Anxiety', p. 84.

49. Baer, 'Cinematheek' [illegible]
50. Kolker and Abrams, *Eyes Wide Shut*, p. 118.
51. Jack Stillinger, *Multiple Authorship and the Myth of Solitary Genius* (Oxford: Oxford University Press, 1991), p. 175.
52. Peter Cowan, 'Persistence of Vision: Film Authorship and the Role of the Cinematographer' [illegible] a case study of Giuseppe Tubaldi', unpublished PhD thesis, Manchester Metropolitan University, [illegible], p. 65.
53. Mullen, *Sound and Meaning in the Cinema*, p. 105.
54. [illegible] R. [illegible], 'Collective Intentions and Actions', in [illegible] Cohen, J. Morgan and M. E. Pollack (eds), *Intentions in Communication* (Cambridge, MA and London: MIT Press, 1990), pp. 401–415.
55. [illegible] Collaborative Authorship, pp. [illegible]
56. [illegible] *Sociality and Responsibility* (Lanham, MD: Rowman & Littlefield, 2000).
57. [illegible] Thomas, *The Auteur* [illegible] (London: Wallflower, 2001), p. [illegible]
58. [illegible] Authorship and the [illegible], p. [illegible]
59. [illegible] Collective Intentions and Actions, p. [illegible]
60. [illegible] Collective Intentions and Actions, p. [illegible]
61. [illegible] Collaborative Authorship [illegible], p. [illegible]
62. [illegible] *Sound and Meaning in the Cinema*, p. 105.
63. [illegible] *Eyes Wide Shut*, p. 72.
64. [illegible] and *Authorship* (London: Wallflower, [illegible])
[illegible] p. [illegible]
65. [illegible] and Sons Harper (eds) [illegible] New York and [illegible]
[illegible]
66. [illegible] Authorship, p. [illegible]
67. [illegible] p. 11.
[illegible]

PART TWO:
THE FILM

4

'If You Men Only Knew': Stanley Kubrick's Attempt to Explore Female Sexuality in *Eyes Wide Shut*

Catriona M. McAvoy and Karen A. Ritzenhoff

Co-written and directed by Stanley Kubrick, *Eyes Wide Shut* (1999) is an adaptation of Arthur Schnitzler's 1926 *Traumnovelle* [*Rhapsody/Dream Story*]. The story focuses on a male lead, the surprising revelation of his wife's sexual fantasies and the exploration of his own erotic desires. His feelings towards his wife, their relationship and his assumed place in society are all challenged by her unexpected confessions. The fundamental difference between reality and fantasy, and the crisis this rift evokes, are central to Schnitzler's and Kubrick's narratives. The filmic adaptation attempts to engage further with a distinctly female perspective but ultimately the dated, misogynistic source material draws the viewer back to the subjective male point of view and its reductive, neurotic fear of female sexuality and expression.[1]

This chapter suggests that the film, like the book, is an exploration of marriage and fidelity from a resolutely male perspective. We argue that Kubrick *did* try to find ways to portray female desire but ultimately did not achieve this aim. Most previous analysis of the film also takes a male point of view, generally framing the male protagonist's journey as the focus;[2] there are however a few notable examples of more balanced perspectives we can draw on.[3] We posit that the narrative arc of the film can be examined as the initial crisis in the marriage followed by three confessions (or therapy sessions) and then the couple's resolution. This approach allows for a more feminist interpretation of the film and perhaps reveals more about what Kubrick was trying to explore: the relationship between husband and wife.

By comparing the on-screen presentation to the original text and considering other books used by Kubrick for research and archival documents such as sketches and letters relating to these scenes, we can explore the underlying themes, Kubrick's motivation for the adaptation and the interventions he made. Finally, we can consider *Eyes Wide Shut*'s somewhat problematic legacy, particularly relevant to current discussions around the #MeToo movement, male privilege, the rise of the involuntary celibate (INCEL) movement and far-right misogyny.

The set up

Schnitzler's novella begins with Fridolin, Albertine and their daughter; in the film adaptation these figures are transformed into Bill (Tom Cruise), Alice (Nicole Kidman) and Helena (Madison Eginton). The child is reading aloud a section from *One Thousand and One Nights*:[4]

> 'Twenty-four brown slaves rowed the splendid galley that would bring Prince Amgiad to the Caliph's palace. But the prince wrapped in his purple cloak, lay alone on the deck beneath the deep blue, star spangled night sky, and his gaze –' Up to this point the little girl had been reading aloud; now, quite suddenly, her eyes closed. Her parents looked at each other with a smile …[5]

This version of events was in the screenplay from drafts dated early 1995 but after a discussion between co-screenwriter Frederic Raphael and Kubrick, the text was changed to the Rudyard Kipling poem 'I keep six honest serving men':[6]

> I KEEP six honest serving-men
> (They taught me all I knew);
> Their names are What and Why and When
> And How and Where and Who.
> I send them over land and sea
> I send them east and west;
> But after they have worked for me,
> *I* give them all a rest.[7]

The poem was written by Kipling for his daughter. It marvels at a child's curiosity, in contrast to an adult who has become complacent and no longer explores and asks questions. While it removes the blatant references to slavery, it retains the theme of exploring; the 'serving men' metaphor refers to the child's act of asking questions. In the final drafts and the completed film this scene and the poem were not used;[8] however, the allusions to slavery, and women as chattels, remain. The introduction to the film presents Alice as an object of beauty and the first exchange between Bill and Alice – 'Honey have you seen my wallet?' 'Isn't it on the bedside table?' – makes the connections between money and sex within the marital contract implicit, as discussed by essayist Tim Kreider.[9]

Schnitzler's original reference to *One Thousand and One Nights* sets this story up as a fable, a morality tale of a man's adventures, here that of Fridolin/Bill whose 'gaze' is the focus of the film. It is his adventure under the 'star-spangled night sky' that we follow. The novella begins with a jump from fantasy to reality, 'a story within a story', as noted by Patrick Webster.[10] In the film, we leap from a 'dream space',[11] a stylized cinematic view of Alice in her Raphaelesque beauty, nude in front of a mirror, framed perfectly by two *faux* roman pillars, to the film's title card, then to an establishing shot of a New York street and the Harfords' apartment block, followed by a realist depiction of marital life. We see Bill looking for his wallet and then Alice again; this time, instead of elegantly poised in her dressing room, she is sitting on the toilet, talking to her husband. A letter from Raphael to Kubrick underlines the film's deliberate blurring of fantasy and reality:

> Variety of tone and a mixture of farce and solemnity are typical in my experience of dream and 'dreamy' episodes in 'reality'. I take it that the heart of the matter is that we should eventually not 'know' any more than Bill does, where objective reality and subjective fantasy begin and end, always assuming that there is a neatly patrolled frontier, which there is not any more than there is between tragedy and farce.[12]

During the adaptation process, Raphael also suggested several different titles including 'Woman Unknown',[13] underlining the originally intended focus of the film. The final title *Eyes Wide Shut* echoes the child closing her eyes in the first few lines of the book and underlines the gaze of the main character Bill. Webster suggests it could refer to a quote from Benjamin Franklin: 'keep your eyes wide open before marriage, half shut afterwards'.[14] It can also be seen to refer to the dream/reality questions that the film invokes. These initial changes and omissions give some clues to the intertextual layers Kubrick was trying to incorporate in order to tell a more nuanced story.

The ball: a marriage in crisis

At an opulent holiday party in the house of Bill's rich client Victor Ziegler (Sydney Pollack), Alice is approached by Sandor Szavost (Sky du Mont) who invites her to dance and then tries to seduce her. 'Did you ever read the Latin poet Ovid on the *Art of Love*?' he asks. Alice is familiar with the text and jokes about Ovid's sad fate: 'didn't he wind up all by himself crying his eyes out in someplace with a very bad climate?' (He was exiled by Augustus to Tomis, now Romania.) Szavost knowingly replies 'but he also had a good time first, a very good time'. The deliberate inclusion of this early Roman poet's seduction guide for the man about town is full of allusions to extramarital affairs.[15] Its presence in this scene demonstrates that little has changed over the centuries, from Ovid's manipulative tips to today's Pick-up Artist (PUA) seminars and books.[16] Though a modern woman like Alice may be aware of this, she still struggles to resist Szavost's somewhat sleazy charms. Ultimately, Alice follows Ovid's advice on how a woman should rebuff such advances. Szavost paraphrases another famous cad, Lord Henry Wotton from Oscar Wilde's *The Picture of Dorian Gray*, saying 'one of the charms of marriage is that it makes deception necessary for both parties'.[17] Alice remains unmoved and eventually displays her wedding ring, twirling her finger provocatively in front of Szavost, to remind him that she is indeed married. Does she wish that Bill, with all his self-pity and neuroses, were more like this suitor? Szavost's character is certainly set up as a foil to Bill, a glimpse for Alice of what she could have if she were not committed to her marriage.

Kubrick also had copies of the eighteenth-century Venetian adventurer and author Casanova's two-volume *Histoire de Ma Vie [Story of My Life]* and Shepherd Mead's 1957 *How to Succeed with Women Without Really Trying* in his library.[18] Mead's book is a satirical look at male–female relationships and this suggests Kubrick had an ironic interest in the sort of man confident and crass enough to employ these 'pick-up' techniques. Neither Ovid nor Szavost are mentioned in Schnitzler's text. In early drafts of the screenplay, Alice has flirty conversations with several men but no dialogue is noted. Szavost is named in the screenplay as 'CHARMER' and his discussion of Ovid doesn't appear until a later draft.[19] This addition to the story shows how Kubrick attempts to present a female perspective whilst highlighting the deceptive charms of predatory men.

Confession 1: Alice's fantasy

The following night, Alice and Bill relax in their bedroom together by smoking a joint and making love. They talk about the night before and get into a heated discussion about the various temptations they encountered, and potential threats to their monogamy. Alice rebuffs her husband's smug complacency in her fidelity with the statement 'if you men only knew', mocking his confidence with cynical laughter, before emasculating him by recounting her past desire for another man. Alice describes how, when on a family vacation, she glimpsed a naval officer and found him so attractive that she imagined leaving her safe and regulated domestic life as a mother and wife behind to escape with him. *Eyes Wide Shut* deals with this simplified dichotomy between whore and mother/wife and the insecurity that is evoked when Bill learns that his partner is not entirely who he presumed her to be. Although he is depicted in various tempting situations with women, Bill is ultimately immune to such advances. Contrary to Szavost and Ziegler, the wealthy host of the party who we see cheating on his wife Ilona (Leslie Lowe) with a prostitute (Julienne Davis), Bill has no double life and is not framed as sleazy or predatory.

This ambivalence of men – willing to be tempted but deciding whether or not to act on seduction – is at the core of Arthur Schnitzler's *Traumnovelle*. Male sexual desire is contrasted with the erotic imaginations of women, who are regarded as property in a bourgeois, binding, marital arrangement. At the beginning of the film, Bill lives an idyllic, domestic, middle-upper-class life that provides him with comfort and financial security. Kubrick establishes with the party scenario at the outset that men of influence and wealth will seek sexual pleasures outside marriage, even in their own homes. While Ziegler has sex with Mandy upstairs, his wife entertains the guests below. Bill, by contrast, does not intend to bring sexual transgressions into his home or workplace. However, the idea that Alice could have left her family to be with another man haunts Bill to the point where those images invade his life, and he feels deeply unsettled while returning to his office, formerly familiar apartment and even the marital bedroom.[20]

Kubrick cuts from the shared bedroom after the marital argument to a wide shot of Bill in a cab, rushing to the apartment of one of his wealthy patients who has passed away that night. The timing could not be worse. Rather than stay with his wife and resolve their conflict, Bill leaves the suddenly unfamiliar and unstable home to begin a nocturnal quest, still in disbelief about his wife's testimony of her desire for another man, a uniformed naval officer no less. Four increasingly drastic fantasies, perhaps of what Bill imagines Alice's desire to be, filmed in short, blue-tinged black-and-white clips, of Alice and the naval officer (Gary Goba) having sex, are injected into the film. The audience never sees Alice's fantasy from her point of view. Bill visualizes what she has merely hinted at. There could hardly be a more corny cliché for female lust than depicting a tall white male in a white military outfit, adorned with medals. This is a male vision of what female erotic fantasies could look like, presented in slow motion and not in full colour. In Bill's mind, his wife is making out with a stranger. This scene could also be interpreted as Bill's (homoerotic) fantasy of intercourse with a male suitor. One can tell from the dark expression on his face as it cuts from his imagination to reality, that this vision troubles him deeply, it does not fit into his idealized life. The mother figure turns into a slut who gives herself to other men, breaking the promise of the wife to be faithful, domesticated and undoubtedly reliable. Each of Bill's later visions of his wife becomes more and more sexually explicit as Alice reaches a climax. All of these visions fill him with jealousy and insecurity and each triggers a vengeful transgression and a step further on his journey beyond the confines of his marriage. Kubrick did not accompany Alice's recounting of her fantasy with images and instead, the viewer sees her desires only through Bill's imagination, a male projection of female sexuality and desire.

Confession 2: Alice's dream

Later in the film, after he has attended and been ejected from a late-night clandestine orgy, Bill returns home and finds Alice dreaming in their bed. She seems to be sleeping but can be heard giggling and then laughing. Bill wakes her and holds her, as she is visibly disoriented and upset, contrasting with the previous laughter. However, when Bill listens to Alice recount her 'horrible dream', he lies on the bed turned away from her. She gets to a point in the story at which she sees the naval officer from her earlier confession, and then begins crying. Bill sits up and looks at her; he then prompts his wife to tell him her entire dream, his voice full of hatred. Contrary to Alice's initial confession the second confession is more intimate and not triumphant. She describes her dream as being filled with 'weird things' and warns her husband that the images are 'too awful'. He assures her 'it's only a dream', encouraging her to continue with the descriptions. Alice seeks closeness and embraces her husband while she continues to narrate: 'he was kissing me, then we were making love'. Her language subsequently becomes cruder and more explicit: '[t]hen there were all these other people around us, hundreds of them, everywhere, everyone was fucking'. She continues to talk while leaning against her husband who listens to her with a blank stare:

> [a]nd then I … I was fucking other men. [Bill looks horrified.] So many, I … I don't know how many I was with. And I knew you could see me in the arms of all these men. Just fucking all these men! And I … I wanted to make fun of you. To laugh in your face. And so, I laughed as loud as I could. That must have been when you woke me up.

While Alice is crying and clearly upset about this memory, Bill and the audience heard her laughter at the beginning of the scene, joyful and abandoned. Alice continues to caress her husband and whimpers while he stays silent. He stares over her shoulder at the wall. The book and the screenplay describe his thoughts: 'It's like a sword between us. We're lying here like mortal enemies. But are we? Are we not?'[21]

As with the earlier recounting of her fantasy, Alice narrates her dream with no on-screen representation of what she describes. However, Kubrick, with the help of the concept artist Chris Baker, did try to find a way to illustrate the female lust and desire recounted in this scene. The Stanley Kubrick Archive houses evidence that they explored the idea of showing Alice's dream with her in various stages of bliss. Sketches by Baker depict a broad meadow where naked figures emerge from the ground. They vary from sensual close-ups to expansive orgy scenes. In one, Alice is opening her mouth in a pose that suggests that she is leaning over her lover, her eyes are closed and her curly hair is framing her head. Another shows her receiving cunnilingus from an anonymous lover, her head leaning back in pleasure. A wide shot depicts Alice naked, stretched out on a field. Baker wrote underneath the image, '[s]tretching out on the grass, Alice seems to melt into and become one with the meadow'. The image's head is bent backwards and her mouth is open. She is alone, suggesting a type of auto-eroticism since she seems to be sensually electrified. Several sparks emanate from her body into the air. In another sketch, the illustrator builds an erotic accumulation of bodies, nestled into each other. The figures are erect and their eyes cannot be seen, insinuating that their individuality does not matter. Masculine figures grab the body of a nude woman whose head is bent back with her long hair touching different male suitors. In this sketch, the woman is fairly small, positioned in the middle of the frame and touched by at least three anonymous men. The cutline states 'this plays around with scale. Also, the way the images are treated could be quite interesting to give it an otherworldly feel the [*sic*] appear to be moving paintings.' Baker's description below the image suggests that he was interested in creating tableaus that are similar and reminiscent of the orgy scenes that Bill experiences at the height of his nocturnal explorations. Contrary to the orgy scene, the woman in the frame seems to be the focus and have some agency and more personality than the loosely sketched men. Baker writes about a scene where a woman is placed in the middle of a vertical picture, surrounded by four male heads and hands that grab her naked body. 'Here the lovemaking is a complete overlapping of distorted images writhing around Alice. Although the effect would be quite subtle, it would also be suggestive without being vulgar.' A close-up of two heads kissing each other on the mouth is added to the lovemaking scene. Baker writes '[h]ere, again, I see their lovemaking an overlapping series of images each one slightly askew to suggest the countless days and nights. Maybe the lighting would constantly be changing as well to suggest the passage of time.' In this scene, similar to the one that Kubrick chose in the first monochromatic scenario that Bill envisions, Alice is on the ground, being animated but not actively caressing her lover. Her body is slightly lifted off the ground but her hands rest next to her body. She is surrounded by grass while her toes are only touching the ground. These are supposedly Alice's erotic fantasies; however, the way the lovemaking is depicted resonates more with the pulsating, mechanical sex of the orgy at the core of *Eyes Wide Shut*. Baker notes how 'a scene like this could easily come across as a mass orgy – a lot depends on how the different elements are treated'.[22] Therefore, when the mother-turned-adulteress narrates the content of her dream, she actually mirrors the scene her husband had just experienced during the exclusive orgy. Alice's fantasies are not her female vision of sensuality but rather a simulacrum of Bill's male experiences.

The contrast between the home environment and the intimate vision of his adulterous wife is created through lighting. Alice is associated with blues when she is confessing her transgressive fantasies and as a sex object. She is basked in warm colours when she is depicted in her role as a mother with a child. During her second confession, the screen is split into blue and orange hues. In the background, a Christmas card can be seen, showing Madonna and Child, the starkest contrast to the group sex Alice is recounting in her nightmare. In a numbered list of notes, Kubrick writes '7. Wife as Whore and Mother' and '13. Bill will never forget the confession and the dream whatever is said between them'.[23] In Schnitzler's book, Albertine's dream goes further and is tied into the reading of *One Thousand and One Nights* from the beginning of the book with a reference to a queen and a boat at sea, ending with Fridolin humiliated and sentenced to be whipped and to die on a cross, as Albertine looks on and laughs.[24] Richard Scholes and Lucy Martin point out that 'a substantial portion of Schnitzler's *Dream Story* is given over to Albertine's description of her intensely erotic and sexually explicit dream'.[25]

It certainly appears Kubrick wanted initially to make more of this scene, as Baker's sketches demonstrate. Understandably, though, the sequence was difficult to realize and went through several iterations during the development process. In early drafts of the screenplay, Bill is killed in the dream, as in the book, although he is thrown into the sea rather than dying on a cross.[26] Kubrick was very keen to keep to Schnitzler's version, writing to Raphael 'I think we should follow every beat of the dream scene as AS [Arthur Schnitzler] wrote it … a lovingly cut-down version … omitting everything about [the] queen's offer of marriage and refusal, all of which seems long and obscure'.[27] Raphael wanted to 'follow the course but not the protracted prosiness of the dream', suggesting it could be 'further shortened, though it would be a shame if it became a mere summary'.[28] A week later he sent another version, stating 'I have done some work on the dream'.[29] In later drafts, the queen and the section with Bill being killed have been removed; it has become 'a mere summary'.[30] This section of the film provided the biggest opportunity to present female erotic desire but Baker's sketches are never realized and we are left with Alice's short, hollow, verbal confession the impact of which on Bill and his reaction are the camera's focus.

Confession 3: Bill's admission

The third and final confession is by Bill and it is not represented in dialogue or images. Rather, the viewer is left to imagine that he recounts the journey that we have followed him on to meet the prostitute Mandy and attend the secretive orgy. Bill returns to his apartment finally, after his adventures have taken a very dark turn. Bathed in blue light, he approaches the decorated Christmas tree, then goes to the kitchen, takes a beer from the fridge and sits at the kitchen table drinking it; he appears to be in shock. Sometime later we see him, a little unsteady on his feet, open the bedroom door. Alice is sleeping on her side of the bed; her hair is curly and angelic-looking, and she is turned towards Bill's missing costume mask from the orgy that we can assume she has placed on his pillow.[31] Bill holds his hand on his heart as if he is in pain, sits down slowly on the bed and starts to cry. His crying wakes Alice up. She looks at him in disbelief, he leans towards her, and she stretches out her arm and cradles him by her chest in a rather motherly and comforting gesture, stroking his hair. 'I'll tell you everything', Bill states through his tears. The next shot is of Alice, smoking, with bloodshot, teary eyes. It is daylight and it appears that, although now more composed, Bill has continued to cry.

During Bill's quest we have seen idealized visions of women and, in the orgy scene in particular, perfection and opulence intertwined, scenes reminiscent of the paintings of Gustav Klimt and the sexualized sketches of Egon Schiele. These two artists were friends and their careers on the Vienna art scene often overlapped, paralleling the relationship between their contemporaries Sigmund Freud and Schnitzler, whose relationship informed the original novella and Kubrick's adaptation of it. Pre-production notes show that the Klimt-adorned hall of the Palais Stoclet in Brussels was an inspiration for the rooms in the orgy scene, albeit with a table replacing the initially considered bed in the middle of the room, seen in early development mockups.[32] A letter from Raphael to Kubrick states: 'I am familiar with the paintings of Klimt and the drawings of Schiele from the catalogue of the Vienna exhibition and from our own books'.[33] This letter suggests that these images were more than just a visual reference for the *mise-en-scène*. They were also an inspiration to the writing and development process, another way to weave the sexual politics of *fin-de-siècle* Vienna from the original text into the script.

Art historian Dijana Metlić has written about the influence of Klimt on Kubrick's imagination. Metlić writes,

> The strongest and the most persistent character in *Eyes Wide Shut* is Alice, who refuses to stay a passive 'household nun', but discloses her sexual drives and erotic fantasies openly to her husband. Even though Klimt's and Kubrick's intelligent and beautiful women cause men to suffer, they eventually save them and release them from their subconscious fears of impotency and death.[34]

As Kubrick film scholars Robert P. Kolker and Nathan Abrams point out, all the women at the secret orgy were conceived as Alice's look-alikes.[35] Bill's nightly extravagance therefore can be seen as a quest to find his wife over and over again. Amongst these clandestine scenes of Bill's transgressions, he remains an outsider, his neuroses blocking him from actively engaging, and his inner thoughts constantly stunting his journey. Kubrick read Karen Horney's *The Neurotic Personality of our Time* (1937) during his pre-production research and highlighted sections in several chapters, namely 'The Basic Structure of Neuroses' and 'Characteristics of the

Need for Affection and Recoiling from Competition'. He also highlighted the sentence '[h]e is like Penelope who unravelled every night what she had woven during the day'.[36] While the reference to Penelope from Homer's epic poem *The Odyssey* appears counterintuitive as compared to, say, Odysseus,[37] a man on a mission who fits better with Schnitzler's reference to another heroic character on a journey, Prince Amgiad from *One Thousand and One Nights*, Penelope is an apt model for Bill, and Kubrick's plan for him. Penelope had many suitors, but she wished only for Odysseus. Promising to make a decision when her weaving was done, she weaved all day but secretly unpicked her work at night to avoid being pushed into choosing. Bill avoids Alice after her confession, not wishing to return home, and his insecurities and fear cause him to unpick the work he has put into weaving his marriage.

Kubrick also explored this idea of neuroses and marital issues in reading Jean-Paul Sartre's 'Intimacy', which was in his book collection.[38] This short story explores a marriage at a breaking point from the perspective of the wife and her female friend. She fantasizes about other men and women, people she knows, brief encounters and affairs she has had. She is happy in her marriage but not in love with her impotent husband. She leaves him, to run away with another man with whom she is having an affair. She has sex with the other man but is left feeling anxious and used. She returns to her husband in the night, cries with him and sleeps next to him, but in the morning she leaves again. However, in the end, she decides she wants to be with her husband, accepting him for his flaws and inadequacies. This story presents an engaging exploration of marriage and desires that in many ways is similar to *Traumnovelle.* The female perspective presented in Sartre's book was something Kubrick grappled with but did not manage to successfully show in his adaptation.

Kubrick also read the work of other experts on female sexuality. This included the work of Simone de Beauvoir, Colette and Anaïs Nin.[39] In her important feminist book *The Second Sex*, Simone de Beauvoir wrote that

> women's autonomy, even if it spares men a good number of problems, will also deny them many conveniences; assuredly, there are certain ways of living the sexual adventure that will be lost in the world of tomorrow: but this does not mean that love, happiness, poetry and dreams will be banished from it. Let us beware lest our lack of imagination impoverish our future.[40]

Such works impacted his consideration of depicting the female perspective in his exploration of relationships.

However, *Eyes Wide Shut* – perhaps unavoidably – follows Schnitzler's misogynistic lead. Schnitzler's text, at its core, is deeply misogynist, reflecting turn-of-the-century Vienna's nostalgic, stereotypical views of women as outlined by Marie Kolkenbrock[41] and Eva Revesz.[42] Bill's equivalent, Fridolin in Schnitzler's novella, hates his bourgeois wife and desires to see her suffer. He wants to 'smile coldly and confess his sins to her, and thus get even for all the bitterness and shame she had brought upon him in her dream'.[43] After her confessions, he continues on his mission to find the woman who sacrificed herself for him as 'he simply could not yet face Albertine'.[44] His brutality is made more clear in the book: 'They're all the same, he thought bitterly, and Albertine no different from the rest – in fact she's the worst of them all. We'll have to part. Things can never be the same between us.'[45]

Schnitzler also presents Fridolin's neuroses as part of the catalyst for his troubled journey. 'He felt helpless and inept, and everything seemed to be slipping from his grasp,' Schnitzler wrote,[46] and 'he felt full of self-pity.'[47] The novella gives us further insights into Fridolin's anxiety and the dichotomy of his feelings towards his wife. Certainly, the story of his inadequacy goes deeper, with the cold feelings he has towards homeless people and the sick, but ultimately he presents as a man whose ego wants him to believe that the woman at the orgy 'very probably preferred him to all those archdukes or whatever they had been'.[48] In the end, Fridolin returns home and sees his wife in bed. 'A feeling of tenderness and of security he had not expected overwhelmed him.' He sees the mask on the pillow and takes it as a 'witty, almost light hearted approach, which seemed to contain both a warning and a willingness to forgive'.[49] But what if she hadn't reacted in this way? What if she had been hurt and angry at the 'real' infidelities to which he confesses? This could have been another opportunity for Kubrick to consider the female perspective and more modern notions of female autonomy, and even divorce, but unfortunately the exploration of the male experience remained his sole focus.

The resolution

In the final scene of the film, a conversation between the couple occurs while they are Christmas shopping in a large toy store with Helena. 'We should be grateful', Alice offers by means of reconciliation and thereby re-establishes the marital equilibrium. She continues to express how they should be 'grateful that we've managed to survive through all of our adventures, whether they were real or only a dream'. Bill looks surprised, but pleased; she reassures him and he justifies his indiscretions further, reminding her '[a]nd no dream, is ever just a dream'. Thus, in the end, as in Schnitzler's version, Alice forgives her husband and allows him his shame and guilt, strangely equating it with her own imagined dreams. There was no premeditated malice in her fantasies and he seems to ignore her comments about her feelings of love towards him, during both her fantasy and her dream; instead of focusing on the imagined infidelities which, in the book, Fridolin admitted to having in their early discussion.[50]

The ending scene also went through several iterations during the development process. Initially, the final conversation took place in bed directly after Bill's confession, as in the Schnitzler novella. Early drafts show a modernized but faithful translation:

> ALICE: 'Fuck me will you please?' He almost resents what he also wants so much. Is he going to refuse her? ... with a sense of returning and of starting something new, BILL begins ... It is as if she were a stranger and his wife, and so she is. THE END.[51]

However, Raphael felt that 'it follows AS quite slavishly'[52] and they looked at ways to break this up. Kubrick and Raphael considered a voiceover from Helena reading the Kipling poem originally considered for the beginning 'as a closing grace note',[53] and Kubrick suggested to Raphael that they incorporate elements from Ernest Hemingway's *A Moveable Feast.*[54] Hemingway's memoir nostalgically and quite romantically ruminates on his first, failed marriage to Hadley Richardson. This intervention could certainly have presented a more regretful Bill and underlined his final realization that his domestic life was more attractive than the pursuit of his fantasies. Hemingway's words speak more clearly than the film's stifled prose lifted from Schnitzler. In his final paragraphs Hemingway reminisces, 'I wished I had died before I ever loved anyone but her'.[55] In the final scene of *Eyes Wide Shut*, it is only Alice who says, 'but I do love you'. Bill does not profess his love, he only asks for a return to the status quo.

Eyes Wide Shut's legacy

The cinematic legacy of *Eyes Wide Shut* is largely problematic. In the late 1970s, Kubrick had considered developing *Traumnovelle* into a story about a porn film actress who wants to be a good wife, with such adult performers as Linda Lovelace and Marilyn Chambers in the role of wife. An explicit videotape of the wife performing was suggested as a replacement for the dream metaphor.[56] Thankfully, Kubrick did not go down this path but, considering the film's wider input into the cultural conversation, we may have still been left with a similar legacy. The masked ball orgy scene and its images of semi-naked women wearing only masks, heels and skimpy underwear has become a cultural shorthand for decadent VIP orgies, swingers, sex clubs and pornography, which have consciously copied the film's aesthetic.[57] *Eyes Wide Shut* has been referenced in relation to Jeffrey Epstein's sex crimes against underage girls and young women. Kubrick's depiction of a wealthy, clandestine sex club has been interpreted as an uncannily prescient warning.[58] When considering the #MeToo movement and the silencing of women by powerful men like Epstein we are also reminded of the plight of Mandy and the ways that the system enables the rich, like Victor Ziegler, to circumvent justice.[59] In the film, part of Bill wanted to do the right thing: he knew women were being exploited and abused, but ultimately he put himself first and kept quiet. Bill's journey, alone and confused, alienated by women's sexuality, also depicts the male frustrations that have warped into the real-life, angry, misogynistic, self-styled 'Involuntarily Celibate', or INCEL community whose hatred of women has resulted in terrible and violent crimes.[60] These themes, explored in the film, make it relevant to the urgent and necessary conversations about culture, sex and society we are beginning to have.

Conclusion

Ultimately, *Eyes Wide Shut* does not explore female sexuality in any depth and rather presents it from an entirely male perspective. Film scholars Robert P. Kolker and Nathan Abrams note that Bill 'is present in almost every shot and, other than brief montages of Alice at home alone or with Helena and her early flirtation with Szavost, what we see throughout the film is what Bill sees and experiences'.[61] Abrams also comments elsewhere that '[t]he women in Kubrick's films are limited to the roles of mothers, children, or whores with minimal subjectivity'[62] but he points out that in *Eyes Wide Shut* it is 'Alice, who drives the narrative, and is unafraid to speak her desires, but who is simultaneously sexualized and compared to a prostitute'.[63] She is still, unfortunately, stuck within Kubrick's simplified female stereotypes. The director may have explored female voices through the work of Karen Horney and Simone de Beauvoir. He may also have considered the relationships of Sartre and de Beauvoir, Hemingway and Richardson, and Penelope and Odysseus. There were great opportunities to reimagine the original text; perhaps to have employed Sartre's shifting of perspectives, de Beauvoir's feminist treatise or even Hemingway's empathy. However, it is the male perspective of Freud, Schnitzler, Klimt and Schiele that we see in this film. Female sexuality eluded Kubrick, at least on screen, but he did *try* to understand and to present a distinctly female perspective. However, as we stated at the outset, ultimately the source material draws the viewer back to the subjective male point of view and its reductive, neurotic fear of female sexuality and expression. Perhaps we can see this analysis as a starting point from which we can assess and discuss *Eyes Wide Shut*, its legacy, its themes and the continued need for female perspectives on these subjects in cinema and in society.

Notes

1 Catriona McAvoy and Karen A. Ritzenhoff, 'Machines, Mirrors, Martyrs and Money: Prostitutes and Promiscuity in Steve McQueen's *Shame* and Stanley Kubrick's *Eyes Wide Shut*', in Catriona McAvoy and Karen A. Ritzenhoff (eds), *Selling Sex on Screen* (Lanham, MD: Rowman and Littlefield, 2015), pp. 153–171.
2 Examples include: Michel Chion, *Eyes Wide Shut* (London: BFI, 2002); Rodney Hill, '*Eyes Wide Shut*', in Alison Castle (ed.), *The Stanley Kubrick Archives* (Cologne: Taschen, 2005), pp. 482–492.
3 Examples include: Robert P. Kolker and Nathan Abrams, *Eyes Wide Shut: Stanley Kubrick and the Making of His Final Film* (New York: Oxford University Press, 2019); Eva B. Revesz, 'Sex, Gender, and the Male Gaze in Arthur Schnitzler's *Traumnovelle* and Stanley Kubrick's *Eyes Wide Shut*', *German Studies Review* 44.2, 2021, pp. 313–333; Dijana Metlić, 'Kubrick's and Klimt's *Femmes Fatales*: *Eyes Wide Shut* and the Crisis of Masculine Identity', in Karen A. Ritzenhoff, Dijana Metlić and Jeremi Szaniawski (eds), *Gender, Power and Identity in the Films of Stanley Kubrick* (London: Routledge, 2023).
4 *One Thousand and One Nights* is a collection of Middle Eastern folk tales compiled in Arabic between the eighth and fourteenth centuries. It was first published in English *c.* 1706–1721 as *The Arabian Nights Entertainment.* Over the years it has been translated in many different versions and has often been known as *The Arabian Nights.*
5 Arthur Schnitzler, *Dream Story* [1926] (London: Penguin Books, 1999), p. 3.
6 Frederic Raphael, to Stanley Kubrick, 23 June 1995, F. Raphael – Drafts, SK/17/1/6, Stanley Kubrick Archive (hereafter, 'SKA').
7 Rudyard Kipling, *Just So Stories* [1902] (London: Wordsworth Classics, 1993), p. 50.

8 Stanley Kubrick and Frederic Raphael, 'Bound Draft', 20 August 1996, SK/17/1/8, SKA.
9 Tim Kreider, 'Introducing Sociology', *Film Quarterly* 53.3, 1999, pp. 41–48.
10 Patrick Webster, *Love and Death in Kubrick: A Critical Study of the Films from Lolita through Eyes Wide Shut* (Jefferson, NC: McFarland, 2014), p. 144.
11 Pam Cook, 'Why Does Nicole Kidman Undress in the Opening Shot of *Eyes Wide Shut*?', 23 March 2012, https://fashionintofilm.wordpress.com/tag/nicole-kidman/. Accessed February 2022.
12 Frederic Raphael to Stanley Kubrick, 12 January 1995, SK/17/1/3, SKA.
13 Frederic Raphael, 'First Draft Screenplay by Frederic Raphael Title – Woman Unknown', 1995, SK/17/1/1, SKA.
14 Webster, *Love and Death in Kubrick*, p. 143.
15 Ovid, *The Art of Love* [2BCE to 2CE] (New York: Vintage Random House, 2012).
16 Examples include Dr Robert Glover, *No More Mr Nice Guy* (New York: Running Press Adult, 2003); Neil Strauss, *The Game* (New York: Harper Collins, 2005); Mystery and Chris Odom, *The Mystery Method* (London: St Martin's Press, 2007). PUA training sessions are offered all over the world; examples can be found on sites such as https://www.bestpuatraining.com/. Accessed February 2022.
17 The original quote reads 'the one charm of marriage is that it makes a life of deception absolutely necessary for both parties': Oscar Wilde, *The Picture of Dorian Gray* [1891] (London: Penguin Classics, 2003), p. 8.
18 Annotated photocopies of the work *Histoire de Ma Vie [Story of My Life]* by Giacomo Casanova, SK/14/2/3/3; 'Shipping Inventory', 1965, SK/11/9/77, SKA.
19 Frederic Raphael, 'Raphael Second Draft', 1 of 3, fax, 17 April 1995, SK/17/1/5, SKA.
20 Contrary to other male leading characters in Kubrick's *oeuvre*, Bill does not respond to female taunting and the expression of sexual desire with violence. In *A Clockwork Orange* (1971), Alex (Malcolm McDowell) clubs to death the Catlady (Miriam Karlin) and thereby seemingly punishes her for her open display of pornographic pop art on her walls. In contrast, interrupted by a phone call from a patient, Bill uses this as a pretext to flee the scene of his wife's revelations.
21 Raphael, 'Raphael Second Draft'; Schnitzler, *Dream Story*, p. 69.
22 Chris Baker, 'Concept Artwork: Alice's Dream', 1996, SK/17/2/10, SKA.
23 Stanley Kubrick, uncatalogued material, SKA.
24 Schnitzler, *Dream Story*, pp. 62–68.
25 Richard Scholes and Lucy Martin, 'Archived Desires: *Eyes Wide Shut*', in Tatjana Ljujić, Peter Krämer and Richard Daniels (eds), *Stanley Kubrick: New Perspectives* (London: Black Dog Publishing, 2015), p. 353.
26 Raphael, 'Second Draft 1 of 3'.

27 Stanley Kubrick to Frederic Raphael, 5 June 1995, uncatalogued material, SKA.
28 Frederic Raphael, 'Second draft 1 of 3', fax, 8 June 1995, SK/17/1/5, SKA.
29 Frederic Raphael, 'Second draft 1 of 3', fax, 14 June 1995, SK/17/1/5, SKA.
30 Kubrick and Raphael, 'Bound Draft'.
31 Alice tells him she 'found the mask on the floor in his study'. Kubrick and Raphael, 'Bound Draft'.
32 'Art Department Props and Location Research', SK/17/2/7, SKA.
33 Frederic Raphael, fax to Stanley Kubrick, 9 May 1995, SK/17/1/5, SKA.
34 Metlić, 'Kubrick's and Klimt's *Femmes Fatales*'.
35 Kolker and Abrams, *Eyes Wide Shut*, p. 41.
36 Karen Horney, *The Neurotic Personality of our Time* [1937] (New York: W.W. Norton, 1964), p. 216. A copy can be found in Kubrick's Research books, SK/17/2/5, SKA.
37 Homer, *The Odyssey* [8th century BCE] (London: Penguin Classics, 2003).
38 Jean-Paul Sartre, *The Wall (Intimacy) and Other Stories,* [1948] (New York: New Directions Publishing, 1975); 'Shipping Inventory'.
39 'Shipping Inventory'.
40 Simone De Beauvoir, *The Second Sex*. Trans. Constance Borde and Sheila Malovany-Chevallier [1949] (New York: Vintage, 2011), pp. 765–766.
41 Marie Kolkenbrock, *Stereotypes and Destiny in Arthur Schnitzler's Prose: Five Psycho-Sociological Readings* (New York: Bloomsbury Academic, 2018).
42 Revesz, 'Sex, Gender, and the Male Gaze', pp. 313–333.
43 Schnitzler, *Dream Story*, p. 80.
44 Schnitzler, *Dream Story*, p. 86.
45 Schnitzler, *Dream Story*, p. 75.
46 Schnitzler, *Dream Story*, p. 82.
47 Schnitzler, *Dream Story*, p. 83.
48 Schnitzler, *Dream Story*, p. 76.
49 Schnitzler, *Dream Story*, p. 98.
50 Fridolin recounts his fantasies relating to a young girl 'no more than fifteen', about whom he had also fantasized during the same holiday that Albertine refers to. Schnitzler, *Dream Story*, pp. 7–8.
51 Frederic Raphael, *Traumnovelle* Draft – William Morris. P.138. SK/17/1/2, SKA.
52 Frederic Raphael to Stanley Kubrick, 27 June 1995, SK/17/1/6, SKA.
53 Frederic Raphael to Stanley Kubrick, 23 June 1995, SK/17/1/6, SKA.
54 Raphael to Kubrick, 23 June 1995 and 27 June 1995.
55 Ernest Hemingway, A *Moveable Feast* [1936] (London; Arrow Books, 1995), p. 126.
56 Kubrick, 'Handwritten Notes', uncatalogued material, SKA.

57 Mike Sagar, 'The Founder of Hollywood's Most Elite Sex Club is Unhappy', *Esquire*, 17 October 2017, https://www.esquire.com/lifestyle/sex/a49636/snctm-sex-club-founder/. Accessed February 2022.
58 Will Pavia, '"Jeffrey Epstein party with Prince Andrew was like *Eyes Wide Shut*", Katie Couric says', *The Times*, 2 October 2021, https://www.thetimes.co.uk/article/jeffrey-epstein-party-with-prince-andrew-was-like-eyes-wide-shut-katie-couric-says-hxz5qdqm9. Accessed 11 April 2023.
59 Alex N. Press, 'Sexual Harassment is Everybody's Problem', in Verso Books (ed.), *Where Freedom Starts: Sex Power Violence #MeToo* (New York: Verso Books, 2018), p. 141.
60 Jia Tolentino, 'The Rage of the INCELS', *The New Yorker*, 15 May 2018, https://www.newyorker.com/culture/cultural-comment/the-rage-of-the-incels. Accessed February 2022.
61 Kolker and Abrams, *Eyes Wide Shut*, p. 175.
62 Nathan Abrams, 'Kubrick's Jewesses: Onscreen and Offscreen', *Shofar: An Interdisciplinary Journal of Jewish Studies* 39.3 (Winter), 2021, p. 210.
63 Abrams, 'Kubrick's Jewesses', p. 235.

5

What about the Daughters? Parenthood in *Eyes Wide Shut*

Joy McEntee

Anecdotal reports suggest that Stanley Kubrick loved his daughters Katharina, Anya and Vivian, yet *Eyes Wide Shut*'s (1999) diegetic 'daughters' are presented ambivalently, particularly in relation to their fathers. There is Marion (Marie Richardson), the engaged daughter who kisses Bill in the presence of her father's corpse. Then, shockingly, there is the unnamed daughter (Leelee Sobieski), who is alternately chastised and prostituted by her father, Milich (Rade Sherbedgia). Ambiguity even hangs over Bill's (Tom Cruise) and Alice's (Nicole Kidman) parenthood of Helena (Madison Eginton). She is apparently loved and cosseted, but Alice confesses to fantasizing about abandoning her permanently. Robert P. Kolker and Nathan Abrams assert that Helena foregrounds Bill's status as a father by bookending the movie and appearing in the middle,[1] but Michel Chion, by contrast, says that we 'forget that Bill is himself a father'.[2] Daughters' relationships with fathers, then, are problematic. Abrams writes how Kubrick's cinematic dealings with children 'foreground fatherhood and absent fathers',[3] and childhood yields two themes: 'the sacrifice of children, and their precocious sexualization or brutalization'.[4] In his view,

> [f]rom the mid-1950s onwards, … the interrelated themes of children abandoned by their fathers, an innocent child confronted by an adult world of danger, an alienated child lost in an adult world, and childhood abuse/separation were at the core of Kubrick's work … In short, Kubrick typically represented children as sacrificed in pursuit of the needs and desires of their figurative filmic fathers.[5]

This chapter will explore father/daughter relationships in *Eyes Wide Shut* in terms of key economies of childhood and patriarchal parenthood, to unpack the meaning in Kubrick's ambivalent and contradictory representations of daughters, which were simultaneously nostalgic and disturbing. It demonstrates the film's uneasy equivalencies between daughters and sex workers, who are at opposite ends of the spectrum between innocence and experience.

Positioned in 1999, these children arose from an era when writers like Anne Higonnet and Neil Postman were presaging the end of innocence and the disappearance of childhood, respectively.[6] Both authors discussed the rise of the 'knowing' child, the child acquainted with adult knowledge. These prognostications about the end of innocence notwithstanding, Hugh Cunningham asserted that, as late as 2006, adults were 'still hooked on the main tenets of the romantic view of the child ... that children have a right to a childhood, and that means a time in life when we are protected and dependent and happy'.[7] Helena, clearly, is protected, dependent and happily oblivious to her parents' troubles. Milich's daughter presents a less edifying picture.

Daughters in *Eyes Wide Shut* and the 'little white girl'

In *The Child in Film,* Karen Lury discusses a figure she refers to as the 'little white girl', citing figures like Lilian Gish as Lucy in *Broken Blossoms* (D.W. Griffith, 1919), Jodie Foster in *Bugsy Malone* (Alan Parker, 1976) and *Taxi Driver* (Martin Scorsese, 1976), and Shirley Temple in multiple roles.[8] Where Gish's role illustrates the dangers of the adult male world for girl children, Jodie Foster's characters raise the spectre of the child who may prefer exposure to the world of adult knowledge.[9] Shirley Temple is an ambivalent figure: her cuteness is weaponized and exploited in ways that do not, now, appear as innocent as they once may have done. Helena and Milich's daughter are both among Lury's 'little white girls' but are contrasted. Where Helena remains cute, innocent and paternally protectable from the adult world of danger, Milich's daughter is sexually experienced and 'dirty'. Where Helena is the virgin girl studying to be her mother, Milich's daughter is motherless, sexualized and exploited.

Helena and Milich's daughter also belong to different economies. Helena belongs to an economy Viviana Zelizer describes as emerging at the end of the nineteenth century and the beginning of the twentieth: she is the economically 'worthless' but sentimentally 'priceless' and 'sacrilized' child; the child who should not be put to economically useful work, but who should be preserved for education and family life.[10] Milich's daughter, on the other hand, is exposed to another economy which Gayle Rubin described as the patriarchal 'traffic in women'.[11] In Rubin's analysis, girls and women are tokens in economies of gift exchange that bind men to one another. Women are not the agents in the economy of sexual traffic.[12] Certainly, Milich's father offers his daughter in exchange to other men. According to Rubin, the traffic in women depends on the incest taboo to ensure exogamy.[13]

Eyes Wide Shut can be productively read in terms of this incest taboo, especially in connection with the contrast between Victor Ziegler (Sydney Pollack) – a character who does not exist in *Traumnovelle/Dream Story* – and Bill. Bill initially acquiesces to the older man's cavalier treatment of Mandy (Julienne Davis), which is, as Ari Ofengenden observes, 'part of the "use and discard" character … of patriarchal capitalism'.[14] Abrams labels Ziegler a 'dark father',[15] although, as he says, we do not know whether Ziegler has biological children. He is not a literal father but a metaphorical one who exists to instruct Bill in the ways of male power, as Chion states in discussing his analysis of Ziegler's paternalism towards Bill.[16] Despite Bill's early eagerness to conform to Ziegler's expectations, as the drama evolves Bill finds himself prohibited – or inhibited – from sleeping with the array of women he encounters during his wanderings. He demonstrates that he is unable to predate women in the same way as Ziegler. This may be more by luck than good management, but to read Bill's failure to exploit women more charitably, two inhibitions stymie him. One is the incest taboo. As a father himself, he sees a potential daughter in each woman he encounters. Where Ziegler is willing to sleep with figurative daughters, Bill is not. Bill's other inhibition is the one against paedophilia. He refuses to take advantage of girls (Ziegler calls Mandy 'kiddo', emphasizing her youth). This means he is caught in a patriarchal double-bind. Where he starts the drama eager to please Ziegler, he ends up being expelled from the world of male privilege Ziegler represents because he fails to play the patriarchal game involving the sexual exploitation of women. So, Bill is contrasted with Ziegler and, as a father, with Milich, who also conducts himself according to the patriarchal economy of the traffic in women. In *Eyes Wide Shut* Bill flirts dangerously with Ziegler's toxic brand of masculinity. As Abrams says, Bill's 'odyssey takes him into the heart of his manliness and masculinity'.[17] He emerges on the side of '*menschilkayt*',[18] or virtuous masculinity. Bill is tested as a man and a father, and ends up, if not a spectacularly good father, then certainly not a bad one: he proves himself a good enough father. Bill represents a final reworking of the father figure, a softening, a retreat from the 'the roll call of bad father figures' that populate Kubrick's work.[19] This, I suggest, has autobiographical connections with Kubrick's relationships with his own daughters, who had grown up by the time he was making *Eyes Wide Shut* in the years approaching 1999.

Kubrick and parenthood

In a 1968 *Playboy* interview, Kubrick commented on the nature of fatherhood:

> You may stand outside your wife's hospital room during childbirth muttering, 'My God, what a responsibility! Is it right to take on this terrible obligation? What am I really doing here?'; and then you go in and look down at the face of your child and – zap! – that ancient programing takes over and your response is one of wonder and joy and pride. It's a classic case of genetically imprinted social patterns … Perhaps man has been too 'liberated' by science and evolutionary social trends … If he is going to stay sane … he must have someone to care about, something that is more important than himself.[20]

However, it is questionable whether Kubrick respected other fathers' obligations. As Abrams says, 'ironically, given the demands of Kubrick's perfectionism, one wonders how much time he and his staff spent with their own children'.[21] Certainly, Emilio D'Alessandro recalls spending more time with Kubrick's children than Kubrick did, and more time with Kubrick's daughters than his own children.[22] Also, the documentary *Filmworker* (Tony Zierra, 2017) suggests that Leon Vitali sacrificed time with his children to his career with Kubrick. In *Full Metal Jacket Diary*, Matthew Modine recalls the bitter struggle he had with Kubrick over getting time off filming to attend the birth of his first child in 1985:

> *Kubrick:* Why do you want to go, anyway?
> *Modine:* To help Cari.
> *Kubrick:* Help her? She's having the baby. Not you. You're not a doctor. You'll be in the way … There is nothing you can do for Cari. And the baby? Doesn't need you for a long time. The first year, the baby doesn't even want to have anything to do with you.[23]

This is in marked contrast to what he said earlier about his own paternity. Kubrick, then, may not have respected paternal attachment in other fathers. And what is not accounted for in his description of being smitten by fatherhood during the birth process is the perspective of the mother. And as in his interview, so in his cinema. As Mick Broderick remarks, 'Kubrick's cinema rarely questions "what does a woman want"'.[24] That said, he does periodically and passingly question what a mother may want. For example, in *Lolita* (1962) Charlotte Haze (Shelley Winters) plans to sends Lolita (Sue Lyon) off to Camp Climax and ultimately to banish her to boarding school. In *Barry Lyndon* (1975), Kubrick attends to Lady Lyndon's (Marissa Berenson) grief for Bryan (David Morley). In *Eyes Wide Shut,* Kubrick returns to that question with greater focus. What does Alice want? As a wife? As a mother? Alice is problematic, as she is susceptible to being drawn away from parenthood. Elsa Colombani has written about the growth in self-assertion in Kubrick's cinematic women as they evolve from *Barry Lyndon*, through *The Shining* to *Eyes Wide Shut*.[25] She describes the 'slow rise of women' through Kubrick's work. Lady Lyndon is silent and long-suffering. Ultimately, she triumphs, but that triumph is equivocally framed, as she signs Barry's cheque under the surveillance of Bullingdon. She does not escape patriarchal control. Wendy (Shelley Duvall) asserts herself as a protective mother in *The Shining,* swinging a baseball bat at Jack Torrance (Jack Nicholson) – albeit without a great deal of assurance – and locking him in a larder. The culmination of this movement from passivity to self-assertion is Alice, who stands up to Bill – psychologically – in a way no other Kubrick heroine does, throwing his complacency back in his teeth. But Alice's self-assertion as a wife has a disturbing concomitant: her willingness to walk away from being a mother. Towards the end of Kubrick's career, it appeared he feared that it was women, and mothers, who might become 'too liberated'.

However, it is not as if Alice's relationship with Helena is fully developed in the film. The narrative of *Eyes Wide Shut* is intercut with shots of Alice interacting with and caring for Helena but, as Abrams points out, Helena 'is never explored in her own right. She is merely a cipher for Bill's status as a father and what his wife, Alice, is willing to give up in pursuit of a fantasy with a naval officer she didn't even know'.[26] So what is Helena for? In Catherine Driscoll's account of girlhood, the daughter is the 'necessary foundation' for the heterosexual family.[27] Helena then, is warrant for Bill and Alice's heteronormativity and for their paternity and maternity. But what is her function in *Eyes Wide Shut* for the extra-diegetic spectator? In *Childhood and Cinema*, Vicky Lebeau asks 'what does cinema *want* of the child?'[28] Lury opines 'the child figure is frequently over-determined by the priorities of interested adults – of the director, of the writer, of the other adult actors and the adult audience'.[29]

One of the things that Kubrick's film does not want is Helena's perspective. This is not a film that imagines Helena's point of view, nor is her perspective on her parents' dilemmas sought. She is not one of the child witnesses of adult behaviour that Neil Sinyard describes in *Children in the Movies*,[30] still less the witness to adult sexual infidelity of Kubrick's unrealized project *The Burning Secret*.[31] As in Lebeau's discussion of Carol Reed's *The Fallen Idol* (1948), sex, jealousy and death fall beyond Helena's ken.[32] And it is with sex, jealousy and death that *Eyes Wide Shut* is largely preoccupied, so Helena, because she remains a touchstone of childhood innocence for the audience throughout the drama, is largely outside its main orbit.

If Helena is a touchstone for the audience, she is not for Bill and Alice, who are more concerned with exploring the state of their marriage than with parenthood over the period of a few days depicted by the film. As Kolker and Abrams observe, 'the couple's mundane daily routine', in which 'Kubrick crosscuts between Bill at his doctor's office and Alice at home with Helena', showing details of her domestic interaction with her daughter, serve only as 'a transitional unit', the 'calm before the impending storm that is to befall Bill and the Harfords' marriage'.[33] Caring for Helena is not an end in itself: it is 'dull' detail to be escaped by both parents.[34] Alice escapes into fantasy; Bill into the hunt for the spectacle offered by the ironic password 'fidelio'.

These interludes also provide opportunities for what Lury calls the 'good touch' by which parents care for children, as opposed to the 'bad touch' by which children are abused.[35] However, Alice does very little touching of Helena. She brushes Helena's hair, but apart from that the body that is curated is Alice's, not Helena's. We see Alice dress herself and apply deodorant. Perhaps these scenes denote Helena's witnessing how to become a woman; they seem primarily to offer further opportunities to explore the juxtaposition, set up in the film's opening frames, between sublime and abject spectacles of Nicole Kidman's body. Indeed, we see more evidence of 'good touching' in Bill's handling of his patients' bodies than in Alice's interaction with Helena.

Bill is drawn away from Alice (and Helena) by his night-time adventures in a world of sexy but death-laden women (Marion, Domino, Mandy) and secretive men (Nick Nightingale [Todd Field], Ziegler and Red Cloak [Leon Vitali/Russell Trigg]). At the Somerton orgy, Bill is in more danger than he knows, and more than the spectator of Kubrick's final film might suspect. Richard Rambuss reports that Kubrick's production notes speculate about Bill's being subjected to 'buggery',[36] and as Kolker and Abrams report, Alice's dream about cuckolding him is 'a far cry from the visions of torture that appear in the novel and in early versions of the screenplay and are reflected to some extent in Fangorn's preproduction sketches'.[37] Something more than undressing and expulsion were threatened, but Bill is mercifully spared thanks to the invention of the unnamed woman. Possibly this merciful release results in his unwise resilience the next day when he sets out to investigate the Somerton mystery.

Bill retraces his night-time journey, encountering things subtly altered, changed and doubled. One of the things he finds changed is the relationship between Milich and his daughter. On Bill's first visit to the Rainbow Costume Shop, Milich catches his daughter sexually entertaining two older, Japanese, cross-dressed men (Togo Igawa and Eiji Kusuhara). Milich immediately chastises her brutally, yelling at her and sending her to her room. Bill is taken aback by this violence. Milich locks his daughter's seducers in the back room, threatening them with the police. The daughter, meanwhile, whispers seductively in Bill's ear, Lolita-like, which he seems to find as disturbing as her father's conduct. She clings to him, touching him – 'bad' or suggestive touching. As Lury observes 'children constantly touch things they shouldn't and poke fingers into places they ought not to go. Their "little hands" get everywhere. The exuberant tactility of children provokes adult tenderness, irritation, excitement, anxiety and fear.'[38]

Lury discusses sexualized girl children in Kubrick's *Lolita*, as well as two other films that I assert form a cinematic background to *Eyes Wide Shut: Broken Blossoms* and *Taxi Driver*. The Rainbow Costume Shop menage recalls the situation in *Broken Blossoms* where the white brute father (Donald Crisp) disrupts the sexualized encounter between the little white girl Lucy and the 'yellow man' Cheng Huan (Richard Barthelemess).[39] On Bill's second visit to the costume shop, however, Milich appears to have arrived at a mutually convenient arrangement with the Japanese gentlemen, and even offers his daughter to Bill: he is pandering her. Again, Bill is not sure how to react. The situation would appear to call on him to behave like Travis Bickle (Robert de Niro) in *Taxi Driver,* who 'rescues' Iris (Jodie Foster) from Scout (played by Harvey Keitel, who was originally to play Ziegler in *Eyes Wide Shut*). I extend Lury's discussion of the connections between Lucy, Iris and Lolita to Milich's daughter. *Broken Blossoms*, *Taxi Driver*, *Lolita* and *Eyes Wide Shut* imagine parallel situations, but have different outcomes for the male protagonists. Cheng Huan fails to save Lucy but at least exacts revenge for her death on Battling Burrows. Travis Bickle succeeds in sending a reluctant Iris home to her parents, despite evidence that this is the last thing she would wish. Humbert Humbert (James Mason) loses Lolita to Quilty (Peter Sellers) and ultimately to humdrum matrimony.

Bill may be concerned for Milich's daughter, but he conspicuously fails to rescue her. He is ineffectual. He fails to challenge Milich's bad fatherhood. And in the process, to apply Lury's argument to *Eyes Wide Shut*, Bill's 'white masculinity' is 'queered' or 'threatened', here by the intertextual 'confusion of illicit desires – of incest, miscegenation and paedophilia' represented by Milich's daughter and her cinematic antecedents.[40] If Helena is the warrant for Bill's heteronormativity, Milich's daughter complicates and destabilizes it. And Bill also fails to enter into the exchange Milich offers: he fails to play his part in the patriarchal traffic in women. He flirts with danger, but emerges, equivocally, on the side of virtuous masculinity.

So, Bill's heteronormative masculinity is implicated in the scene with Milich's daughter. The extra-diegetic audience are also implicated. As Lebeau might ask '[w]hat do cinematic spectators want of her?'

> Adults *want* something from the image of the child, something that can break through in their acts of watching – filming, photographing – children. But to understand that wanting in terms of a resolutely adult sexuality that can be denied in the child is … one of the effects, and limitations, of the discourses of childhood innocence and, in other modern legal and social rhetoric, child protection. What, after all, is sex for a child?[41]

This is a question Kubrick asks in *Eyes Wide Shut* and *Lolita*. Milich's daughter and Lolita are not without sexual agency.[42] However, both raise the question of the age of consent, the age at which children can properly become sexually knowing, as well as presenting problematic relationships between daughters and fathers. As Lawrence Ratna says of *Lolita*, 'considering that Kubrick was an overprotective parent to his daughters, his reconstruction of a child molester as a sympathetic figure reflects his predilection for the dark side of human nature'[43] – to say nothing of the dark side of fatherhood, as Humbert is Lolita's stepfather. However, Gilles Menegaldo sounds a note of caution, pointing out that Lolita's final plight is one of exploitation and victimization.[44] As Ritzenhoff says, one cannot gloss over the facts that 'incest, criminal sex with a minor, and rape are the focal point of [*Lolita*]'.[45] If Kubrick goes some way to imagining what sex might be for this child in Milich's daughter's shocking forwardness, the discourses of childhood innocence cannot be denied. She is exploited after all, as is registered by Bill's outrage when he finds Milich has come to an arrangement with the Japanese gentlemen and is prepared to extend the same bargain to him.

In *Eyes Wide Shut*, as in *Traumnovelle/Dream Story* and Nabokov's *Lolita*,[46] the extreme youth of the seductive daughter is insisted upon. She is precociously sexualized.[47] The relationships between Milich's daughter, Milich and the various 'funny uncles' he would recruit for her recall relationships between Lolita, her stepfather Humbert and her fake uncle Quilty. The suggestions of paedophilia and incest that hang over *Lolita* also hang over *Eyes Wide Shut*. If all the women Bill encounters in his night-time adventure are versions of Alice, Milich's daughter is one of them. Kolker and Abrams draw attention to the parallels between Bill's situation and that of Humbert, calling Quilty a 'proto-Ziegler' and pointing to *Lolita*'s road trip as a 'larger-scale foreshadowing of Bill Harford's solo walk through the streets of Greenwich Village'.[48] But Bill, unlike Humbert, cannot realize his sexual ambitions. Unlike Ziegler, he cannot sleep with random women, including much younger women. He is prohibited – by chance or internal inhibition – from sleeping with any of the daughters or sex workers he encounters. Here I note an interesting omission in Kubrick and Raphael's adaptation of *Traumnovelle/Dream Story*: the young girl Fridolin encounters on the beach; his rejoinder to Albertine's confession about Denmark.[49] Kubrick and Raphael also raise the age of the waifish and girl-like sex worker Mizzi,[50] with Vinessa Shaw playing Domino as being in her mid-twenties. These changes sanitize Bill's conduct to an extent. While children like Milich's daughter may offer themselves to him, Bill, unlike Fridolin, is not tempted by paedophilia. He even forestalls the approaches of the young, but clearly not pre-pubescent, Nuala (Stewart Thorndike) and Gayle (Louise J. Taylor) at Ziegler's party. After her confession, Bill may seek revenge on Alice, but he finds nothing but inhibition. As McAvoy and Ritzenhoff say, *Eyes Wide Shut* 'may appear to be about male sexuality', but is 'perhaps more about male vulnerability and the fear of female sexual power'.[51] As Kolker and Abrams say, 'the ascent of the feminine' seems to be one of the abiding fears in *Eyes Wide Shut*, even though that ascent is 'still – in the person of Ziegler – under the rule of the patriarch'.[52]

Daughters and sacrifice

McAvoy and Ritzenhoff observe that money, sex and prostitution connect almost all the women in the film, including Alice the kept wife, as well as Domino and Mandy, who is dismissed as a 'hooker' by Ziegler.[53] But a specific connection between prostitution and the film's daughters comes together in the figure of Milich's daughter. This connection has been suggested earlier, by Bill's transition from being kissed by Marion over her father's corpse to being kissed by the ill-fated Domino. Daughters, sex workers and sacrifice are connected: Marion has sacrificed herself to her father; Milich is sacrificing his daughter 'for money and advancement',[54] and finally the unnamed woman at the Somerton orgy – unnamed, like Milich's daughter – will sacrifice herself for Bill. The unnamed woman is a martyr, as Ritzenhoff and McAvoy say, who pays the ultimate price for a man's sins.[55] Confused with Mandy by Bill and Ziegler,[56] this woman perhaps represents the Baroness D. who commits suicide in Schnitzler's *Traumnovelle/Dream Story*.[57] As Abrams points out, Kubrick had discovered that Schnitzler's daughter Lilli killed herself on the day of his own birth, so the unnamed woman/Mandy too represents a daughter.[58] To complete this circuit connecting Marion to Mandy there is Bill's visit to the morgue. He hovers over Mandy's body and seems ready to plant an inverted kiss on those dead lips, a necrophiliac gesture, before he takes himself in hand. This brings us back to Marion's passionate embrace over her father's corpse, and it is a scene that mirrors and doubles that one. If adult and teen daughters are uncomfortably connected with prostitution and death through Bill's night-time adventures in *Eyes Wide Shut*, what is the future for Helena? Will she, too, be sacrificed? But to ask this question this way overlooks how Helena serves adult needs for innocence to counteract the corrupt world of Milich and Ziegler: Bill's diegetic need, and the extra-diegetic audience's need, for innocence to counteract the corruption of that world; for an asexual, child-like other to the sexualized women, daughters among them, whom Bill encounters. *Eyes Wide Shut* does not, in the end, challenge Helena's imagined innocence. She is not, in the end, sacrificed.

But did Mandy really sacrifice herself for Bill? McAvoy and Ritzenhoff ask

> [i]s it Bill's fantasy that this woman sacrificed herself for him or did it really happen? It is the ultimate compliment to his damaged ego, revenge, and retribution for his humiliation by Alice; he is important enough that a woman would die for him.[59]

Mandy's death certainly doesn't seem to dent Bill's self-involvement: he is not dissuaded from pursuing the Somerton mystery until Ziegler explicitly threatens him and sends him home. He is perhaps being punished for having lost his moorings and become 'too liberated' from his role as a husband and father, but it is failing to find purchase in a masculine sphere rather than finding his child 'more important than himself' that drives him home.[60] Kolker and Abrams write that 'Bill goes straight to his daughter's room after returning home, emphasizing his paternity and the bond he shares with her ... Only then does he walk into the bedroom to hear Alice murmuring in her sleep.'[61] What I would point out here is that Helena is unconscious and unaware of Bill's attentions, and that ultimately he has returned to Alice rather than to his daughter. What is endangered in the aftermath of Bill's intrusion in Somerton is not his status as a father, but as a husband: the menacing mask appears on Alice's pillow, not Helena's. Bill does not have to make a choice about sacrificing Helena: it is Alice he stands to lose.

Alice and motherhood

After Bill wakes Alice and confesses, weeping,[62] we see the aftermath: Alice's sullen face, showing the first signs of ageing. There follows the family's reconstitution for Helena's sake in the final toy store scene. Kolker and Abrams say the toy store gives us a scene of innocence to counter the corrupt and cynical world of Ziegler.[63] Helena is also innocent of her parents' troubles, throwing herself into the retail environment with glee. Running among the shelves, she admires an oversized, apparently very expensive teddy bear and other toys aimed at her age and gender: a Barbie doll in an enormous pink tutu and a doll's pram. Helena is revealed in this setting in her role as Bill and Alice's 'lonely status symbol and parental toy',[64] one among their other empty possessions. The contrast between Helena's enthusiasm and Alice's indifference to the toys Helena identifies itself highlights the limits of the joys of consumerism and possession, foregrounded by the commercialization of Christmas, which is here a ritual evacuated of meaning.

In this scene Helena represents Zelizer's 'economically "worthless" but emotionally "priceless" child' who is sentimentalized and also 'very expensive'.[65] As Zelizer outlines, this child emerged between the 1870s and the 1930s as children were moved out of exploitative work environments and into education, and as they became a badge of their parents' consuming power. However, when Zelizer was writing in 1985, children were moving back in the direction of 'usefulness' – the 'useful' child contributes in kind or in cash to the household.[66] Kubrick, then, would appear to be appealing to a rather nostalgic idea about what the idealized daughter can be in his 1999 figuration of Helena. She is relieved of the adult burden of being 'useful', in contrast to Milich's daughter who is used in an economy of exchange that benefits her father. Helena remains 'useless' but 'sacred', purely indulged in sheer consumerism.[67]

But here, as elsewhere in the film, Helena's activities quickly become irrelevant as we focus on the conversation between Bill and Alice. The tracking shot that has traced the progress of the family group through the store settles down into a shot/reverse shot focusing on Bill's and Alice's faces. Their dialogue is ambiguous: perhaps nothing has changed, or perhaps there is reconciliation. Somewhat fancifully, Chion projects beyond the film's closure to the birth of another child, the result of the 'fuck' Alice demands. This implies, Abrams says 'not only a regenerated marriage but also more children in the future'.[68] It looks forward to the birth of a loved child, in other words, rather than Helena – a son rather than a daughter, according to Chion.[69] This is another way of reading the Christmas scene: as a potential nativity. Kolker and Abrams say that *Eyes Wide Shut* 'ends with resignation', but also in 'an unsteady state of hope'.[70] However, Miriam Jordan and Julian Jason Haladyn say that Alice's rejection of the pram Helena favours signals her disinterest in becoming a mother again.[71] Specifically, Alice declares the pram 'old-fashioned', inviting speculation that she finds the business of motherhood itself tedious and old-hat. While *Eyes Wide Shut* may explore marital infidelity from a typically Kubrickian, androcentric point of view – that of Bill – it does at least go some way to exploring what a mother may want, or not want. She does not want Bill's 'forever'.

The Shining

The Shining bears comparison with *Eyes Wide Shut* as Kubrick's '*other* family film'.[72] Bill's 'forever', which frightens Alice, echoes Jack Torrance's 'forever and ever', which is, of course, the invitation to madness in *The Shining*. And if *Eyes Wide Shut* ends in family reconciliation rather than fracture, that linguistic echo illustrates how much *Eyes Wide Shut* has in common with its dark double. *Eyes Wide Shut,* Rambuss says, 'can be taken in part as a restorative rewriting of [*The Shining's*] horror show'.[73] The fate of children is key to this conversion: 'note that the traumatized young boy who sees things in *The Shining* has been exchanged in *Eyes*

Wide Shut ... for a standard-issue adorable little girl, who remains mercifully oblivious throughout to the travails of her parents'.[74] And the gender of these children is also important. As William Paul and Tony Magistrale observe, it is the deadly Oedipal tension between fathers and sons that *The Shining* dramatizes.[75] Father/daughter relationships do not fare better, however. Danny (Danny Lloyd) is not the only child in *The Shining*. As Abrams points out, 'the murdered twin Grady sisters [Lisa Burns and Louise Burns], central to the film's imagery but not the novel, reinforce [the] theme of child as victim'.[76] In Kubrick's *The Shining*, as in *Eyes Wide Shut*, daughters are represented in unsettling ways. This is the film in the Kubrick canon that most directly thematizes the sacrifice of children and their brutalization – first that of the Grady girls and then that of Danny.

Some critics have detected a vein of incestuous abuse in the father–son relationship in *The Shining*, which bears examination in the light of *Lolita* and the Milich/Milich's daughter narrative of *Eyes Wide Shut*. Specifically, there is the infamous cover story of the *Playgirl* Jack reads while waiting for Ullman: 'Incest: why parents sleep with their children'.[77] This is certainly suggested by the creepy cuddle scene in the apartment, in which Jack draws Danny onto his lap and talks about staying in the hotel 'forever and ever'. Milich has the look of *The Shining*'s bad father about him, 'an aging and disheveled version of Jack Torrance, complete with lank graying hair, a balding pate, and a threadbare checked dressing gown'.[78] Milich and Jack also both resembled Kubrick himself, suggesting all kinds of disturbing paternal doublings.[79] Bill Harford's tidiness contrasts with the slovenly disorder of Milich and Jack. Where they are sloppy, he is a relative model of propriety in every way.

The Shining contrasts with *Eyes Wide Shut* in another way. Jack achieves what Bill can only dream of (although perhaps this is something that scares Bill too much for him to realize it): Jack ends up liberating himself from the obligations of family and fatherhood, and escapes 'into an ecstatic bachelor space'[80] represented by the photo that appears at the end of the film. Since the caption reads July 4th, 1921, this is evidently Jack's independence day. Jack has apparently been incorporated into the permanent past tense of the ball in the Overlook's Gold Room. The *mise-en-scène* of the Gold Room bears comparison with Ziegler's Christmas party, and the occasion of the Overlook ball bears comparison with the Somerton orgy, in the exclusivity of its guests: only those who are invited by the mysterious call of the hotel are allowed in. In *The Shining*, Kubrick permanently 'liberates' the father from paternal responsibility, but he simultaneously problematizes the idea of liberation. Jack would appear to be the result of becoming 'too liberated'. It is quite apparent that fatherhood has not kept Jack 'sane'. In *Eyes Wide Shut*, by contrast, Bill is only temporarily liberated, only temporarily goes a little mad, and returns chastened.

It matters how Jack frees himself from paternity. *The Shining*'s conclusion is one of Kubrick's most important emendations of Stephen King's novel.[81] In the final chase scene, when Jack is hunting Danny down to kill him, Kubrick's Jack shuffles after his son without check. However, King's Jack relents briefly, remembering that he loves Danny, and allows him to escape. Where Kubrick releases the spectre of the murderous father who would brutally sacrifice his son to advancement in the hotel's hierarchy (as represented by Grady [Philip Stone]), King recoils sentimentally from damaging paternal trust. Kubrick has no such inhibitions.

In Kubrick's film, Wendy and Danny do escape the Overlook, as much because of Danny's ingenuity in defeating the monster in the maze as because of Wendy's attempts at asserting herself as a protective mother. However, we are not necessarily reassured by their fate. Wendy's heroism is equivocal and,[82] as Abrams says, Danny, like Lolita and unlike Helena, 'prematurely loses his childhood'.[83] While Wendy may be a more assertive mother than Lady Lyndon, she is not yet Alice Harford. However, even then, Alice does not assert herself *on behalf* of Helena, but on her own behalf, and potentially at the risk of sacrificing Helena. Is Alice, then, 'too liberated' relative to Wendy Torrance?

Conclusion

Eyes Wide Shut was Kubrick's last realized project. Bill Harford was his last diegetic father; Alice his last mother; Helena his last daughter. What are we to make of these characters as final statements about the status of daughters and parents? As Abrams points out, children in Kubrick's films tend to be sacrificed by their fathers, but while Helena may be marginalized by Bill and Alice, she is not sacrificed. That said, it is a near thing. The modern mother may fantasize about abandoning her child. This fear is mercifully not realized in *Eyes Wide Shut*. However, if one projects beyond Kubrick's realized projects, the sacrifice is realized in Monica's (Frances O'Connor) abandonment of David (Haley Joel Osment) in Steven Spielberg's *A.I. Artificial Intelligence* (2001). Given Kubrick's career-long pattern of confronting children with adult worlds of corruption and danger, perhaps his abstaining from exposing Helena to sordid adult realities was an index of a final mellowing. Or perhaps not, if one again considers *A.I.*, which exposes David to the perils of the Flesh Fair. While the innocence of small girls like Helena was to be preserved, small boys like Danny and David, it appears, remained vulnerable to exposure to the dangerous world. But if Kubrick lets Helena off the hook in *Eyes Wide Shut*, she is the one lucky daughter in a film full of less fortunate ones. Marion is rendered pitiful and Milich's daughter is frankly offered in trade. What is at stake in these representations of daughters is Bill's place in patriarchal structures. Ironically, his being a father to Helena inhibits him from making his way in the patriarchal power structures represented by Ziegler and Milich. He fails to engage in the exploitative economy in which women and girls are trafficked. Perhaps Helena, for all that she is marginal to his everyday existence, does give Bill something to care about that is more important than fitting in with other men. If one contrasts Bill with Milich, Humbert, Jack and Grady, he is not, in the end, one of Kubrick's bad fathers. While he may not be a conspicuously good father, Bill is at least a good enough father.

Anya said of Stanley,

> [h]e wasn't a remarkable father. He was a remarkable filmmaker. He was a very nice, good, rather Jewish father – probably over-protective but no more so than many. He would always be there for us and he was fantastic in a crisis. He could be impatient with you if he thought you weren't dealing with things properly, but if you fell, he was there.[84]

Unremarkable as his paternal skills may have been, Kubrick doted on his daughters. Jon Ronson reports on a 2010 interview with Christiane Kubrick, in which she says that 'when Stanley was alive, he kept her and their daughters cosseted from stress, from life's legal and financial arrangements, allowing them to float through Childwickbury without worries'.[85] Kubrick kept his daughters close to him, as Katharina remarked: 'he could easily have sent us off to boarding school, but instead we had tutors and goodness knows who else travelling with us. We had an incredibly interesting childhood and he was interested in almost every aspect of our lives.'[86] Kubrick was reluctant to let his daughters have their independence as adults,[87] although Katharina has said he probably wasn't strict enough with her as a teen.[88] He also kept his daughters close by involving them in his films, including *Barry Lyndon*, *The Shining*, *Full Metal Jacket* (1987) and *Eyes Wide Shut*, in which Katharina appears, for example, as the mother of one of Bill Harford's (Tom Cruise) patients (with her son Alex).[89]

Kubrick cultivated Vivian's interest in filmmaking in particular. She directed the *Making of the Shining* and scored *Full Metal Jacket*, as well as shooting behind-the-scenes footage of that film for another planned documentary. She also appears in *Barry Lyndon*, and famously as 'Squirt' in *2001: A Space Odyssey* (1968), via a video link with her indifferent, detached and affectless diegetic father Floyd (William Sylvester). Vivian was ever a vivid personality, or even a volatile child according to Emilio D'Alessandro.[90] The rift between Vivian and Kubrick began during the filming of *Eyes Wide Shut*, which she was to score.[91] As Christiane Kubrick says:

> [Vivian and Stanley] had a huge fight. He was very unhappy. He wrote her a 40-page letter trying to win her back. He begged her endlessly to come home from California. I'm glad he didn't live to see what happened [the death of Anya and Vivian's conversion to Scientology. Elegiacally, Christiane recalls] We had fights. But [Vivian] was hugely loved. And now I've lost her … I've lost hope. So. She's gone.[92]

Eyes Wide Shut, then, was created against the background of the loss of Vivian: Kubrick's loss of a dearly beloved daughter. Helena may have been a way of sentimentally cathecting that loss. Helena helps redeem Bill at the end of *Eyes Wide Shut.* She also may have helped Kubrick imagine his own redemption as a father. As Jane O'Connor says, '[w]e see our children grow up and away from their vulnerable, young selves and there is a tendency to sentimentalise and idealise childhoods past and lost'.[93] Helena, who appears in the final scene of Kubrick's final realized film about children, suggests a certain nostalgic desire to return to a time of childhood innocence, if only for his own sake as a father.

Notes

1 Robert P. Kolker and Nathan Abrams, *Eyes Wide Shut: Stanley Kubrick and the Making of His Final Film* (New York: Oxford University Press, 2019), p. 156.
2 Michel Chion, *Eyes Wide Shut*, trans. Trista Selous (London: BFI/ Palgrave MacMillan, 2002), p. 56.
3 Nathan Abrams, 'Kubrick and Childhood', in Nathan Abrams and I.Q. Hunter (eds), *The Bloomsbury Companion to Stanley Kubrick* (London: Bloomsbury Academic, 2021), p. 282.
4 Abrams, 'Kubrick and Childhood', p. 290.
5 Abrams, 'Kubrick and Childhood', p. 281.

6 Anne Higonnet, *Pictures of Innocence: The History and Crisis of Ideal Childhood* (London: Thames and Hudson, 1998); Anne Higonnet, 'Picturing Childhood in the Modern West', in Paula S. Fass (ed.), *The Routledge History of Childhood in the Western World* (Abingdon and New York: Routledge 2013), pp. 296–312; Neil Postman, *The Disappearance of Childhood* (New York: Vintage, 1994 [1982]).
7 Hugh Cunningham, *The Invention of Childhood* (London: Random House, 2006).
8 Karen Lury, *The Child in Film: Tears, Fears and Fairy Tales* (London and New York: I.B. Tauris, 2010).
9 Lury, *The Child in Film.*
10 Viviana A. Zelizer, *Pricing the Priceless Child: The Change Social Value of Children* (Princeton, NJ: Princeton University Press, 1994 [1985]), pp. 3, 11.
11 Gayle Rubin, 'The Traffic in Women: Notes on the "Political Economy" of Sex', in Rayna R. Reiter (ed.), *Toward an Anthropology of Women* (London and New York: Monthly Review Press, 1975), pp. 157–210.
12 Rubin, 'The Traffic in Women', pp. 175, 177.
13 Rubin, 'The Traffic in Women', pp. 171–176.
14 Ari Ofengenden, 'Agency, Desire, and Power in Schnitzler's *Dream Novel* and Kubrick's Adaptation *Eyes Wide Shut*', *CLCWeb: Comparative Literature and Culture* 17.2, 2015, p. 5.
15 Nathan Abrams, *Stanley Kubrick: New York Jewish Intellectual* (New Brunswick, Camden and Newark, NJ and London: Rutgers University Press, 2018), p. 257. See also p. 262.
16 Chion, *Eyes Wide Shut*, pp. 76–78.
17 Abrams, *Stanley Kubrick: New York Jewish Intellectual*, p. 261.
18 Abrams, *Stanley Kubrick: New York Jewish Intellectual,* p. 261.
19 Richard Rambuss, *Kubrick's Men* (New York: Fordham University Press, 2021), p. 162.
20 Stanley Kubrick, '*Playboy* Interview: Stanley Kubrick', in Gene D. Phillips (ed.), *Stanley Kubrick: Interviews* (Jackson, MS: University Press of Mississippi, 2001), p. 67.
21 Abrams, 'Kubrick and Childhood', p. 286.
22 Emilio D'Alessandro with Filippo Ulivieri, *Stanley Kubrick and Me: Thirty Years at His Side*, trans. Simon Marsh (New York: Arcade Publishing, 2012), p. 70.
23 Matthew Modine, *Full Metal Jacket Diary* (New York: Beacon Audiobooks, 2014 [2005]).
24 Mick Broderick, 'Kubrick, Gender and Sexuality', in Nathan Abrams and I.Q. Hunter (eds), *The Bloomsbury Companion to Stanley Kubrick* (New York and London: Bloomsbury, 2021), p. 263.
25 Elsa Colombani, 'Through a Glass Darkly: The Slow Rise of Women in *Barry Lyndon, The Shining* and *Eyes Wide Shut*', in Elsa Colombani (ed.), *A Critical Companion to Stanley Kubrick*, (Lanham, MD: Lexington Books, 2020), pp. 179–192.

26 Abrams, 'Kubrick and Childhood', p. 288.
27 Catherine Driscoll, *Girls: Feminine Adolescence in Popular Culture and Cultural Theory* (New York: Columbia University Press, 2002), p. 93.
28 Vicky Lebeau, *Childhood and Cinema* (London: Reaktion Books, 2008), p. 9.
29 Lury, *The Child in Film*.
30 Neil Sinyard, 'The Children are Watching Us', in his *Children in the Movies* (London: B.T. Batsford, 1992), pp. 97–116.
31 Stefan Zweig, *Burning Secret*, trans. Anthea Bell (London: Pushkin Press, 2011).
32 Lebeau, *Childhood and Cinema*, p. 26.
33 Kolker and Abrams, *Eyes Wide Shut*, p. 161.
34 Kolker and Abrams, *Eyes Wide Shut*, p. 161.
35 Lury, *The Child in Film*.
36 Rambuss, *Kubrick's Men*, pp. 158–159.
37 Kolker and Abrams, *Eyes Wide Shut*, p. 176.
38 Lury, *The Child in Film*.
39 Lury, *The Child in Film*.
40 Lury, *The Child in Film*.
41 Lebeau, *Childhood and Cinema*, p. 75.
42 Karen A. Ritzenhoff, 'Kubrick and Feminism', in Abrams and Hunter (eds), *The Bloomsbury Companion to Stanley Kubrick*, pp. 251–252. Similarly, Rambuss, Ritzenhoff and Abrams also associate Milich's daughter with Lolita: Rambuss, *Kubrick's Men*, p. 154; Ritzenhoff, 'Kubrick and Feminism', pp. 259–260; Abrams, 'Kubrick and Childhood', p. 409.
43 Lawrence Ratna, 'Kubrick and Madness', in Abrams and Hunter (eds), *The Bloomsbury Companion to Stanley Kubrick*, p. 265.
44 Gilles Menegaldo, 'Adapting *Lolita:* Hybridizing and Subverting Genre Conventions', in Colombani (ed.), *A Critical Companion to Stanley Kubrick*, p. 75.
45 Ritzenhoff, 'Kubrick and Feminism', p. 252.
46 Vladimir Nabokov, *Lolita* (London: Penguin, 2015 [1958]).
47 Abrams, 'Kubrick and Childhood', p. 290.
48 Kolker and Abrams, *Eyes Wide Shut,* p. 7.
49 Arthur Schnitzler, *Dream Story* (London: Penguin, 1999), pp. 18–19.
50 Schnitzler, *Dream Story,* pp. 29–32.
51 Catriona McAvoy and Karen A. Ritzenhoff, 'Machines, Mirrors, Martyrs and Money: Prostitutes and Promiscuity in Steve McQueen's *Shame* and Stanley Kubrick's *Eyes Wide Shut*', in Karen A. Ritzenhoff and Catriona McAvoy (eds), *Selling Sex on Screen: From Weimar Cinema to Zombie Porn* (Lanham, MD, New York and London: Rowman and Littlefield, 2015), p. 154.
52 Kolker and Abrams, *Eyes Wide Shut,* p. 185
53 McAvoy and Ritzenhoff, 'Machines', p. 164.

54 Abrams, 'Kubrick and Childhood', p. 289.
55 McAvoy and Ritzenhoff, 'Machines', p. 154
56 This isn't helped by Kubrick replacing one actress with another and then having her voiced by a third.
57 Schnitzler, *Dream Story*, pp. 74–75.
58 Abrams, *Stanley Kubrick: New York Jewish Intellectual*, p. 240.
59 McAvoy and Ritzenhoff, 'Machines', p. 162.
60 Joy McEntee, 'Kubrick, Marriage and Family', in Abrams and Hunter (eds), *The Bloomsbury Companion to Stanley Kubrick*, p. 199.
61 Kolker and Abrams, *Eyes Wide Shut*, p. 176.
62 *Eyes Wide Shut* is, as Rambuss points out, another one of Kubrick's male melodramas or male 'weepies': Rambuss, *Kubrick's Men*, p. 160.
63 Kolker and Abrams, *Eyes Wide Shut*, p. 181.
64 Abrams, 'Kubrick and Childhood', p. 288.
65 Zelizer, *Pricing the Priceless Child*, p. 3.
66 Zelizer, *Pricing the Priceless Child*, pp. 208–228.
67 Conspiracy theorists postulate that Helena is abducted while her parents are distracted at the end of *Eyes Wide Shut*. They base this idea on the presence of two extras in the toy store scene whom Kubrick had reused from Ziegler's party. This idea was connected to theories about Hillary Clinton running a child sex-trafficking ring. However, the presence of the extras is more likely to be a sign of directorial parsimony than anything sinister, so the contrast between Milich's daughter as trafficked child and Helena as sacred child stands. See Kolker and Abrams, *Eyes Wide Shut*, pp. 143–144.
68 Abrams, 'Kubrick and Childhood', p. 288
69 Chion, *Eyes Wide Shut*, p. 17.
70 Kolker and Abrams, *Eyes Wide Shut*, pp. 9, 10.
71 Miriam Jordan and Julian Jason Haladyn, 'Carnivalesque and Grotesque Bodies in *Eyes Wide Shut*', in Gary D. Rhodes (ed.), *Stanley Kubrick: Essays on His Films and Legacy* (Jefferson, NC: McFarland, 2008), p. 194.
72 Rambuss, *Kubrick's Men*, p. 164; my emphasis.
73 Rambuss, *Kubrick's Men*, pp. 162–163.
74 Rambuss, *Kubrick's Men*, p. 164.
75 William Paul, *Laughing Screaming: Modern Hollywood Horror and Comedy* (New York and Chichester: Columbia University Press, 1994), pp. 342, 344; Tony Magistrale, 'Paternal Archetypes: *The Shining*, *Pet Sematary*, *Apt Pupil*', in Tony Magistrale (ed.), *Hollywood's Stephen King* (Basingstoke: Palgrave Macmillan, 2003), p. 100.
76 Abrams, 'Kubrick and Childhood', p. 287.
77 Rambuss, *Kubrick's Men*, p. 166.
78 Kolker and Abrams, *Eyes Wide Shut*, p. 170.
79 Abrams, *Stanley Kubrick: New York Jewish Intellectual*, p. 244.
80 Joy McEntee, 'Paternal Responsibility and Bad Conscience in Adaptations of *The Shining*', *Journal of Adaptation in Film and Performance* 9.2, 2016, p. 178.

81 Stephen King, *The Shining* (London: Hodder and Stoughton, 1977).
82 McEntee, 'Kubrick, Marriage and Family', pp. 195–196.
83 Abrams, 'Kubrick and Childhood', p. 288.
84 Nick James, 'At Home with the Kubricks: "Stanley Was Amazingly Tolerant in Taking the Most Extraordinary Abuse"', *Sight and Sound*, 27 November 2019, https://www2.bfi.org.uk/news-opinion/sight-sound-magazine/interviews/stanley-kubrick-family-christiane-anya-katharina-man-mythology. Accessed 18 October 2021.
85 Jon Ronson, 'After Stanley Kubrick', *The Guardian*, 19 August 2010, https://www.theguardian.com/film/2010/aug/18/stanley-kubrick-christiane. Accessed 18 October 2021.
86 James, 'At Home with the Kubricks'.
87 D'Alessandro, *Stanley Kubrick and Me*, p. 150.
88 James, 'At Home with the Kubricks'.
89 Abrams, 'Kubrick and Childhood', p. 286.
90 D'Alessandro, *Stanley Kubrick and Me*, p. 70.
91 Ronson, 'After Stanley Kubrick'.
92 Ronson, 'After Stanley Kubrick'.
93 Jane O'Connor, 'Childhood and Celebrity: Mapping the Terrain', in Jane O'Connor and John Mercer (eds), *Childhood and Celebrity* (London and New York: Routledge, 2017), p. 13.

6

'Lucky to Be Alive': Clockwork Models and the Logic of the Inanimate in Stanley Kubrick's *Eyes Wide Shut*

Ohad Landesman

Stanley Kubrick's *Eyes Wide Shut* (1999), adapted from Arthur Schnitzler's phantasmagoric *Traumnovelle* (1926), chronicles a few days in the life of a perfectly wealthy, healthy and beautiful high-society couple, Alice and Bill Harford (played respectively by Nicole Kidman and Tom Cruise). Transposed from Schnitzler's early-twentieth-century Vienna to *fin-de-siècle* New York City, Kubrick's nocturnal 'after hours' experience takes place in the aftermath of a Christmas party, during which a husband's inability to contain an excessive obsession and sexual jealousy places a seemingly ideal marriage on the verge of collapse. *Eyes Wide Shut*, I will argue in this chapter, is a film saturated with statuesque and death-like performances, thus oscillating between stillness and movement to depict a critical account of a modernized civilization losing its moral values by the end of the twentieth century. High society's empty manners, socially constructed behaviours and treatment of sex as a mechanized and passionless ritual that becomes a consumerist commodity, are all aestheticized in the film, I will show, through a continuous effort to *inanimate the animate*. Thus, *Eyes Wide Shut* emphasizes corpse-like and defunct human behaviours, and exhibits emotionally devoid facial expressions that invite further exploration of the analogy between humans and inanimate machinery in Kubrick's films.

Kubrick always tells a similar story, about an individual being victimized and mechanized by modernity, a fable about the efforts of mankind to contain and overcome irrational and instinctual human desires. The blurry boundaries he draws between the normal (human) and abnormal (machine) often call into question the idea of being liberally recognized as human in a modernized world. Consequently, the end of the millennium in his last film is similarly evoked in apocalyptic and dystopian terms, as a moment when individuals lose their souls and become shadowy ghosts victimized by a mechanizing society.

Kubrick's multiverse: from humanized machines to lifeless humans

In a compelling analysis of the narrative structure in Kubrick's *Dr. Strangelove* (1964),[1] William G. Simon turns to the theory of warfare outlined by Manuel DeLanda in *War in the Age of Intelligent Machines*.[2] DeLanda's work focuses on new computerized weapons and surveillance technology in the aftermath of the first Gulf War, marking a historic shift in the relation of human beings to machines and information. It describes an advanced paradigm that integrates human and machine components into a 'coherent "level" machine'.[3] As a cutting-edge creation of human rationalism in the age of robotic intelligence, the weaponry model outlined is a supposedly perfect system in which the accumulation of elements becomes more than the sum of its parts while the use of human instrumentality is slashed to the bare minimum. This framework provides Simon with a useful explanation for how a nuclear military machine designed to work flawlessly in *Dr. Strangelove* begins to malfunction shortly after activation. By theorizing how each component within the apparatus has restricted knowledge of the activities of the others, making the machine intrinsically self-destructive and unreliable, Simon shows that 'the very premise of the machinic paradigm as applied to warfare is demonstrated to be fallacious'.[4]

DeLanda's descriptive schema, I argue, can be extended beyond *Dr. Strangelove* and applied to other Kubrick films. Ultimately, the Kubrickian project is enmeshed in a tragic contradiction of the perfect functionality of machine-like qualities by the inevitable, though quite unexpected, fatal human mistake. This is an unavoidable collapse based on contingency and it is presupposed by the indeterministic nature of progress as a whole: when one component of an otherwise perfect system breaks down, the entire machine falls apart. The failure of one constituent part, often a human factor that goes 'astray', attests to the flawed structure of the apparatus in its entirety, and to its inability to remain stable and predictable, despite the efforts to make it so. Therefore, what is so captivating in Kubrick's films is how they all explore the nature of mankind and its irrationally violent dispositions. Human beings, Kubrick shows us again and again, are perpetually animated by the death instinct, thus making any effort to mechanize or automate their behaviour entirely futile. Accordingly, the psychotic violence of Alex in *A Clockwork Orange* (1971) cannot be contained and alleviated; the perfectly constructed space-travel machine HAL 9000 in *2001: A Space Odyssey* (1968) is still capable of making fatal mistakes; and the Marine Corps's disciplined and torturous training in *Full Metal Jacket* (1987) can only animate the animalistic instincts in its human subjects.

In 'Clockwork Violence', Kenneth Moskowitz compares *2001*, *A Clockwork Orange* and *Barry Lyndon* (1975), and argues that all three films constitute a coherent, imaginative vision that supersedes their *prima facie* diversity of setting, characters and ideas. What is striking, he argues, is that 'all of these movies contrast a disordered human energy, which is violence, with social forces that build a structural organization upon this slippery foundation and seek to deny, disguise or repress the violence by formalizing or rationalizing it in some way'.[5] By focusing on society's attempts to contain the violent act and its failure to comprehend the importance of the instinctual and the unconscious, Kubrick is looking to undermine and problematize any attempt to mechanize the human. Can the irrational and destructive human instinct be contained and restrained by the façade of social manners in the enlightened period of *Barry Lyndon*? How absurd are the consequences of mentally conditioning an irrational violent criminal in *A Clockwork Orange*? In addition, is it not ironic that even though man can build spaceships and travel to the moon, such progress is still nullified time and again by violence in *2001*?

With the imaginary apparatus of space and time travel in *2001*, Kubrick returns to his interest in creating devices that mimic and enhance human intelligence, as he had previously explored in *Dr. Strangelove*. HAL 9000, a seemingly indispensable machine that self-consciously takes pride in its inability to make mistakes, becomes the only entity in the spaceship with genuine, visible emotions. Ironically, the fatal error that HAL 9000 makes (and that leads to his disconnection) occurs because of his humanness, and stems from a psychological malfunction that he experiences. HAL 9000 suffers a nervous breakdown of sorts, and so becomes arguably more human than the impassive astronauts on the spaceship. Similarly, both HAL 9000 (the humanized machine) and Clockwork Alex (the mechanized human) are polar opposite examples of failure, typical of a Kubrickian world characterized by human hubris and emotional blindness.

Kubrick's last film *Eyes Wide Shut* can be seen in this larger, 'machinic' context as well. Bill, struck by his wife's confession of an old sexual fantasy that was never put into action, leaves the domestic safety and marital cosiness behind for a night of surreal sexual adventures. From that point on, the film oscillates between reality and dream, life and death, and depicts a critical picture of the nuclear family. Kubrick continues to explore the conflictual and turbulent sphere of the family, as he previously had in *Lolita* (1962) and *The Shining* (1980), here functioning as a system that is incapable of containing and restraining the libido and jealousy of one individual, trapped within the social rituals of modernized civilization by the end of the twentieth century.[6]

Characters in Kubrick's films often act in a mechanized and non-human manner. Faulty explanations that critics usually provide for this focus on bad directing skills, failure to work with actors, or even just sheer misanthropy. As Kent Jones notes, many critics have found all kinds of reasons to dislike Kubrick by equating his private profile with misanthropy, linking it to 'the tone of monumental remove in his last six films'. But is the remove really his, or is he merely dramatizing the remove he feels between people and the beyond? 'People are alone in very different ways in movies,' observes Jones, 'but they are scarily alone in Kubrick, bouncing around an echo chamber of uncertainty.'[7] Tom Cruise, according to this line of criticism, delivers an expressionless performance in *Eyes Wide Shut*; Kidman's character exists for merely exhibitionistic reasons; and the film, surprisingly and unexpectedly, is just not erotic enough.[8]

What these accounts fail to address, though, is not merely the intentionally grotesque and alienating quality that any typical Kubrickian performance usually offers, but also the inseparable synthesis between theme and aesthetics towards which these performances strive. Kubrick's films, and particularly *Eyes Wide Shut*, I argue, explore the destructive effects of modern culture on individuals in their various guises, thus inviting a certain statuesque or death-like performance. In a world where individuals lose their identity and become lifeless ghosts victimized by the norms and rules of behaviour of modern society, an insentient appearance becomes the appropriate form of representation. Take, for example, Bill's stoic expression in the four reverse-shot close-ups, showing him listening to Alice's confession about the naval officer. Those, as James Naremore notes, are 'underrated reactions' that expose Bill mostly from the outside without ever revealing what is really going on in his head, thus contributing to 'the feeling that Bill is being carried away impassively, rather like someone in a dream'.[9] Once Alice's story is interrupted by a phone call, and Bill goes out into the night for adventure, his facial expression remains static and frozen even in the taxi. It reveals nothing of his inner self to us and is therefore supplemented by a mental image of Alice's sexual fantasy.[10] Such a unique filmic strategy, unprecedented in Kubrick's *oeuvre*, attests to how Bill suddenly becomes alienated from his wife and illustrates how she becomes abruptly unfamiliar to him.

Social critique in *Eyes Wide Shut* is continuously embedded with surface-like appearances, lifeless characters with stoic expressions, inanimate human beings. Kubrick, of course, is also known for attributing human qualities to non-human objects, thereby achieving the opposite effect, *animating the inanimate*. In *2001* spaceships waltz together to the sounds of Strauss and HAL 9000 takes on certain mannerisms that are characteristic of individuals, while in *The Shining* the Overlook Hotel becomes a living organism with nerves and blood vessels. Michel Ciment observes that 'puppets, robots, dolls and statues [in Kubrick's films] connote a world in which man has become no more than a docile machine, a toy in the society of empty forms, a servile being in the universe of semblances', and he highlights, as examples, the quasi-mechanical gestures of both Lloyd the barman and Grady the caretaker in *The Shining*.[11] Respectively, I argue, further exploration of Kubrick's powerful evocation of a supernatural world could better explain the essence of representing the macabre and the (almost) living dead in his films, and particularly in *Eyes Wide Shut*.

Unlike *The Shining*, in which supernatural elements are hermetically contained within the logic of a fantasy, there is never quite a clear distinction between reality and fantasy in *Eyes Wide Shut*. It opens with a decadent, high-society, New York soirée that rhymes quite suggestively with Jack's creepy *déjà vu* of a classy 1920s ball in *The Shining*. While the latter is *literally* a ghost show, it is the similar décor and frame composition, the statuesque photographic quality, and the ironic remark made by Bill about not knowing a 'soul' in the party, that become suggestive of how the contemporary bourgeoisie at Ziegler's party are also participating in a phantom-like theatre of death.[12] Following Steven Spielberg's observation that 'some of his [Kubrick's] movies are like stylized theatre – as ritualized as kabuki', it is interesting how Kubrick wishes to stage here, right from the outset, the metaphorical space of a bourgeois society that is already dying.[13]

'Life goes on. It always does, until it doesn't': death, sex and the uncanny

A little later in the party, when two beautiful women approach Bill and offer to take him 'where the rainbow ends', he is suddenly instructed to go meet Victor Ziegler (Sydney Pollack) upstairs. To his surprise, he finds Victor in the bathroom with a prostitute named Mandy lying naked on the couch, unconscious after a drug overdose. Mandy's body, not unlike the bodies of the other women in the film, is immaculately shaped and appears like a mannequin. She is reduced in this scene to nothing but a sex object that has somehow stopped functioning.[14] Bill, who is constantly being 'looked at' by women trying to captivate him sexually and seduce him during his nocturnal journey, uses his own, active, male gaze here to revitalize a completely passive female object. As Mandy returns his gaze, she gradually becomes reanimated and is brought back to life. *Eyes Wide Shut*, we soon realize, is a film that meditates on what it means to look at something or someone, and asks a question that is central to both its characters and viewers: what is it really that we see when we are watching?[15] It is, as Lehmann observes, a film about 'the meaning and implications of "the act of seeing" in the psychological reality of the human being'.[16]

Coinciding with Bill's paranoid explanation for the events he experiences during the night, the film offers us a narrative proposition that supposedly solves the mystery: Mandy (the woman in Ziegler's bathroom), the nameless statuesque woman offering to 'redeem' Bill during the orgy and Amanda Curran, the beauty queen who is found dead in a hotel room, are all in fact the same woman. It is unclear whether this is true or not (the film remains vague on this point),[17] but all three appear lifeless or dehumanized, and two of them lack sight. When Mandy opens her eyes for the first time, we see only two black holes instead of eyes; the woman who offers to redeem Bill in the party is wearing a mask; and Amanda Curran, lying dead in the morgue, has her eyes wide open but without the ability to see any more (perhaps suggesting a possible meaning for the film's title).[18] When Bill pays a visit to the morgue to check on the body of Amanda Curran, we find him gazing sexually again at a flawless, passive body, this time even leaning down to almost kiss her. This could only be a gesture of gratitude to the woman who saved his life during the orgy trial, but it also rhymes with the slow-paced body language with which Bill reaches out to kiss the prostitute Domino shortly before his phone rings. Ironically, the latter would be as close as Bill would ever get to having sex that night.

In his seminal book *The Uncanny*, Sigmund Freud forms the ambivalent idea of something latent and repressed coming back to life, the familiarly 'homey' (*Heimlich*) joining together with the weirdly unfamiliar (*unheimlich*). He writes: 'for this uncanny is in reality nothing new or foreign, but something familiar and old-established in the mind that has been estranged only by the process of repression.'[19] The uncanny is very much present in *Eyes Wide Shut* and defines its main narrative structure. After listening to his wife's sexual confession, Bill begins an uncanny adventure into the night. While his wife remains both homey and strangely unfamiliar to him after revealing her fantasy, the events that unfold retain this ambivalence as well giving Bill the unchaining experience of a *déjà vu*, a journey that is both unearthly, peculiar and vaguely familiar. The dreamlike voyage becomes in many ways a response to an unconscious wish, a repressed sexual fantasy, and weirdly rhymes with earlier events that Bill experienced (the prostitute and her reappearance in the party, the masked ball and its resemblance to Ziegler's soirée, and meeting the devilish pianist Nick again).[20] In fact, the same experience of *déjà vu* would further characterize Bill's process of 'running errands' the day after returning to the Somerton location to receive the warning letter, revisiting Milich's shop to return the costume, and coming back to Domino's apartment to hear from her friend that she had been infected with HIV.

Kubrick has always been fond of mirror-structured narratives that create an uncanny feeling. Everything that Jack Torrance sees or dreams about in *The Shining* produces for him a sensation of *déjà vu*, a vague recollection that he had been the caretaker of the Overlook Hotel in the past ('you have always been the caretaker', he is told by Grady, presumably the ghost of the previous caretaker). Another example would be the second half of *A Clockwork Orange*, in which the 'rehabilitated' Alex meets his vengeful victims again, only to be victimized by them as a punishment. Freud's theory of the uncanny, written during the nineteenth century in an age of enlightenment, not only criticizes religious ideas but also challenges a conception of reality based solely on material and rational means with its emphasis on the double. Kubrick was so fascinated by this essay that it actually served as the basis for the screenwriting process he adopted, along with Diane Johnson, for *The Shining*.[21] The essay, I believe, provides the theoretical backdrop for Kubrick's social critique of seemingly perfect apparatuses and his emphasis on the shortcomings of rationalism and modernity.

Like Freud, Kubrick does not situate the uncanny exclusively within the realm of the supernatural, but rather oscillates between the fantastic, the imaginary and concrete reality. Michel Ciment, while analysing *The Shining* and *2001* (with explanations taken from Tsvetan Todorov), suggests that in both films the spectator, when confronted with a supernatural event, lacks the rational reasoning needed to make sense of her experience.[22] The fantastic, he explains, can only originate from a background of strongly defined 'realism', where 'the framework of reality must be scrupulously respected'. Such an aesthetic tradition, embraced by authors 'from Hoffmann to Gogol, from Balzac to Maupassant', treats the fantastic in a realistic or even naturalistic manner.[23] In *Eyes Wide Shut*, Kubrick consistently aligns with this literary tradition and with the development of science, to portray ghosts (or implied apparitions) more tangibly, never privileging non-realistic depictions of the fantastic. As the uncanny in the film becomes more associated with death, corpses and ghosts, it materializes aesthetically with a corporeal quality. Kubrick makes his ghost characters appear real, refusing to bend to any convention of the fantastic in cinema (such as using a hazy background to make the figure half-invisible or framing it with an auratic glow.)

The orgy in the Somerton mansion involves unnaturally flawless women, who cannot be distinguished from each other. These women are represented as masked, empty-eyed, dehumanized figures who are sent to sexually serve the men at the party. 'The perfect nudes remain disenchanted commodities', suggests Jayamanne, 'plastic bodies molded to the desire of late twentieth-century mediatized beauty'.[24] As the party heats up, couples gather and copulate in a mechanized rhythm. The sexual act becomes aesthetically de-eroticized, shot from a typical Kubrickian, disembodied, God-like vantage point. Keeping their movements and dialogue to a minimum, the women are reduced to soulless objects, and their surreal masks, as Tim Kreider suggests, become 'harbingers of death'.[25] The fetishization of body parts in these immaculately composed human dolls is reminiscent of the brutal fight sequence at the end of *Killer's Kiss* (1955), in which dismembered limbs of female mannequins are used as weapons.

Death and sex are constantly intertwined in *Eyes Wide Shut*, from the very moment that Victor's infidelity in the bathroom almost turns to a tragic death. Shortly after Alice confesses to Bill an unfulfilled sexual fantasy she had about a complete stranger a year earlier (a potentially fatal moment in their marriage), Bill learns of the death of Lou Nathanson. As soon as he arrives at Lou's house to pay his condolences, Marion, Lou's daughter, passionately declares her love for him in the presence of her dead father. Shortly thereafter, the HIV-positive Domino almost seduces Bill to have sex with her. Lastly, Bill's involvement in the orgy, which has already put his own life at risk, ends in the killing of Amanda Curran, a prostitute attending the event. This sex/death analogy is laced with implicit criticism of contemporary society's failure to refine its decadent moral values. Nonetheless, Kubrick's exploration of the erotic as a celebration of death does not refer simply to the exploitation of women,[26] but also to what he intentionally does not wish to show us, and to his continuous reluctance to represent the sexual act.

When the new and 'healthy' Alex in *A Clockwork Orange* is shown publicly to the government members, a typically perfect 'Kubrickian' woman, seemingly taken from the orgy scene in *Eyes Wide Shut*, approaches him. Suddenly, as Alex is reaching out to her, a terrible sickness takes hold of him, a side effect of the mechanizing treatment he has been undergoing, and he becomes immobile, incapable of fulfilling his sexual desire. Since Alex, Kubrick's agent for scopophilia, has been paralysed, the spectator is consequently deprived of his erotic pleasure immediately. This coincides not only with how something always stands in Bill's way throughout the night in his desperate efforts to get laid (a phone call, a service call upstairs, or simply being busted for not having a password), but also with how eroticism is visually blocked from the viewer during the orgy scene in *Eyes Wide Shut* (in the censored version sexual acts are concealed by extra naked bodies). This is reminiscent of the bathroom scene in *The Shining*, where both Jack and the spectator are punished for their perverse voyeurism by encountering a young, naked woman transformed into a horrific corpse, a scene designed to play with our physiological responses to the erotic. Kubrick's camera is generally incapable of revealing events, so instead of allowing vision, it denies it. When the sexual turns deadly, the event becomes unrepresentable.

Film as a grave of motion: between movement and stasis in *Eyes Wide Shut*

Eyes Wide Shut creates a dialogue with other art forms, including photography and painting. Thus, death and stillness are associated in it not only with sex, but also with artificiality, repetition and simulacra. The meeting between film and painting in *Eyes Wide Shut* (not unlike *Barry Lyndon*, for that matter) intentionally slows down the narrative flow in order to create a pictorial effect and draw attention to the visuality of the image. According to Jayamanne, the Symbolist movement in painting is evident in the film through a 'self-conscious aesthetic awareness of the simulacral commodity form of the cinematic image'.[27] The film is set in a simulated setting of New York City, has a married couple playing Bill and Alice (thereby blurring the boundaries between reality and fiction) and includes an orgy scene in which 12 identical prostitute models are similarly masked to overcome any sense of identity. The Kubrickian aesthetics of repetition and simulation correspond to the process of reification, where duplicable human beings function as merely things that move, objects that are animated. In more Freudian terms, this repetition implies an unexpressed desire for death and attests to society's drive towards self-destruction (thus building on Freud's two fundamental drives, Eros[28] and Thanatos).[29]

Kubrick's focus on the static, painterly image is counterpart to his fascination with cinematic movement. In *The Shining*, suggests Brigitte Peucker, 'the static image as photograph does much to evoke the uncanny and the supernatural'; photographs in the film become 'material', and function as the imaginary, 'as a return of the repressed'. Jack and Danny, she points out, have a 'visionary' capacity that helps them animate photographs from the past (the twin sisters, the bartender or the caretaker), an ability to 'animate them [the photographs] narratively in the manner of cinema'.[30] In the final sequence of the film, when the camera zooms in on a group picture of the hotel's guests in 1921, Jack becomes a still image on the wall. 'Now himself a ghost,' Peucker writes, 'Jack has been exorcised into the space of photography.'[31] What she does not indicate about this peculiar sequence, though, is the striking incompatibility formed between the balanced camera movement in it, zooming in to centralize on a photograph of death, and the photographic stillness in the preceding shot, where a flesh-and-blood human body is depicted frozen. Kubrick is exploring here the photographic and painterly qualities of the cinematic image to represent death, the same variation of medium that will be present in his final film.

As part of an ambitious scholarly effort to re-evaluate the assumption that photographs are synonymous with death, Garrett Stewart uses literary modernism to explore cinema's fixation with photography. 'Whereas photography engraves the death it resembles,' he writes, 'cinema defers the death whose escape it simulates. The isolated photo or photogram is the still work of death; cinema is death always still at work.'[32] As the camera tracks in on a dead subject in *The Shining*'s final sequence, penetrating with superimposition and close-ups through the time–space coordinates of the photograph, it shows us, according to Stewart, how its fluid movement is only an illusion: '[o]nce again photography comes forward as the grave of motion, film (through editing as well as through the rudiments of projection) as the never better than artificial resuscitation of any such movement, any change whatever over time'.[33]

Kubrick, who had initially worked as a photographer for *Look* magazine, and carries a definitive photographic quality in his cinematic style,[34] treats the medium of film as also a 'grave of motion' in *Eyes Wide Shut*. During the orgy scene, for example, characters are lifelessly posing as frozen statues in an impeccably constructed composition. Differently decorated erotic positions and South Indian vocal music break the sequence into seemingly separable images reminiscent of pages taken from a copy of the *Kama Sutra*. Both here and in the final shot of *The Shining*, Kubrick's camera adopts a God-like point of view, perpetually gliding into or hovering above insentient characters, and delivering deadly cinematic movement to already anaesthetized images. Cinema and photography join forces as two artistically similar media that can meditate notions of mortality.

Kubrick depicts women in *Eyes Wide Shut* in a deadly and inanimate manner that inevitably evokes the analogy between women in modern society and figures of robots and automatons. In several classic works of nineteenth-century literature, women are depicted and imagined as sex workers or automatic love dolls meant to serve men.[35] While numerous films, especially within the science fiction genre, deal with the perfection of a woman's body through technology and directly address such literary origins in their diegesis, Kubrick has never voiced explicit references to these science fiction tales.[36] Nonetheless, the border between the normal (human) and the abnormal (machine) in his *Eyes Wide Shut* calls into question what is liberally recognized as human in a modernized society. Kubrick's attraction to both inanimate objects and representations of deadpan human beings reaffirms that for him it becomes dangerous to be a subject within the vital order of the simulacra.[37] One of those inanimate objects that is infused with unexplained kinetic quality is Bill's mask from the orgy. The reason for the sudden reappearance of the mask in the marital bedroom remains unclear in the film. Was it magically animated to move on its own, or did someone else place it there to scare Bill?

Capitalism dictates the power structures of prostitution and social hierarchy throughout the film. Respectively, it is very symbolic that *Eyes Wide Shut* is bookended by two references to money and exchange value. The film begins with Bill asking Alice whether she has seen his wallet and ends with a stroll through a toy shop. Coinciding with the absurd logic of sexual exploitation within the Somerton orgy palace or the artificial New York City set, the F.A.O. Schwarz toy shop becomes, as Jayamanne notes, another perfectly controlled environment of late capitalism in which all things and the relations between them are under the reign of standardized exchange of commodities as signs.[38] Thirty years after Floyd's little daughter in *2001* had asked for a bushbaby for her birthday, Helena expresses her desire for a Christmas gift; she wants a teddy bear or a Barbie doll, perhaps. As Michel Chion accurately observes, 'we will not find out whether she has received the object of her desire'.[39] 'You're gonna have to wait and see', Alice tells Helena in reply to her request, an answer that rhymes perfectly with Floyd's response to his own daughter's wish: 'a bushbaby? Well, we'll have to see about that.' The fact that human 'puppets' in the film, whether model prostitutes or even Mr Milich's daughter, an underwear-clad teenage doll, are much more available to play with than real dolls becomes terribly ironic.

Conclusion

In his discussion of Auguste Villiers de l'Isle-Adam's *Tomorrow's Eve* and E.T.A. Hoffman's 'Automata' and 'The Sandman', Tom Gunning points to the dialectical moment in these tales, when 'the technological simulacrum of life ... ultimately produces animated corpses, rather than a living human being'.[40] Modernity, he observes, deprives the industrial worker of her soul so that 'she becomes nothing but the tool of the machine and the factory system'.[41] Kubrick, I argue, always tells a similar story, of an individual being victimized and mechanized by modernity, a telling fable about the efforts of mankind to contain and overcome irrational and instinctual human desires. The voyages through which Kubrick takes us become impossible quests to locate the reasons behind irrational terrors, trips to the unconscious that leave us with more puzzling questions than absolute certainties. From the mannequins in *Killer's Kiss*, through the deranged machine-like *Dr. Strangelove*, the human-like HAL 9000 computer in *2001* and finally the clockwork models in *Eyes Wide Shut*, the threatening hybridity between technology and the organic, along with the anxiety of uncertainty it produces, become a theme not fully explored yet in Kubrick's *oeuvre*, an important topic that calls for much further research.

Notes

1 William G. Simon, '*Dr. Strangelove*, or: The Apparatus of Nuclear Warfare' in Richard Allen and Malcolm Turvey (eds), *Camera Obscura Camera Lucida: Essays in Honor of Annette Michelson* (Amsterdam: Amsterdam University Press, 2003), pp. 215–229.
2 Manuel DeLanda, *War in the Age of Intelligent Machines* (Cambridge, MA: MIT Press, 1998).
3 DeLanda, *War in the Age of Intelligent Machines*, p. 4.
4 Simon, '*Dr. Strangelove*', p. 222.
5 Kenneth Moskowitz, 'Clockwork Violence', *Sight and Sound* 46.1 (1976), p. 22.
6 'Throughout his films', observe Kolker and Abrams, 'the family is a nightmare of bad choices and violent ends, of unbearable mistakes and

deplorable decisions.' *Eyes Wide Shut*, thus, becomes 'a *summa* of Kubrick's concern with domesticity and its discontents …' See Robert P. Kolker and Nathan Abrams, *Eyes Wide Shut: Stanley Kubrick and the Making of His Final Film* (New York: Oxford University Press, 2019), pp. 8, 10.

7 Kent Jones, 'David Thomson & Cinephilia', *Film Comment* (Jan/Feb 2003), p. 36.

8 Several critics have found Kidman's performance much more convincing than Cruise's, despite her relatively short screen time. J. Hoberman, for example, sarcastically points out that 'the actress [Kidman] is not only a more assured performer than her husband, but an incomparably greater showboat, almost absurdly comfortable acting without clothes (a year spent shooting and reshooting this material must have propelled her into *The Blue Room*).' See J. Hoberman, *The Magic Hour: Film at Fin de Siècle* (Philadelphia, PA: Temple University Press, 2003), p. 69. Laleen Jayamanne even equates Kidman's ornamented performance and the way she is framed in the film with Kubrick's affinity for the Symbolist movement in painting: see Laleen Jayamanne, 'The Ornamentation of Nicole Kidman (*Eyes Wide Shut*) and Mita Vashisht (*Kasba*)', *Senses of Cinema* 23 (2002), https://www.sensesofcinema.com/2002/the-female-actor/ornament/. Accessed 18 October 2021.

9 James Naremore, *On Kubrick* (London: BFI, 2007), p. 237.

10 Lehmann brilliantly observes that the 'Blue Movie' we watch from Bill's perspective is in fact a mental image of Alice's fantasy. It creates an interesting embodiment through which we oddly watch her own desire through Bill's eyes. See Hans-Thies Lehmann, 'Film/Theatre: Masks/Identities in *Eyes Wide Shut*', *Kinematograph* 20 (2004), p. 238.

11 Michel Ciment, *Kubrick: The Definitive Edition* (New York: Faber & Faber, 2001), p. 136.

12 The masked ball during the Somerton orgy rhymes again with Ziegler's party and the Golden Room ball in *The Shining*. The naked and masked dancers grant the implied connection between sex and death a peculiarly perverse aspect.

13 Quoted in Lehmann, 'Film/Theatre: Masks/Identities', p. 236.

14 A woman Bill is treating in his clinic has the same flawless figure as Mandy's, as do the 12 prostitutes featured in the orgy sequence. This, of course, is also reminiscent of the unattainable and impeccable woman who stands above the poor mechanized Alex during his rehabilitation show in *A Clockwork Orange*.

15 When Alice asks Bill 'is my hair OK?' before they go to Ziegler's party, he immediately replies 'it's great', to which she rightly answers 'you're not even looking'. Kubrick, I argue, addresses the viewers here by giving them advance notice of how crucial it is to carefully observe every part of the *mise-en-scène* in the film.

16 Lehman, 'Film/Theatre: Masks/Identities', p. 234.

17 In fact, in the reality outside the film's diegesis, the three women are not the same person. Mandy (and Amanda Curran) are both played by Julienne Davis while the mysterious woman is played by Abigail Good. What are we to make of this extra-diegetic piece of information? Does it further blur the boundaries between fiction and reality in the film by inviting us to pay attention to physiognomic differences and become sceptical of Victor's explanation?

18 Freud discusses the uncanny in the context of E.T.A. Hoffman's 'The Sandman' and relates the idea of being robbed of one's eyes to an uncanny anxiety and the fear of going blind. Not unrelated, Freud also addresses the fear that a lifeless body might suddenly become alive and animated. See Sigmund Freud, *The Uncanny* (New York: Penguin Books, 2003).

19 Freud, *The Uncanny*, p. 394.

20 The act of tracing Freudian elements in the original story, Schnitzler's *Traumnovelle*, is further substantiated by the famous analogy often drawn between the two authors in relation to psychoanalysis. Freud famously wrote to Schnitzler in 1922 that he had always been terrified of meeting him: 'I will make a confession and ask you to keep it to yourself, in consideration for myself, and not to share it with any friend or stranger. A question disturbs me: why, in fact, during all these years, I never frequented and conversed with you …? I think I have been avoiding you for some kind of fear of meeting my double. Not that I have the tendency of easily identifying myself with another person or that I have wished to minimize the difference of talents which separate us; but, when plunging into your splendid creations I always thought I would find – behind the poetical look – the hypothesis, the interests and the results that I knew were mine.' Sigmund Freud, 'Letter 197 to Arthur Schnitzler, Vienna IX Berggasse 19.14.15. 1922', in E.L. Freud (ed.), *Letters of Sigmund Freud: 1873–1939*, trans. T. Stern and J. Stern (London: The Hogarth Press, 1961), p. 344.

21 It is well known that Kubrick asked Johnson to read the essay before writing the screenplay for the film.

22 Ciment, *Kubrick*, p. 125.

23 Ciment, *Kubrick*, p. 125.

24 Jayamanne, 'Ornamentation', p. 4.

25 Tim Kreider, '*Eyes Wide Shut*: Review', *Film Quarterly* 53.3 (2000), p. 46.

26 Considering *Eyes Wide Shut* 'Kubrick's Marxist finale', Herbert J. Gans regards the film as a Marxist analysis of the place sex serves in Western societies. In the Kubrickian world of *Eyes Wide Shut*, explains Gans, sex is freely available but only to the ruling class and only at a carefully hidden orgy in which the lower class is only a servant. The 'professional class' (to which Bill Harford belongs) is never able to actually have sex, but is nonetheless constantly busy talking or fantasizing about it. See Herbert J. Gans, 'Kubrick's Marxist Finale', *Social Policy* 30.1 (1999), p. 61.

27 Jayamanne, 'Ornamentation', p. 4.
28 Kolker and Abrams observe that when Bill talks to Milich at the entrance to his store, the viewer can recognize a red sign with the word 'Eros' over his shoulder. See Kolker and Abrams, *Eyes Wide Shut*, p. 191.
29 In order to explain how human necessities such as love and sex can lead to a path of either destruction or self-destruction, Freud combines Eros, the life, love or sexual instinct, with Thanatos, the death instinct. While Eros is a positive force that innocently yearns for love, unity and companionship, it is constantly challenged by Thanatos, a death instinct that seeks to dissolve those units and reduce them back to their primeval, inorganic state. Thanatos indulges in pleasure, tends to repeat desirable acts and, if the ego is unable to restrain them, Thanatos can lead it to a path of destruction. See Erich Fromm, *The Anatomy of Human Destructiveness* (New York: Fawcett Crest Books, 1973).
30 Brigitte Peucker, 'Kubrick and Kafka: The Corporeal Uncanny', *Modernism/Modernity* 8.4 (2001), p. 666.
31 Peucker, 'Kubrick and Kafka', p. 667.
32 Garrett Stewart, *Between Film and Screen: Modernism's Photo Synthesis* (Chicago: The University of Chicago Press, 1999), p. xi.
33 Stewart, *Between Film and Screen*, p. 184.
34 On Kubrick's early photographic work see Rainer Crone, *Stanley Kubrick Drama & Shadows: Photographs 1945–1950* (London: Phaidon Press, 2005); Philippe D. Mather, *Stanley Kubrick at Look Magazine: Authorship and Genre in Photojournalism and Film* (Bristol: Intellect, 2013); and Donald Albrecht and Sean Corcoran (eds), *Through a Different Lens: Stanley Kubrick's Photographs* (Cologne: Taschen, 2021). One can trace many similarities between the early photographs and Kubrick's later preoccupations in his films, such as his inclination towards the absurd. Most importantly, though, these photographs attest to Kubrick's ongoing fascination with the tension between movement and stasis, as explored further in *Eyes Wide Shut*.
35 See, for example, August Villiers de l'Isle-Adam, *Tomorrow's Eve*, trans. and ed. Robert M. Adams (Urbana: Illinois University Press, 1982), or E.T.A. Hoffman, 'The Sandman' in E.F. Bleiler (ed.), *The Best Tales of Hoffmann*, trans. J.T. Bealby (New York: Dover Publications), p. 196. Both of these works, which focus on the fabrication of an ideal female android, are also cited by Freud in his essay 'The Uncanny'.
36 The ultimate example in this sense would be *The Stepford Wives* (Bryan Forbes, 1975), a film that questions the image of the wife-as-servant-robot with close resemblance to the ideas discussed by Betty Friedan in her influential 1963 book *The Feminine Mystique* (New York: Norton, 1963).
37 *A.I. Artificial Intelligence*, one of Kubrick's unrealized projects that was turned into a Steven Spielberg production in 2001, returns to similar motifs of robots and the simulacrum (though developing them much further) and addresses more thoroughly the question of what it means to be human.

38 Jayamanne, 'Ornamentation', p. 5.
39 Michel Chion, *Eyes Wide Shut* (London: BFI Publishing, 2002), p. 58.
40 Tom Gunning, 'The Ghost in the Machine: Animated Pictures at the Haunted Hotel of Early Cinema', *Living Pictures* 1.1 (2001), p. 14.
41 Gunning, 'The Ghost in the Machine', p. 16.

7

Eyes Re-opened: Elucidation and Enlightenment through Music in *Eyes Wide Shut*

Marie Josephine Bennett

Introduction

The employment of pre-existing classical music within a film's soundtrack was not something new for Stanley Kubrick when he decided to include sections from several such works in what was to be his final film. Perhaps the most famous usages of classical works in his movies are the inclusion of Richard Strauss's *Also Sprach Zarathustra* and *The Blue Danube* waltz by Johann Strauss II in *2001: A Space Odyssey* (1968).[1] From the directing of this 1968 film onwards, Kubrick highlighted pre-existing music in the scores of his movies.[2] Indeed, Claudia Gorbman argues that his 'strength as an auteur lay in his inspired handling of pre-existing music',[3] while Chris Chang suggests that Kubrick 'had a knack for irreversibly wedding sound and image'.[4] As well as choosing pieces by Franz Liszt, Wolfgang Amadeus Mozart and Dmitri Shostakovich for the movie, Kubrick selected a composition by György Ligeti – the second piece from *Musica Ricercata*, a set of piano pieces written between 1951 and 1953.[5] Kubrick had used music by Ligeti previously, in both *2001: A Space Odyssey* and *The Shining* (1980). Christine Lee Gengaro suggests that 'the Ligeti piece made a huge impression on filmgoers … becoming indelibly intertwined with *Eyes Wide Shut*'.[6] Indeed, as I suggest in the scenes analysed, music and the moving image become interconnected in the narrative of *Eyes Wide Shut*. The film's soundtrack also includes pre-existing non-classical works, along with music composed for the film by the English composer Jocelyn Pook.

In this chapter, I will focus in particular on how the inclusion of sections of the second piece from *Musica Ricercata* can be interpreted within the movie's narrative, although I will also reference the employment of music from Mozart's *Requiem*, as this is heard in one of the scenes in which Ligeti's music also features. Mervyn Cooke has proposed, of the employment of *Musica Ricercata* II in *Eyes Wide Shut*, that 'whether viewers will find [the music] tensely threatening ... or merely mind-numbingly repetitive will depend on the extent to which they have identified with the thin psychological content of this sex melodrama'.[7] However, I will argue that, every time, the Ligeti piece is employed adeptly as a way of indicating musically a connection between Dr Bill Harford (Tom Cruise) and the orgy scene at the Somerton mansion. Furthermore, the usages combine with the narrative to suggest moments of elucidation or enlightenment for Bill, the movie's central character, especially in a role in which the lead actor 'gives little away'.[8] They are linked to the male protagonist in ways that figuratively disclose his thoughts and actions, in a film in which pretence and masquerade play an important role.

György Ligeti and *Musica Ricercata*

György Ligeti was born to Jewish parents in 1923 in 'one of many Hungarian enclaves in what had recently become Romanian Transylvania'.[9] He was sent to a labour camp in 1944; his father and brother both died at the hand of the Nazis in concentration camps. He fled to Vienna as a result of the Hungarian Revolution in 1956, later becoming an Austrian citizen, and died there in 2006.[10] While at the Academy of Music in Budapest, Ligeti was influenced by the works of Béla Bartók and Igor Stravinsky,[11] and on leaving the Academy in 1949 he 'appeared on the Hungarian musical scene almost exclusively as a composer of folk song arrangements'.[12] However, he was keen to find 'his own voice as a composer'[13] and *Musica Ricercata*, a set of 11 pieces composed for solo piano, can be seen as innovative in that respect. Ligeti stated that 'in 1951, I started to experiment with simple structures of rhythm and sound in order to build up a new music from nothing',[14] and Richard Steinitz suggests that the aim of the composer 'was to derive, concisely yet ingeniously, the maximum result from the minimum material' when writing this work.[15] John Caldwell describes a *ricercare* or *ricercata* as 'a technical exercise either of a practical nature or illustrative of some device of composition'.[16] The first piece of *Musica Ricercata* has only two pitch classes (A and D), the second has three, and so on, with the last piece including all twelve pitches of the chromatic scale. As noted by Márton Kerékfy, the pieces 'were written more or less in the same order as they follow each other in the final score'.[17]

It is the second piece that is pertinent to *Eyes Wide Shut*, which includes sections of the work as underscore. This piece has three pitches, namely E#, F# and – eventually – G, which does not appear until bar 18 of the 33-bar score. These notes are initially unaccompanied and follow a one-bar rest that is marked with a *fermata*.[18] Ligeti indicates that the first section of the piece should be played *mesto, rigido e cerimoniale*, in other words, thoughtfully, inflexibly and with ceremony. The initial tempo is a stately crotchet = 56, or 56 crotchet beats per minute, but this does alter to crotchet = 126 at the point when the Gs are initially heard, and crotchet = 76 at bar 25, before returning to the original tempo at bar 29. When they are first introduced, the Gs are not only marked with an accent but also given the musical direction that they should be played *tutta la forza* (with full force) and *fortissimo* (very loudly).[19] At first, the Gs are isolated, and they gradually die away in bar 24. Following the re-emergence of the theme in the bass clef at bar 25, the Gs re-enter after four beats, only to die away again in bar 28, the two ideas appearing to battle with one another for supremacy. The opening theme returns for four bars, *rigido e cerimoniale* once more, but the Gs are heard again in the final bar as if to usurp and smother the original theme before dying away for a final time.[20]

The initial short motif is varied in the first four bars through the use of different time signatures and note lengths. It alternates between two notes (E# and F#) that are just a semitone apart, creating the interval of a minor second. In his discussion of film music, Kenneth Lafave suggests that 'narrow intervals evoke mystery or even danger',[21] while film composer Lalo Schifrin argues that the minor second is 'the "tension" interval'.[22] Indeed, perhaps the best-known use of a minor second interval as underscore is John Williams' main theme for the film *Jaws* (Steven Spielberg, 1975). The Ligeti piece functions as an underscore in five scenes within *Eyes Wide Shut* and, although not specifically composed film music, the theme's interval of a minor second does indeed appear to suggest the mystery, danger or tension that the writers quoted above propose. This is especially because it occurs frequently in the piece, marked to be played sometimes loudly but at other times very softly and barely audibly.

First use of Musica Ricercata

Given that Ligeti's music features many times in *Eyes Wide Shut*, it is perhaps unusual that the first occurrence does not take place until over an hour into the narrative. Bill has persuaded his friend Nick (Todd Field) to give him the password to a masked orgy that is taking place at a mansion named Somerton. Not long after Bill arrives at the house, although he has the correct password to enter and an appropriate outfit, it appears that a combination of arriving late and in a taxi has aroused suspicion. After a short while, he is told (erroneously) that his taxi driver wants to speak to him at the front door, but he is actually directed into a room where he is questioned by Red Cloak (Leon Vitali), who is surrounded by a number of other masked attendees. Ligeti's music begins as Bill looks across from the doorway at those in the room, and there are then close-ups of some of the masked faces before Red Cloak asks Bill to 'Please, come forward', over the sustained 3½-beat note at the end of bar 4. The theme continues very quietly in octaves, adding to the mystery as Bill walks forwards towards Red Cloak, while some of the bystanders encircle him so that he is completely surrounded. The interrogation of Bill by Red Cloak starts as the music continues, not only operating as underscore but also appearing to support the cross-examination via the high F# that appears from bar 10, especially as the score is marked *quasi parlando* (as if speaking) at this point. Responding to Red Cloak's question regarding the password for the house, Bill replies 'I seem to have … forgotten it' just as the music reaches bar 17, which is a whole bar rest, with the addition of a *fermata*. The entrance of the knell-like note G, marked to be played *tutta la forza* in the following bars, adds to the tension, given Red Cloak's response and his demand that Bill remove his mask, which takes place just as the notes become more rapid before dying away. Red Cloak's request that Bill remove his clothing occurs as the *intenso, agitato* section of Ligeti's work begins at bar 25, before the piece returns to the original tempo and theme (in octaves) at bar 29. The Mysterious Woman (Abigail Good), who had earlier advised Bill to leave the house because he was in danger, then interrupts proceedings by shouting 'Stop!' from the balcony. But she also 'interrupts' the music, which suddenly ceases on the fourth quaver of bar 30. As she is led away, Ligeti's music returns, recommencing at bar 29 and finishing at the *fermata* at the start of the last bar. While almost the whole piece is heard as underscore during this scene, therefore, it does not quite reach its end. Not arriving at its conclusion appears to indicate that the music may be heard again, and certainly leaves Bill's fate open.

Ligeti's music appears to be questioning and commenting on the action that is taking place in this scene. Bill is out of his depth, having waded into a situation in which he does not belong. Even though all the attendees are masked, still somehow he has been exposed as an interloper, and that exposure involves the removal of the mask that is concealing his identity, while the isolated Gs of the piece add to the suspense. The exposure almost includes that of his naked body as well, and this is prevented only by the intervention of the Mysterious Woman. Her call of 'Stop!' ceases both the music and any further humiliation of Bill.

While it is strange that her plea terminates what is presumably non-diegetic music – in other words, there is no visible source – the fact that Kubrick appears to toy here with which music is heard by those within and without the filmic narrative also occurs earlier in the film; the opening scene of the movie similarly illustrates a seemingly deliberate aural deception. Shostakovich's Waltz No. 2 from his *Suite for Variety Stage Orchestra* is heard when the opening credits are shown, and this music continues during the film's first scene, in which Bill and Alice are getting ready to go to a Christmas party being held by Victor Ziegler (Sydney Pollack).[23] However, just before the couple leave, Bill turns off the stereo in the apartment, indicating that the music has been emanating from this source, even though it could not have originated from the stereo when heard over the film's opening credits.[24] The fact that Ligeti's music pauses when the Mysterious Woman shouts from the balcony, only to restart as she is led away, thus again playfully questions the music's source.

Second use of Musica Ricercata

Although Ligeti's music is not heard initially until around halfway through the narrative of *Eyes Wide Shut*, there is not too long to wait before it is heard a second time. Once more, the music is connected to the Somerton mansion. Bill has been retracing some of his steps from the previous day, while also trying to find out what has happened to Nick, who was shown being led away from the house during the orgy sequence. Back at his surgery, Bill decides to cancel his afternoon appointments and drives back to Somerton. As Bill parks outside the gates of the mansion, Ligeti's music is heard as underscore during the remainder of the scene, once more appearing to 'comment' on the actions, especially given that there is no verbal dialogue during this scene. The first four bars of the piece are heard as Bill looks through the gates, and the octaves section that starts at bar 5 enters as he becomes aware that a security camera positioned above is tracking him. He then hears and sees a car approaching from

Figure 7.1 Bill is filmed as if behind bars
(*Eyes Wide Shut*, Stanley Kubrick, Stanley Kubrick Productions).

the house. It stops just before the gates and a stern-faced elderly man, all dressed in black, gets out of the car and walks towards Bill, pushing an envelope towards him through the grilled gates. During the one-bar rest in Ligeti's score, Bill takes the letter from the man and looks at the front of the envelope. Tension builds regarding what might be in the envelope when the accented Gs enter in bar 18 and the man turns away without a word, returning to the car to be driven back to the house. The solitary Gs continue and grow in frequency as Bill sees that the envelope is addressed to him and takes out the letter inside. There is a close-up of the typed message, which warns Bill not to make any further enquiries, and the *intenso, agitato* section of the piece begins. Given the pre-prepared letter, there was clearly an expectation that Bill would return to Somerton for more information about what had happened there the night before, and the agitation of the music provides an apt accompaniment to the warning written in the letter.

The music also reminds the filmic audience of the first time it was heard at the orgy scene, but now, instead of Bill being inside the mansion, he stands outside it, unable to enter. He is filmed in a way that illustrates his otherness by seeming to be behind bars, the gate literally and figuratively a barrier to him becoming part of this different world (see Figure 7.1). The music is also linked to Bill trying to find out more information and seek clarification about the previous night's events. Reading the letter he has been given, he becomes aware that he is being warned against making any further enquiries, with Ligeti's music accompanying these moments of realization. The isolated Gs again augment the tension, while the *intenso, agitato* section reveals Bill's enlightenment about his predicament as he looks up from the typed warning letter. Once again, the piece does not reach its conclusion, finishing on this occasion at bar 28.

Third use of Musica Ricercata

Bill returns to the home of Domino (Vinessa Shaw), a prostitute with whom he had spent some time the previous evening, although they did not sleep together. Domino is not at home, but her flatmate Sally (Fay Masterson) answers the door and invites Bill inside. During their conversation, she informs Bill that Domino had received some bad news that morning: she is HIV-positive. The scene that follows starts suddenly and is once more underscored by Ligeti's music. Bill is walking along an empty road, possibly thinking about his potentially lucky escape with Domino. Something makes him turn around and, on the other side of the road, he sees a man who is walking in the same direction. Bill appears uneasy and gradually becomes aware that the unknown man is following him. The repetitive semitone intervals and occasional octave leaps of Ligeti's music can be heard as providing a menacing accompaniment to the visuals at this point, as Bill tries to get away from his pursuer by hailing a cab but has no luck.

As the first of the repeated Gs sounds, this coincides with the appearance of the mysterious man halting at the corner of the street, hands in pockets. The notes sound like ominous tolling bells as they gradually accelerate, suggesting aurally that Bill is in danger. Bill stops at a nearby newsstand when he sees that the stalker is stationary on the street corner opposite, all the while looking towards Bill, who buys a newspaper at the stand. This action is seemingly more to keep an eye on the man who has been following him than because it is something he needs. However, as will be seen, the purchase of the newspaper is to prove eventful. The stalker then crosses the road, observing Bill the whole time, but he does not approach him. He stands somewhat ironically near a clearly visible red 'Stop' sign, as if this is another warning message to Bill, before continuing to walk in the same direction until out of sight (see Figure 7.2). Breathing

Figure 7.2 The stalker pauses near a red traffic sign
(*Eyes Wide Shut*, Stanley Kubrick, Stanley Kubrick Productions).

heavily, the anxious Bill turns away and spots a café a few doors along. As he enters the café and goes up the stairs, the music of Ligeti stops, three bars short of the piece's end, thereby suggesting once more that it may be heard again.

As in its previous usage, the music appears to provide a quizzical and perplexed 'commentary' in a scene in which there is no dialogue (apart from the few words exchanged between Bill and a taxi driver). Once again, it is used in a manner that indicates some form of illumination for Bill, who appears to connect the stalker with the warning letter he had received earlier that day at Somerton and thereby to Red Cloak's words of caution regarding the events that he had witnessed at the orgy. This is because, although no words are spoken between the two men, and even though the stalker does not actually directly approach Bill, the latter is clearly and visibly shaken by the experience.

Fourth use of Musica Ricercata and Mozart's Requiem

As Bill enters Sharky's café to compose himself, the 'Rex Tremendae' from Mozart's *Requiem* can be heard as diegetic music in the coffee shop. Yet a *Requiem* is an unusual piece to be playing in such a venue, even more so in the run-up to Christmas; although Mozart's music is often used as filmic background music in this type of scene, it seems incongruous that the café should be playing a section from this particular work. Initially, it appears that Kubrick may be using the music to reference the news Bill has recently heard about Domino. It could thus be an ironic allusion to the 'Lucky to be Alive' headline on the front page of the newspaper Bill has just purchased; as Gorbman notes, 'many of Kubrick's placements of pre-existing music produce irony'.[25] The music could be suggesting that Bill's life is still in danger, however, given the warnings he has received about his presence at the orgy both from Red Cloak and in the typed letter, especially as he has just been followed by a suspicious-looking individual.

Melanie Lowe similarly notes that the *Requiem* is an 'unusual choice for coffeeshop Christmas-time background music' and argues that the music is used here to inform the audience that 'this film should be ending soon'.[26] She suggests that, in *Amadeus* (Miloš Forman, 1984), the use of the *Requiem* informs viewers not only that Mozart's life is coming to an end, but also that the end of the movie is approaching. She argues that through the work's 'subsequent uses in the penultimate and ultimate scenes of several other films' the piece 'acquires an extramusical cinematic meaning: the beginning of the end'.[27] Although Lowe states that *Eyes Wide Shut* is an example of such a film, her hypothesis about the reason for employing excerpts from Mozart's *Requiem* both here and in other movies seems somewhat extreme. *The Big Lebowski* (Ethan and Joel Coen, 1998), for example, uses the *Requiem*'s 'Lacrimosa' roughly 22 minutes into the film rather than towards its end, whilst in *Primal Fear* (Gregory Hoblit, 1996) the 'Lacrimosa' is likewise heard not long after the start of the movie, although the piece is also used again during the end credits.

The fact that the *Requiem* stops abruptly mid-scene here, being interrupted and superseded by the Ligeti piece, is arguably of more significance. Gorbman suggests that the *Requiem* seems to be 'preparing for Bill's imminent discovery in his newspaper that … Mandy has died of a heroin overdose'.[28] At this point, however, Bill knows only that Mandy has taken an overdose.[29] He does not discover that she is dead until he goes to the hospital to visit her. As Gengaro explains, 'it should be noted that Bill is reading about a girl who is still alive, as far as he knows'.[30] It can be argued, therefore, that the *Requiem* is used here in a prophetic fashion, as a way of alerting the filmic audience to the fact that Mandy has not survived, so that viewers become aware of this information ahead of Bill.

Interestingly, Michel Chion suggests that the use of the second piece from *Musica Ricercata* in the café scene is a 'superfluous repetition'.[31] However, the employment of the piece is noteworthy here in that it links the newspaper's outer headline to the original use of the music in the orgy scene, where Bill is an 'odd man out' or 'other' amongst the members of a secret and strange sect and is apparently 'lucky to be alive' after being 'saved' by a mysterious woman. His isolation within a crowd in that location is repeated in the café scene; despite the room being very busy with customers chatting amiably, and the choral singing in the background, the piano music interrupts and 'silences' both the ambient sounds and the Mozart piece. This indicates that Bill is so caught up in his own thoughts about what he has just read regarding Mandy's overdose that he has become unaware of the diegetic music. Raising his eyes as the music changes from solitary notes to octaves, the sound and image reflect his realization that Mandy was the woman who was at Ziegler's party – the woman whose life he potentially helped to save. Having just been followed himself, he also presumably suspects that the overdose had not been self-inflicted. Consequently, it can be argued that, whilst the diegetic Mozart piece is employed in a predictive fashion, the non-diegetic use of the Ligeti composition reflects Bill's subjectivity.

The disparity between the solo instrument, highlighting Bill's isolation and self-absorption, and the polyphonic singing that blends with the chattering customers is one of a number of contrasts between the compositions of Mozart and Ligeti that are prevalent here, and the contrast between the two pieces is insightful. First, one piece is a work written for a group of people, while the other is for a soloist. Second, a sacred work is juxtaposed with a secular one. Third, Mozart's work was written in the late eighteenth century in a baroque style, whilst the Ligeti piece is a twentieth-century modernist work. Fourth, one usage is diegetic, whilst the other is non-diegetic. Finally, the *Requiem* has a text, but the Ligeti composition is instrumental.

Indeed, the text is arguably significant here, in that it is just after the sopranos sing the words 'qui salvandos, salvas gratis' that the 'Rex Tremendae' is interrupted by the piano piece. These Latin words can be translated as 'who freely saves those worthy'. Bill at this point believes he had 'saved' Mandy and in turn been 'saved' by a mysterious woman at the orgy – possibly, Mandy. The tenors and basses are simultaneously singing 'rex tremendae majestatis', which translates as 'king of tremendous majesty'. This tells of an all-powerful being, and a person, like Red Cloak, with the power to save. Ligeti's music thus seems to question the worthiness of Mandy and Bill, and also whether they will be 'saved', by silencing the Mozart work.

Ligeti's piece could be described once again as a metadiegetic usage here, representing Bill's thoughts, as the music begins with the visual close-up of the article about Mandy in the newspaper, and the *pianissimo* octaves of bar 5 synchronize with the moment Bill raises his eyes from the newspaper, deep in thought. There are thus visual echoes of the scene in which the piece was heard when Bill was outside Somerton, in the way that he reads something and raises his eyes from the text. In this scene, the music then continues in a fashion that is common in filmic underscore, aurally linking the scene in Sharky's café to the one that follows, in which Bill is shown getting out of a taxi and walking through the revolving entrance doors of the hospital to which Mandy had been taken. Gorbman describes underscore used in this way as a classical Hollywood practice that provides continuity 'between shots, in transitions between scenes'.[32] However, one can argue that the music is doing more in this instance than simply providing continuity, as it additionally connects the person named in the article that Bill has just read in the café with his reason for visiting the hospital.

In this penultimate usage, it is significant that Ligeti's music interrupts the diegetic music of Mozart that is playing in the coffee shop just as the text mentions both a powerful figure and the salvation of those that are worthy. That the music is from a requiem, a mass for the dead, also emphasizes the 'Lucky to be Alive' headline clearly visible on the front of the newspaper Bill has purchased, while the polyphonic singing of the 'Rex Tremendae' blends with the many voices of the customers in the busy café that he enters. Bill makes the assumption that the model reported in the newspaper as taking an overdose is the woman who had 'saved' him from an unknown fate at the orgy, and that she is the same woman that he had 'saved' at Ziegler's party. In addition, the Ligeti music appears to represent Bill's thoughts and concerns as he looks up from the newspaper, oblivious to the 'real' music being played in the café. Only eight bars of the second piece from *Musica Ricercata* are heard on this occasion, but the final usage is longer.

Final use of Musica Ricercata

As he is leaving the hospital, having discovered that Mandy has died, Bill receives a telephone call asking him to visit Victor Ziegler. Upon Bill's arrival, Victor explains that he had also been at Somerton the previous night, saw what happened and arranged to have Bill followed. Bill shows Victor the newspaper article about Mandy but Victor is already aware of the model's death and he confirms that she was the woman who had taken an overdose at his party. The first shot after this scene is a close-up of the mask Bill had worn – and mysteriously somehow later mislaid – when he was at the orgy at Somerton. A few seconds after the mask is shown, the opening piano notes of the second piece from *Musica Ricercata* are heard once more. It transpires that the mask has been placed on Bill's pillow in his bedroom as, during the second bar of the piece, the camera pans across to the pillow next to it, revealing the sleeping figure of his wife Alice (Nicole Kidman). As the third bar commences, Bill is shown entering his home, unaware of the mask's re-emergence. The music continues as the camera tracks Bill walking slowly through the apartment, clearly very tired, stopping to turn off the Christmas tree lights and then going into the kitchen, where he gets himself a drink from the refrigerator and sits down to drink it. The purpose of the underscore accompanying Bill's actions before he enters the bedroom appears to be to escalate the tension and increase the suspense as to what his reaction will be once he eventually sees the mask.

There is an ellipsis when the music reaches the whole-bar rest with *fermata* at bar 17, and the next shot is of Bill opening the door to the bedroom. When the first G of bar 18 sounds, Bill's facial expression changes as he finally sees the mask. The camera quickly and dramatically pans across from Bill to the mask on the pillow and Alice sleeping next to it, and the second G is heard. The visuals then switch between this view and Bill's startled face, while the Gs continue forebodingly as underscore, musically illustrating his shocked reaction. As the *intenso, agitato* section of the piece begins at bar 25, Bill sits down on the bed, looking towards his wife and the mask, and starts to weep uncontrollably. When the music begins to die away in bar 28, her husband's crying wakes Alice. The following bars, marked *pianissimo*, are barely perceptible beneath Bill's audible and inconsolable expressions of grief, and he says to Alice that he will 'tell her everything'. Once more, as in its first usage, the music ceases at the *fermata* that begins the last bar, thereby stopping just short of the piece's completion.

The final use of Ligeti's piece once again connects Bill to Somerton and the orgy, this time through the reappearance of the mask he had worn, and had to take off, at the event. Seeing the mask prompts Bill to tell Alice about his activities. However, no explanation is given for how the mask fell out of the carrier bag in which Bill had placed the costume he had hired for Somerton or – assuming that Alice found it in the apartment – why she would place it on her husband's pillow. Ligeti's music accompanies the scene in a way that adds a further level of anticipation for the filmic audience about how Bill will react when he finally sees the mask and appears to denote through music his thoughts and anxieties, while also augmenting his decision to confess all to his wife.

Conclusion

Music from the second piece in György Ligeti's composition *Musica Ricercata* is heard five times during *Eyes Wide Shut*, each time in some way connected to the orgy scene at Somerton, and it is therefore pertinent that the piece is not heard as underscore before this scene. While the first hearing takes place during the interrogation at the mansion, all subsequent hearings link back to Bill's infiltration into the party and his subsequent unmasking as an intruder. The second hearing is when Bill returns to Somerton, only to be given a typed letter warning him not to pursue his enquiries. The piece is next heard when Bill is walking along the street at night and is followed by an unknown man who, it is later revealed, had been hired by Victor Ziegler, who was also at the orgy and saw what had taken place. The next hearing takes place in Sharky's café when Bill reads about Mandy's overdose and suspects that she was the woman who had come to his rescue at Somerton. Finally, the music is heard when Bill returns home from his visit to Ziegler and sees that the mask from the outfit that he had worn to the orgy has been placed on his pillow.

The inclusion of music from Mozart's *Requiem* is also of significance, as it is sandwiched between two hearings of the Ligeti piece. Even though fragments of pieces by Mozart are often used in film as underscore for social gatherings, such as at parties and in restaurants, the fact that the piece chosen here as diegetic background music is from the *Requiem* gives an extra layer of depth and significance within this short scene. Far from being a clichéd and stereotypical usage, the incongruity between the cheery social milieu and the powerful 'Rex Tremendae' with its connections to death provide a surprising juxtaposition. Because the choice of piece is unusual in this type of setting, the text of this part of the *Requiem* is brought more into focus. The fact that the piece is also positioned between two hearings of the stylistically contrasting music of Ligeti helps to focus the minds of the filmic audience on what they are seeing and hearing at this point in the storyline. As well as being used to predict what is going to be discovered shortly within the narrative, Mozart's music suggests that Bill's life may be in danger, especially as it is used in parallel with the visual pointer of the newspaper headline.

Even though the Ligeti piece is instrumental, the music still appears to pass comment on or analyse the action. It is of particular interest that, after its first usage, all the scenes in which the work is subsequently heard have little or no dialogue, so that the music seems to provide an aural commentary on the visuals. This allows the composition to be perceived as directly elucidating the events taking place. The piece heralds Bill's awareness of and realization about his situation and the potential danger he faces, through providing an accompaniment to his interrogation by Red Cloak, his receipt of a written warning during his second visit to Somerton, his awareness that he is being followed, the newspaper article about Mandy's overdose and seeing the mask on his bedroom pillow. In each case, no words are needed; the music does 'the talking', accompanying moments of enlightenment and illumination for Bill regarding his predicament. These moments are heightened and framed through the use of Ligeti's music, given that all five uses of sections from *Musica Ricercata* are associated with Bill's experience at the orgy.

Furthermore, it is of note that the piece is never heard to its conclusion, despite featuring in five different scenes, thereby creating a feeling of uncertainty and ambiguity. While this gives the impression in part that it may return in subsequent scenes, it also suggests that Bill's dilemma may not actually be over, especially as, on the two occasions the piece reaches the final bar, it stops on a *fermata* or pause mark rather than concluding. This indicates an incompleteness of some sort, perhaps suggesting that there will be further consequences from Bill's experience at the orgy and that his unwelcome attendance may come back to haunt him at a later date. But the score being constrained in this way may also allude to shortcomings in the Harfords' relationship; as noted by Robert P. Kolker and Nathan Abrams, the couple's final conversation is 'troubling rather than comforting',[33] indicating that both parties have been affected by what has happened. In many ways, then, *Eyes Wide Shut* provides a good example of a movie in which the incorporation of pre-existing classical music in a filmic narrative is open to a wider number of interpretations than may initially be evident, via the single hearing of Mozart's *Requiem* and, particularly, the five hearings of Ligeti's *Musica Ricercata*.

Notes

1 *The Blue Danube* is the title commonly used for *An der schönen blauen Donau*, composed in 1866. Regarding the film's inclusion of pre-existing music, it is of note that composer Bernard Herrmann argued that it 'shows vulgarity … when a director uses music previously composed. I think that *2001: A Space Odyssey* … is the height of vulgarity in our time.' See 'Bernard Herrmann: A Lecture on Film Music (1973)' in Mervyn Cooke (ed.), *The Hollywood Film Music Reader* (Oxford: Oxford University Press, 2010), p. 213.
2 Claudia Gorbman, 'Ears Wide Open: Kubrick's Music' in Phil Powrie and Robynn Stilwell (eds), *Changing Tunes: The Use of Pre-existing Music in Film* (Aldershot: Ashgate, 2006), p. 4.
3 Gorbman, 'Ears Wide Open', p. 4.
4 Chris Chang, 'Hot Ice: Sophie Mennes, Anselm Kiefer, and György Ligeti together at last', *Film Comment* 47.2 (2011), p. 16.
5 The Liszt piece is *Nuages Gris* and the Shostakovich work is his Waltz No. 2 from *Suite for Variety Stage Orchestra*.
6 Christine Lee Gengaro, *Listening to Stanley Kubrick: The Music in His Films* (Lanham, MD: Rowman & Littlefield, 2012), p. 230.
7 Mervyn Cooke, *A History of Film Music* (Cambridge: Cambridge University Press, 2008), pp. 447–448.
8 Michel Chion, *Eyes Wide Shut* (London: BFI, 2002), p. 27.
9 Richard Steinitz, *György Ligeti: Music of the Imagination* (London: Faber & Faber, 2003), p. 3.
10 See Amy M. Bauer, 'György Ligeti' in Alfred W. Cramer (ed.), *Musicians and Composers of the 20th Century*, Vol. 3 (Pasadena, CA: Salem Press, 2009), pp. 855–859.
11 Márton Kerékfy, 'A "new music from nothing": György Ligeti's *Musica ricercata*', *Studia Musicologica* 49.3/4 (2008), p. 205.
12 Kerékfy, 'A new music from nothing', p. 207.
13 Benjamin R. Levy, *Metamorphosis in Music: The Compositions of György Ligeti in the 1950s and 1960s* (Oxford: Oxford University Press, 2017), p. 12.
14 Quoted in Robert W. Richart, *György Ligeti: A Bio-Bibliography* (Westport, CT: Greenwood Press, 1990), p. 4.
15 Steinitz, *György Ligeti: Music of the Imagination*, p. 54.
16 See John Caldwell, 'Ricercare', Oxford Music Online, https://www.oxfordmusiconline.com/grovemusic/view/10.1093/gmo/9781561592630.001.0001/omo-9781561592630-e-0000023373. Accessed 1 February 2021.
17 Kerékfy, 'A new music from nothing', p. 210.
18 A *fermata* indicates a pause of unspecified length.
19 Ligeti stated in the documentary *Stanley Kubrick: A Life in Pictures* (Jan Harlan, 2001) that 'when I composed it … it was a knife in Stalin's heart'. This comment is taken to refer to the Gs that sound in the piece, with their repetitive 'stabbing' motion. Joseph Stalin died in March 1953.

20 The musical direction is *perdendosi*, which means fading away in terms of dynamics (and sometimes tempo).
21 Kenneth Lafave, *Experiencing Film Music: A Listener's Companion* (Lanham, MD: Rowman & Littlefield, 2017), p. 77.
22 Lalo Schifrin, *Music Composition for Film and Television* (Boston, MA: Berklee Press, 2011), p. 35.
23 The same music is heard over the closing credits.
24 Robert P. Kolker and Nathan Abrams suggest that Kubrick 'blurs the boundaries between diegetic and nondiegetic worlds in the film'. See their *Eyes Wide Shut: Stanley Kubrick and the Making of His Final Film* (Oxford: Oxford University Press, 2019), p. 156.
25 Gorbman, 'Ears Wide Open', p. 6.
26 Melanie Lowe, 'Claiming Amadeus: Classical Feedback in American Media', *American Music* 20.1 (2002), p. 110.
27 Lowe, 'Claiming Amadeus', p. 109.
28 Gorbman, 'Ears Wide Open', p. 17.
29 Like Gorbman, Amy J. Ransom states that Bill 'reads of a woman's death from cocaine overdose'. See her 'Opening *Eyes Wide Shut*: Genre, Reception, and Kubrick's Last Film', *Journal of Film and Video* 62.4 (2010), p. 35.
30 Gengaro, *Listening to Stanley Kubrick*, p. 247.
31 Chion, *Eyes Wide Shut*, p. 89, n. 17.
32 Claudia Gorbman, *Unheard Melodies: Narrative Film Music* (Bloomington and Indianapolis, IN: Indiana University Press, 1987), p. 73.
33 Kolker and Abrams, *Eyes Wide Shut*, p. 183.

PART THREE: RECEPTION

8

Eyes Wide Shut: A Late-1990s 'Quality' Blockbuster

Eddie Falvey

Is it appropriate to call *Eyes Wide Shut* a blockbuster? It is certainly true that if one considers Stanley Kubrick's final film today, especially in light of the global franchise filmmaking that has come to dominate the American film market, it is far removed from the current paradigms that illustrate the industry's most lucrative commodity, the blockbuster. Released in the United States on 16 July 1999, and thus arriving in the same summer as, among other films, a glossy update of *The Mummy* (Stephen Sommers, 1999), the *Zeitgeist*-baiting sci-fi actioner *The Matrix* (Lana and Lilly Wachowski, 1999) and a much-anticipated return to a galaxy far, far away (*Star Wars: Episode I – The Phantom Menace*, George Lucas, 1999), *Eyes Wide Shut* is clearly of a markedly different mould to more typical blockbusters. Kubrick's swan song, an adaptation of Arthur Schnitzler's *Traumnovelle/Dream Story* (1926), is a dark, thematically complex, adult-oriented work that invites close reading, toys with perspective and invokes middlebrow genres – such as the marital drama – that are rarely favoured in large-budget studio fare. And yet the notion that *Eyes Wide Shut* is a blockbuster corresponds with many of its salient features. By virtue of its primary production characteristics – it was financed and produced by Warner Bros. (Warners hereafter), a major studio, with a budget of $65 million (equal to *The Matrix* and more than $100 million in today's money, adjusting for inflation) – the film satisfies Sheldon Hall and Steve Neale's open-ended rubric that defines blockbusters as 'unusually expensive productions designed to earn unusually large amounts of money'.[1]

Naturally, the term 'blockbuster' carries the weight of certain expectations. Charles R. Acland acknowledges both the term's ubiquity and its vagueness as an indicator of content, writing that 'we refer to a movie as a "blockbuster" and assume that others will understand what we mean … the movie will be loud, bright, dynamic, and familiar'.[2] The term blockbuster has been invoked to refer to a variety of different dimensions for 'big' (and/or expensive), prestige, studio films. Beginning with aesthetic tendencies,[3] the term also delineates an industrial (and, especially, studio) 'mindset';[4] it accounts for a film's size;[5] its adoption and application of new film technologies;[6] and offers a framework for responding to the attractions and sensations it offers its audience.[7] I would like to note that Acland's words are not being presented as an unconscious simplification of a complex object in film discourse but intended to address the slipperiness of definitions; he later explains that 'more than a movie, a blockbuster is *a set of ideas* about spectacle, culture, and economy'.[8]

I argue that *Eyes Wide Shut* presents a compelling case study for rethinking the contemporary blockbuster along less clear-cut lines than Acland's loud-bright-dynamic-familiar model allows for. If *Eyes Wide Shut* fails to tick the boxes of a typical tent pole summer blockbuster in the same way that, say, a new *Star Wars* film does, it nevertheless exhibits many criteria illustrative of the format while offering evidence that blockbusters are a flexible category of film. *Eyes Wide Shut* marked the return of an enigmatic auteur adapting a respected if not widely known literary work; coupled with the backing of a major studio and two of the world's then-biggest stars, the real-life couple Tom Cruise and Nicole Kidman. These factors, combined with the expense of the enterprise, illustrate *Eyes Wide Shut*'s claim to the blockbuster title while demonstrating how, following Acland, ideas about spectacle, culture and economy are not fixed to a specific model (for example, the action film) but operate fluidly across various types of film production.

In a later chapter on the blockbuster question, ruffled by overuse of the term, Sheldon Hall further qualifies his and Steve Neale's suggestion that blockbusters include 'films which are not just exceptionally successful box-office hits but those which are specifically intended to be so, and are budgeted, made and marketed accordingly'.[9] For Hall, then, qualifying blockbusters is less about a film's reception and more about production strategy; a staple product of the studio system, blockbusters are 'big' films in scale, spectacle and ambition, designed, made and marketed with box office receipts in mind. Considering the inevitable risk of a film missing the mark with audiences, on the simple basis that no film producer no matter how successful is going to produce a loss leader at the cost of tens or potentially hundreds of millions of dollars, it is reasonable to conclude that *any* studio film boasting a large budget at least partially satisfies the blockbuster's requirement for 'bigness'. Irrespective of box office earnings

– which serve only to reflect a film's commercial reception, and not the structural characteristics of its financing and production – of all the films released in 1999 by major American studios, only the following had larger production budgets than *Eyes Wide Shut*:[10]

Film (director)	*Studio*	*MPAA rating*	*Production budget*	*Global box office*
Wild Wild West (Barry Sonnenfeld)	Warner Bros.	PG-13	$175 million	$221 million
Tarzan (Chris Buck and Kevin Lima)	Walt Disney	G	$145 million	$448 million
The World is Not Enough (Michael Apted)	MGM	PG-13	$135 million	$361 million
Star Wars: Episode 1 – The Phantom Menace (George Lucas)	20th Century Fox	PG	$115 million	£1,027 million
The 13th Warrior (John McTiernan)	Walt Disney	R	$125 million	$62 million
Stuart Little (Rob Minkoff)	Sony Pictures	PG	$105 million	$299 million
End of Days (Peter Hyams)	Universal	R	$100 million	$212 million
Toy Story 2 (John Lasseter)	Walt Disney	G	$90 million	$511 million
The Haunting (Jan de Bont)	Dreamworks	PG-13	$80 million	$180 million
= *The Mummy* (Stephen Sommers)	Universal	PG-13	$80 million	$416 million
Anna and the King (Andy Tennant)	20th Century Fox	PG-13	$75 million	$114 million
= *Inspector Gadget* (David Kellogg)	Walt Disney	PG	$75 million	$134 million
= *Life* (Ted Demme)	Universal	R	$75 million	$74 million
= *Virus* (John Bruno)	Universal	R	$75 million	$31 million
Runaway Bride (Garry Marshall)	Paramount	PG	$70 million	$310 million

Film (director)	*Studio*	*MPAA rating*	*Production budget*	*Global box office*
= *Sleepy Hollow* (Tim Burton)	Paramount	R	$70 million	$207 million
The Insider (Michael Mann)	Walt Disney	R	$68 million	$60 million
= *Mystery Men* (Kinka Usher)	Universal	PG-13	$68 million	$33 million
Entrapment (Jon Amiel)	20th Century Fox	PG-13	$66 million	$212 million
***Eyes Wide Shut* (Stanley Kubrick)**	**Warner Bros.**	**R**	**$65 million**	**$104 million**
= *Fight Club* (David Fincher)	20th Century Fox	R	$65 million	$101 million
= *The Matrix* (Lana and Lilly Wachowski)	Warner Bros.	R	$65 million	$465 million

Table 8.1 Budgets and box-office takings of major American studio productions in 1999.

Retrospective evaluations of the 'winners' and 'losers' of a given year almost always apply ideas about a film's reception, if not assessed by box-office takings, then by ever more slippery notions relating to its cultural value determined by the sort of critical consensus that comes with awards and placement on end-of-year lists. The data in Table 8.1 reflects not only the winners and losers of 1999 on a ratio of cost to profit, but also the fact that, while *Eyes Wide Shut* may be distinguishable from regular examples of the blockbuster format, it can nevertheless be situated within and understood as a part of the big-budget, or 'blockbuster', pantheon of that year.[11] *Eyes Wide Shut* was certainly regarded as a culturally 'big' film at the time. Jaime Estrada Torres of Avid Technology, in a letter to film editor Nigel Galt requesting permission to use footage from *Eyes Wide Shut* for a broadcasting showcase, writes: 'I have received materials from *Star Wars*, *The Mummy*, the new James Bond picture [*The World is Not Enough*], as well as other major European films, but would also like to include the two international trailers available for *Eyes Wide Shut*'.[12] Differences aside, it was in these terms, as a showcase film adjacent to other major studio productions, that *Eyes Wide Shut* was positioned.

I am not first to consider *Eyes Wide Shut* away from its rarefied status as purely a Kubrick film – the last Kubrick film in fact, with all the myth-making and cumulative weight that distinction brings – but as a film belonging to, among other contexts, late-1990s tendencies within studio filmmaking. Linda Ruth Williams, for example, has made the case that *Eyes Wide Shut* 'is essentially an erotic thriller, even if it is a lot of other things too'.[13] Despite the strong impulse shared by critics and scholars to frame Kubrick as an independently operating visionary – which in some ways he undoubtedly was, such was his process and style – he nevertheless had to negotiate a tricky shoot with a major studio applying pressure for a commercially viable product.[14] Bryan Appleyard, writing in 1997, reports:

> One vast project – *Napoleon* – now lies abandoned, but another, *A.I.* – a sci-fi story based on *Pinocchio* and a short story by Brian Aldiss – may still be made, though $100 million would be a conservative estimate for its final cost. Rumours suggest that Warner Bros. insisted he did *Eyes Wide Shut*, a sexy story of two married psychiatrists having affairs with patients, as a relatively low-cost money-spinner before embarking on the high-risk *A.I.*[15]

'Rumour' is the word of the day in this article; however, it nevertheless intimates the operational and strategic considerations for the studio that accompanied making films with Kubrick. These considerations again came to light closer to the film's release, with Shauna Snow reporting that Warners announced on 9 September 1998 that 'the film will be ready for release in early 1999, but we don't want to go out with it until summer when we can globally position it in the period of maximum admissions'.[16]

While I do not aim to divorce Kubrick from *Eyes Wide Shut*'s status as a studio film, it is one ambition of this chapter to reposition it in a way that acknowledges different facets of its identity. Moreover, I contend that while *Eyes Wide Shut* can be renegotiated as a prestige, blockbuster-like production, it is nevertheless an atypical text and therefore important for signalling what was taking place within the American film industry at the end of the 1990s. Adjacently, then, this chapter will observe how large-scale, yet markedly 'highbrow' productions such as *Eyes Wide Shut* reflect one type of aftermath for the independent boom that occurred in the earlier part of the decade, while anticipating, or indeed illustrating, the emergence of what Geoff King has referred to as the 'quality' studio film.[17] And yet it is notable that even King finds it tricky to fit Kubrick comfortably into the 'quality' model without further qualification, noting that 'while much of the Hollywood quality tradition – historical and more recent – has been located in a cultural region often labelled disparagingly as "middlebrow", Kubrick's *oeuvre* has been accorded higher status … including association with venerated established "high art" traditions of modernism' over what might be called more regular 'quality' fare.[18] Despite the critical enigma that Kubrick poses, which has largely accorded him an 'inside/outside' status with respect to the wider culture of studio productions, *Eyes Wide Shut* is exactly the sort of film King is discussing. In the shadow of the new millennium, *Eyes Wide Shut* represents a moment of change for studio filmmaking, in which studios, producers and filmmakers had no choice but to respond to various industrial forces while renegotiating their staple product around new and evolving cultural and commercial modalities. I contend the 'blockbuster' framework sheds light on both *Eyes Wide Shut* itself and the business surrounding it, drawing especially on the circumstances of the studio film industry at a crucial point of transition.

The Kubrick factor: discursive interference in the reception of *Eyes Wide Shut* as a studio film

'Prophet. Progenitor. Godfather. Good influence. Bad example.'[19] These are the terms with which Hannah McGill describes Kubrick in the opening lines of her December 2019 *Sight & Sound* article to coincide with the twentieth anniversary of *Eyes Wide Shut*'s release. In that same article, she writes of Kubrick as 'a big directorial beast who insisted upon his vision, wilfully eclipsed writers and other collaborators, and was formidable with actors[;] Kubrick – or at least the myth that clings about him – embodies the excesses enabled by reverence for the auteur director'.[20] McGill's words express (and, indeed, in their own way contribute to) Kubrick's exalted, near-mythic status in film discourse, intimating the cultist veneration to which his body of work has been subjected in recent years. Kubrick's *oeuvre* has already been the subject of millions of words of biography, journalism and scholarship, as well as dedicated symposia, multiple home releases, documentaries and so forth. Each of his films has received dedicated book-length studies, which often position him as something of a father figure to modern American cinema. Film scholar Michel Chion, for example, conceptualizes *2001: A Spacey Odyssey* (1968) as 'the absolute film' and frames *Eyes Wide Shut* in similarly exalting terms.[21] Elsewhere, James Naremore contends that Kubrick 'belongs both to Hollywood and to the twilight of international modernism' and therefore to a realm of artists that transcend film specifically, including the likes of James Joyce and Samuel Beckett, among others.[22]

Following a certain type of auteur-led film scholarship that centres on the director as the chief structuring principle, Kubrick has arguably been afforded certain discursive powers and privileges over co-existing filmmakers of his era. Indeed, even opposite Cruise and Kidman, Kubrick is positioned on the film's poster as equal among stars; the three are graphically rendered in such a way as to collapse the hierarchical distinction usually offered to on-screen performers over directors. As such, Kubrick's placement on the poster corresponds with a pervasive star image that conveys once again his reputation as the archetypal auteur who presides over everything. Indeed, King has written that Kubrick's reputation 'lies at the upper end of the Hollywood quality spectrum, probably as close to its summit as that of any filmmaker of the post-classical studio era'.[23]

It is important to note that, despite his reputation as an outlier, Kubrick absolutely belongs within an American studio context. As James Fenwick notes, 'Kubrick was very much a part of the Hollywood system upon which he relied', even as he vied for control within it.[24] Kubrick's first three features (*Killer's Kiss* [1955], *The Killing* [1956] and *Paths of Glory* [1957]) were all distributed by United Artists, followed by collaborations with Universal [*Spartacus* [1960]), MGM (*Lolita* [1962] and *2001: A Space Odyssey*) and Columbia (*Dr. Strangelove or: How I Learned to Stop Worrying and Love the Bomb* [1964]) before sticking it out with Warners for the remainder of his career (*A Clockwork Orange* [1971], *Barry Lyndon* [1975], *The Shining* [1980], *Full Metal Jacket* [1987] and *Eyes Wide Shut*). Even *2001*, as Peter Krämer writes, was backed by MGM operating on the expectation of a blockbuster:

> [The] studio's investment in *Journey Beyond the Stars* [the working title for *2001: A Space Odyssey*] was based on the perception that what Kubrick and [Arthur C.] Clarke had outlined in their 'film story' was an innovative movie that was nevertheless grounded in recent trends in Hollywood entertainment. *Journey Beyond the Stars* was going to be a roadshow attraction for the whole family; a big-budget historical epic and futuristic Cinerama travelogue which promised to take audiences on the most spectacular journey of their lifetime …; the latest work of a young director who was increasingly perceived as one of the great masters of Hollywood Cinema.[25]

According to Krämer, it is within a precise industrial framework guided by principles relating to the Hollywood blockbuster, here referred to as a 'roadshow attraction', that *2001: A Space Odyssey* was strategically positioned.[26]

Indeed, despite his status as a 'great master', Kubrick was nevertheless centrally located within the wider Hollywood firmament with a design to make commercially viable films. Fenwick discloses the admiration Kubrick held for commercial auteurs such as Steven Spielberg and George Lucas, noting that:

> [i]n the early 1980s [Kubrick] became interested in an adaptation of Henry Rider Haggard's *The Saga of Eric Brighteyes* (1890), sensing it could be filmed as a children's action adventure story. The idea was explored shortly after the release of *E.T.* [Steven Spielberg, 1982], demonstrating how Kubrick wanted to produce a film with broad family appeal like Spielberg's films.[27]

Kubrick would never enjoy the commercial success of Spielberg or Lucas, but has in other ways acquired a legacy that arguably outstrips them both.[28] When comparing Kubrick to Spielberg in a chapter on *A.I. Artificial Intelligence* (Steven Spielberg, 2001), King refers to the latter as a 'highly popular sentimentalist', but differentiates Kubrick as the 'more rigorously artistic' of the two, whose work 'significantly push[ed] the boundaries of ... quality within the studio environment', referring to films that include *Dr. Strangelove, 2001: A Space Odyssey* and *A Clockwork Orange*.[29]

All in all, Kubrick's body of work is often invoked as a high benchmark for auteur-led American (or, indeed, any form of) filmmaking despite being embedded within Hollywood from nearly the beginning. Nevertheless, Kubrick is often distinguished from the staple New Hollywood pack (Spielberg, Lucas, Martin Scorsese, Brian De Palma, etc.) for producing films that pushed the boundaries of 'quality', *per* King, and showcased significantly more aesthetic daring than those of many of his contemporaries. In choosing to focus on the artfulness of Kubrick's films over the circumstances of their production, such analysis covets above all else how his cinema inverts, undermines and challenges pre-existing notions about aesthetic uniformity at the cost of situating his work within prominent industrial paradigms.[30] Bearing in mind what I have referred to here as 'the Kubrick factor', which accords him power and privilege for the fact of being Kubrick, my argument is that, by reinstating *Eyes Wide Shut* within industrial paradigms, we not only dispel the rarefied status that his films assume for being his but also come to understand how his work figures within the wider industrial landscape.

A studio in search of a blockbuster: selling sex in the marketing of *Eyes Wide Shut*

It is relatively clear from the outset that Warners was hopeful that *Eyes Wide Shut* would at least resemble a blockbuster of sorts. At the very least, Warners' studio executives were encouraging Kubrick to make a marketable product with the cultural capital of A-list stars ready to adorn the red carpet when the time came. In an oft-recollected exchange, after Warners had given *Eyes Wide Shut* the go-ahead, then-president Terry Semel appealed to Kubrick, saying that 'what I would really love you to consider is a movie star in the lead role; you haven't done that since Jack Nicholson' (in reference to *The Shining*).[31] However, aside from a couple of early collaborations with then-stars Kirk Douglas and Peter Sellers, *The Shining* was arguably his only truly star-led production in decades.[32] Enter Cruise and Kidman.

Due to the lengthy shoot, at the time of *Eyes Wide Shut*'s release, Cruise had been absent from screens since 1996 when the combination of *Mission: Impossible* (Brian De Palma) and *Jerry Maguire* (Cameron Crowe) solidified his status as a highly commercial star with acting pedigree – indeed, as the titular star of *Jerry Maguire*, Cruise received his second Oscar nomination for Best Actor after *Born on the 4th of July* (Oliver Stone, 1989). Kidman had not yet achieved the box-office pull of her co-star and then-partner – her biggest hits thus far had been *Days of Thunder* (Tony Scott, 1990), also starring Cruise, and *Batman Forever* (Joel Schumacher, 1995), in which she was fourth lead. Nevertheless, she was an established presence in Hollywood, a status that would only increase in the following years with larger hits such as *Moulin Rouge!* (Baz Luhrmann, 2001) and *The Others* (Alejandro Amenábar, 2001), and an Oscar-winning performance in *The Hours* (Stephen Daldry, 2002). In press briefings for the film's release, Warners was eager to underscore the pair's critical acclaim, emphasizing certain aspects of their star credentials that include Cruise's Oscar nominations and, interestingly, Kidman's stage work.[33]

Faithful to *Eyes Wide Shut*'s thematic investment in sex, power and voyeurism, whatever interest audiences might have had in Cruise and Kidman independently was only amplified by the titillating prospect of getting to see behind the curtain concealing the sex life of a real star couple. In reference to such expectations, in a review of the film for the British film magazine *Empire*, Angie Errigo accordingly warns readers to:

> [b]e aware that the film has been poorly served by advance speculation (most of the widely reported plot titbits prove wrong) and the

> overexposure of the juicy Tom and Nicole snog clip, an outrageous bit of trailer foreplay unconsummated in the event and giving the entirely erroneous impression that this film is a non-stop bonkfest.[34]

Elsewhere, actor Alan Cumming has acknowledged the misdirection spearheaded in the marketing of the film, explaining that 'the whole world was mesmerized by the idea that Tom Cruise and Nicole Kidman were going to be having actual sex on film'.[35] As early as October 1997 – almost two years before the film's release – though armed with next to no facts about the film, Kidman's interviewer for *Vanity Fair* magazine found the secrecy-shrouded project and its effects on her family life to be a major point of interest in a career-spanning panorama of the actor.[36] Other publications were even more salacious with their gossip: *The New York Times* reported in 1998 that 'one studio executive said he believed the film involved a *ménage-à-trois*',[37] while *Time Magazine*, in the week before the film's US release, had the stars pose nude for the cover, accompanied by the promise of 'Cruise and Kidman like you've never seen them'.[38] Consciously collapsing the space between the public and the private, with the support of rumours from studio executives, the discursive utility of Cruise and Kidman's marriage was being invoked by the popular presses as a major source of appeal for the film, especially given its thematic preoccupation with sex in tandem with an implicit promise of explicitness.[39] And it is telling of the film's status as a studio property that Warners were happy to fan the flames of the press brouhaha; it shows, among other things, the lengths to which the studio were willing, or needed, to go to cash in on their substantial investment.

Even the now-infamous poster for the film is structured around a licit invitation to gaze upon the sex of its stars. Note that the couple is framed by a mirror and pronounced, in large block capitals, as Cruise and Kidman themselves and not their fictional counterparts (admittedly, this is as film posters are wont to do, but the design appears more deliberate, especially given the discourse surrounding the film). Moreover, the representational system on display is chiefly aimed at Kidman; as Cruise goes about his business, Kidman gives off the impression of being caught, struck by the glare of a spotlight that catches her off-guard. This iconic image recurs again and again in the film's marketing and is utilized extensively in the extratextual ephemera that accompanied the film's release, from press materials to posters to home-release VHS and DVD packaging, to other items such as Penguin's publication of the film's screenplay (accompanied by a reprinting of *Dream Story*) in September 1999 to tie in with the film's UK release.[40] This particular item comes with the promise of original stills from the film: of these, eight include Kidman; of the eight, six feature Kidman in intimate clothing (including two images in which her nipples are visible). By contrast, only one image of Cruise (out of thirteen) features any form of nudity and, in that image, he is mostly blocked by Kidman's more visible body. It suggests that the film is being consciously and deliberately framed in such a way that its core iconography is being constructed out of its erotic content, which prioritizes the presentation and exploitation of the star couple's sex in general, and Kidman's body specifically.

Richard Dyer, who has written at length on the cultural economy of film stardom regarding sex, says the following about Marilyn Monroe:

> In line with these wider trends in society, sexuality was becoming increasingly important in films. One of the cinema's strategies in the face of the increasingly privatised forms of leisure … was to provide the kind of fare that was not deemed suitable for home consumption – hence the decline of the family film and the rise of 'adult' cinema.[41]

While half a century separates Monroe from Kidman, it remains interesting if unsurprising that sex as a signifying strategy remains a key aspect of the creation, commoditization and export of film stardom as a sellable asset. Though various forms of 'adult' media had entered the home life by 1999, courtesy of the internet, *Eyes Wide Shut* was being presented, somewhat anachronistically (and indeed incorrectly), as a peep show marked by extreme, erotic content. And even then, the problems posed by the film's stronger content reveal Warners' prominent role in the structural and strategic make-up of the film's creation and release: Julian Senior recalls '[w]ould they release a $65 million NC-17 movie that many theatres would not play …? Warner is the biggest conglomerate in the world ... an NC-17 movie is just something that we would not have wanted to release'.[42] Elsewhere Jon Lewis has identified the same link between content and risk to the film's status as a studio film, writing that

> the flap over *Eyes Wide Shut* … is not really about the integrity of the film itself … it's about box office and ancillary revenues. It's about the generation of profits and the complex ways cine-regulation … is designed primarily to serve the studios' best interests.[43]

The Stanley Kubrick Archive holds boxes of materials that reflect *Eyes Wide Shut*'s rather complicated critical life,[44] yet it has been well reported that the lack of extreme content in the final product was a major source of disappointment for early critics, with one for the *Washington Post* going as far to say that the film 'boast[ed] far more eroticism in its ad campaign than it ever shows on screen'.[45] Disappointment aside, the marketing campaign nevertheless reveals the commercial strategies at work when a studio is presented with an expensive film in need of a dependable marketing hook. In their biography of the production of *Eyes Wide Shut*, Robert P. Kolker and Nathan Abrams detail indicative elements of the film's tricky post-production, not least Kubrick and Warners' decision to 'market the movie as an "erotic thriller", heavily hyping its supposedly sensational sexual content'.[46] This decision has since been called 'the wrong one' by assistant Anthony Frewin and Julian Senior, then-head of European advertising for Warner,[47] and one that illustrates a discordance between the material facts of the film's content and the director's and studio's commercially minded design for it, who were positioning it as a box office-baiting erotic thriller in the mould of *Basic Instinct* (Paul Verhoeven, 1992) or *Disclosure* (Barry Levison, 1994) before it. The former is used as a point of comparison in an inter-office memo from Bill Ireton,[48] and the latter comes up in the data compiled for Warners' comprehensive and strategic sell-through marketing plans for rentals of the film, where it is referred to as an 'erotic thriller' expected to sell 35,000 units, appearing alongside mentions of *Bram Stoker's Dracula* (Francis Ford Coppola, 1992), *The Piano* (Jane Campion, 1993), *Interview With a Vampire* (Neil Jordan, 1994), *The English Patient* (Anthony Minghella, 1996), *The Devil's Advocate* (Taylor Hackford, 1997), *L.A. Confidential* (Curtis Hanson, 1997), *Armageddon* (Michael Bay, 1998), *City of Angels* (Brad Siberling, 1998), *Enemy of the State* (Tony Scott, 1998), *Lethal Weapon 4* (Richard Donner, 1998), *Saving Private Ryan* (Steven Spielberg, 1998) and *There's Something About Mary* (Bobby Farrelly and Peter Farrelly, 1998).[49]

For Amy J. Ransom, *Eyes Wide Shut*'s awkward positioning as an erotic thriller is most to blame for the film's failure to generate a larger audience. She writes that 'the perceived "failure" of Kubrick's last film can be attributed not to its flaws as a work of art but rather to critics' misplaced expectations about the film's genre and its conventions'.[50] Kolker and Abrams have provided evidence of the film's polarized reception among critics, the film-going public and scholars.[51] What they identify as the style of the film – 'expressive inexpressiveness', 'visual restraint', 'slow, deliberate pace' and a 'focus on domesticity' – comes up in reviews as the basis of complaints about the film.[52] Guided by the powers of retrospective re-evaluation by subsequent scholars and film critics[53] – which, once again, show discursive bias for Kubrick – it is quite clear to anyone who remains interested that *Eyes Wide Shut* was wrongly framed on release as something far more generic than it actually was. I contend that, by using the same terms that Kolker and Abrams do, terms that were often employed against the film by those critics that were hoping for something sexy over something artful, one can understand the tensions surrounding *Eyes Wide Shut*'s identity as a mis-marketed late-1990s studio film with 'quality' features.

Speaking of 'quality': *Eyes Wide Shut* and Hollywood in the shadow of the new millennium

Barry Salt, in a chapter titled 'The Shape of 1999', uses stylistic motifs as a means of tracking what was taking place in American film at the end of the millennium. For Salt, a survey of formal features (such as average shot length) is a means of dispelling what is for him an 'egomaniacal world where nothing but "critical intuition" is used in dealing with the arts'.[54] There are two things striking here. First, how democratic evaluative models are useful for taking stock of internal industrial developments and their characteristics and, second, that critical discourse is pervasively centred around notions of value. As I have outlined earlier in this chapter, for the purposes of thinking more broadly about *Eyes Wide Shut*'s identity within the wider landscape of late-1990s studio filmmaking, I plan to position it as a late-1990s studio film and draw on King's concept of the 'quality' Hollywood film for understanding its industrial and textual components.

King has used the 'quality' rubric to explain the industrial and aesthetic dimensions of a particular type of studio film that emerged in the first decade or so of the twenty-first century – examples that feature in his book *Quality Hollywood: Markers of Distinction in Contemporary Studio Film* include a range of films of different sizes and differing generic persuasions: *Blood Diamond* (Edward Zwick, 2006), *The Assassination of Jesse James by the Coward Robert Ford* (Andrew Dominik, 2007), *Inception* (Christopher Nolan, 2010) and *The Social Network* (David Fincher, 2010) all feature, while *A.I. Artificial Intelligence* also appears, a film that bears more than a few hereditary traces of Kubrick as an unmade film picked up by Spielberg. In his definition of the 'quality' film, King writes:

> Quality at the narrative level might be marked, variously, through slower narrative pace and development or greater complexity of plotting … [it] might, in general, be marked as subtle, low-key

> or nuanced in character – and/or more demanding – requiring closer attention from the viewer than is normally expected in Hollywood. A sense of drift might in some case replace dynamic, character-driven action; or, on the contrary, narrative and/or dialogue might be more rapidly paced and 'smarter' in quality. Characterisation ... might be more ambiguous, presented as more psychologically in-depth, lacking the relatively clear-cut distinctions between 'good' and 'bad' more typically associated with Hollywood and again requiring more cognitive work on the part of the viewer and implying a more complex view of the world.[55]

Though *Eyes Wide Shut* does not feature in King's study (it predates his period of interest), it certainly could have, given the stylistic markers identified above. Indeed, King employs a model flexible enough to be taken in new directions and applied to new texts. Thomas Allen Nelson's reading of the film corresponds with a case to be made for *Eyes Wide Shut*'s figuration as a 'quality' film:

> The narrative design of *Eyes Wide Shut* integrates a series of contrasts, reversals, and paradoxical doublings that recall the schizophrenic structure of *Full Metal Jacket.* As he did for most of his career, Kubrick combines in his final film a number of contrasting story developments, tones, and themes that seem to pull in opposite directions and to cancel each other out rather than meld into narrative unity.[56]

What one might note in Nelson's reading of *Eyes Wide Shut*'s maze-like structure are 'quality' characteristics in keeping with King's definition. Indeed, if one takes the complex narrative structure of *Eyes Wide Shut* and traces its formal properties through other 'quality' productions such as *A.I. Artificial Intelligence*, a notable example for King, one might find that *Eyes Wide Shut* fits relatively comfortably within the recent history of 'quality' studio films.

The failed marketing notwithstanding, there exists a potential to renegotiate *Eyes Wide Shut*'s identity as a studio film amid the strategic prerogatives of the mid-to-late-1990s Hollywood system. Though often thought of as a 1999 film due to its release that year, *Eyes Wide Shut*'s production strategy equally belongs to 1996 as production launched in November of that year. Between 1995 and 1996 Warners alone had mid-sized hits with 'R'-rated films including *Outbreak* (Wolfgang Petersen) and *Heat* (Michael Mann) in 1995, and *Eraser* (Chuck Russell),

Sleepers (Barry Levinson) and *A Time to Kill* (Joel Schumacher) in 1996. Excluding *Eraser*, a straight-up action film, all the other films in this list share at least one characteristic with the 'quality' mode. During the time of *Eyes Wide Shut*'s lengthy production, Warners had further success with archetypal 'quality' film *L.A. Confidential*, *The Devil's Advocate*, a starry 'R'-rated adaptation of a pulp horror novel, and *The Matrix*, released mere months before *Eyes Wide Shut*.

These films of course profess some degrees of variety; accordingly, I would like to contend that a 'quality' film is not determined by textual factors in isolation from a film's industrial positioning, but rather through the interplay of these overlapping discursive referents. King himself observes 1999 as being a particularly important year for the 'quality' mode, calling it a 'year of at least partially quality-oriented studio films including *Fight Club*, *Three Kings* [David O. Russell, 1999] and *American Beauty*'.[57] I would add *Bringing Out the Dead* (Martin Scorsese, 1999), *The Green Mile*, *The Hurricane* (Norman Jewison, 1999), *The Insider* and *Magnolia* (Paul Thomas Anderson, 1999) to that list, which all exhibit 'quality' elements, though to greater and lesser degrees, while not falling under the banner of what is commonly referred to as independent.[58] There is nothing, I argue, beyond the Kubrick factor, that marks *Eyes Wide Shut* as wholly distinct from any of those other films mentioned above – included among the filmmakers is Martin Scorsese, a contemporary of Kubrick's with a similar canon-defining pedigree, as well as heirs apparent, including Paul Thomas Anderson and Sam Mendes. Understanding these films as part of a new strategic orientation for studio filmmaking offers another means of looking at Kubrick's final film amid established and emergent industry paradigms.

So, what is it that these films convey about late-1990s studio filmmaking, exactly? First, how the 'R'-rated market was still being recognized as a significant part of the commercial landscape for major studios. With that being said, even against the success of films such as *The Sixth Sense* and *The Matrix*, the commercial underperformance of expensive 'R'-rated films including *The 13th Warrior, End of Days* and even *Eyes Wide Shut* at the turn of the millennium conveys a twilight for expensive adult films opposite the explosive success of family franchises in the early 2000s. Within this landscape, there are nevertheless distinctions to be made between smaller and larger studio productions. As King writes:

> in the case of the Hollywood film, ... what we find tends to inhabit a place somewhere between the poles suggested by ['art' and 'entertainment]. This space can itself be a broad one, including the realms

> of indie and Indiewood film as well as that of quality production from within the main studio divisions. The most commercially minded mainstream films are clearly engineered quite deliberately, through many decades of evolution, to appeal to the widest possible audience – or to the particular audience segments believed at any time to be the most fruitful Hollywood constituency. The quality film likewise appears to be designed to achieve a particular kind of appeal that might in some cases be a degree more specialised, but that is also usually intended to be capable of achieving broad circulation[.][59]

It is interesting how broad King's schema is, yet it is precisely due to distinctions regarding size that I offer the further category of 'quality' blockbuster for consideration – it is a category that is arguably implied by King but is ultimately absorbed into a schematic that is designed to be inclusive and not exclusive. But exclusivity is precisely what sets little apart from large. Returning to Table 8.1, it is evident that in the case of *Eyes Wide Shut*, *Fight Club* (co-produced by Fox 2000, Regency Enterprises, New Regency and Linson Films) and *The Insider* (co-produced with Touchstone Pictures and Spyglass Media), to isolate just a few examples, that 'quality' dimensions can equally be accompanied by great expense. Wherever these costs manifest, in salaries, the scale of production or elsewhere, they demonstrate a fluctuating openness to serious investment in alternative commercial strategies.

As the basis of a micro-study into the characteristics of late-1990s 'quality' films, I will consider *Eyes Wide Shut* alongside *The Insider*, *Fight Club* and *Bringing Out the Dead* (co-produced by Paramount, Touchstone Picture and Scott Rudin Productions), where certain elements of textual uniformity come to light. Firstly, there is the common element of a star-director in Kubrick, Mann, Fincher and Scorsese, respectively; each being known for their ability to successfully produce serious (synonymous with 'quality') content to moderately large audience bases. Second, there is a reflexive, or even self-effacing, use of stars. From the fourth-wall-breaking coupledom of Cruise and Kidman to the reflexive utilisation of Brad Pitt's sex appeal as a projected id in *Fight Club*, to the method ugliness of Russell Crowe in *The Insider* and Nicholas Cage in *Bringing Out the Dead*, stars are ever-present but put to work in different ways that self-consciously engage with or undermine their primary star images. Thirdly, each work has a pronounced literariness that is marked by its source material. *Eyes Wide Shut* adapts a work of modernist literature, while *Fight Club* and *Bringing Out the Dead* are adaptations of more contemporary cult works.

The Insider, meanwhile, is a dramatization (in a decidedly dialogue-heavy, play-like fashion) of a high-profile *Vanity Fair* segment aimed at the tobacco industry.[60] Fourth, each of the works emphasizes a heavyweight mode of storytelling that is combined with complex characterization. Indeed, all four films are classically and complexly dramaturgical, taking the form of tragedies. Each narrative finds its protagonist descending into one form of mania or another in a way that critiques and invites scrutiny of the wider cultural machinations of living under the spectres of patriarchy, neoliberalism and/or late capitalism. Next, the films equally adopt a conscious artfulness at the level of form. *Eyes Wide Shut* and *The Insider* are both dramatic films with running times outside what might be called the Hollywood 'safe zone', at 159 minutes and 151 minutes respectively. All four films demonstrate stylistic markers consistent with the 'art' film,[61] and employ formal apparatus to differentiate them from more straightforwardly commercial properties, from the palindromic shapes of *Eyes Wide Shut* or *Fight Club* to the chaotic spatiality of *Fight Club* and *Bringing Out the Dead* (and even *Eyes Wide Shut*, if popular psychoanalytic readings of the film are to prevail) to the documentary-realist, new historicism of *The Insider*.

One might find many more corresponding features in these films; however, the central thesis is that each film, both independently and collectively, demonstrates for better or worse a prevailing, post-indie strategy to develop expensive 'quality' films in the era that precedes King's primary period of interest. Of course, the 'success' or 'failure' of these four specific films is easy enough to reduce to money matters, critical algorithms and flighty notions of legacy, but to what end is that helpful to anyone except for an accountant? More useful is to consider how the structural underpinnings of these films facilitate a way of looking at the late-1990s studio system in an enlightening way. Accompanying the success of family-oriented franchises such as *Harry Potter* (various, 2001–2011), *The Lord of the Rings* (Peter Jackson, 2001–2003), *Shrek* (various, 2001–2010), *Spider-Man* (Sam Raimi, 2002–2007) and *Pirates of the Caribbean* (various, 2003–), the early 2000s saw a steady stream of further mature, 'quality' studio films that included, among others, *Traffic* (Steven Soderbergh, 2000), *Gangs of New York* (Martin Scorsese, 2002), *Road to Perdition* (Sam Mendes, 2002), *Munich* (Steven Spielberg, 2005) and *Blood Diamond* (Edward Zwick, 2006),[62] which features as a prominent case study for King.[63] Amid the various shifts and fluctuations taking place, it is equally evident that studios continued to entertain the possibility of films with pronounced narrative complexity akin to *Eyes Wide Shut*. From *Babel* (Alejandro González Iñárritu, 2006) to

The Departed (Martin Scorsese, 2006) to *Zodiac* (David Fincher, 2007), there is clear evidence that, notwithstanding its 'success' or lack of, *Eyes Wide Shut* exists on a continuum of studio risk-taking that encompasses expensive 'quality' films aimed at mature audiences. It is a mode that arguably has roots in New Hollywood – where Kubrick himself operated, albeit at the fringe – moving through the rise of the independents to take hold once again in the modern (post-millennium) studio era.

Studio consciousness of the 'quality' of Kubrick's films, and how that element appeals to certain audiences, arises in the conclusion of Warners' release statement for 'The Kubrick Collection' on DVD in 2001:

> The Kubrick Collection addressed both a demanding quality-oriented audience and a larger audience owing to the diversity of the Kubrick films. In both cases, those are undoubtedly viewed as *absolute cult masterpieces*, which should generate even more awareness among the audience in general.[64]

Clearly, notions of 'quality' are adaptable and have both a prescriptive and retrospective function. This chapter has largely circumvented the question of how one can or, indeed, should read *Eyes Wide Shut*. That is not to say *Eyes Wide Shut* is not a rich, inviting text – quite the opposite, in fact – but rather that tendencies towards textual analysis, while fascinating and often useful, can conceal other methodological pathways. Rather than perpetuate that tradition, I have chosen to offer a new (or newly adapted) framework for understanding *Eyes Wide Shut* as evidence of shifting, stagnating and even newly emerging directions in studio filmmaking during a transition period.

Acknowledgements

In support of the work conducted for this chapter, I paid visits to both the Bill Douglas Centre at the University of Exeter and the Stanley Kubrick Archive held at the University of the Arts, London. I am grateful to those who maintain these collections, which is a great and important service to film studies, and to the staff members who aided me on my visits. I would also like to thank Arts University Plymouth, which provided a research allowance that made possible my attendance at the initial conference *Behind Eyes Wide Shut* (in December 2019, co-hosted by University of the Arts, London and Bangor University).

Notes

1 Sheldon Hall and Steve Neale, *Epics, Spectacles, and Blockbusters: A Hollywood History* (Detroit, MI: Wayne State University Press, 2010), p. 1.
2 Charles R. Acland, *American Blockbuster: Movies, Technology, and Wonder* (Durham, NC and London: Duke University Press, 2020), p. 4.
3 Acland, *American Blockbuster.*
4 Thomas Schatz, 'The New Hollywood' in Jim Collins, Hilary Radner and Ava Preacher Collins (eds), *Film Theory Goes to the Movies* (New York: Routledge, 1993), pp. 3–36.
5 Hall and Neale, *Epics, Spectacles, and Blockbusters.*
6 See Michael Allen, 'Talking About a Revolution: The Blockbuster as Industrial Advertisement' in Julian Stringer (ed.), *Movie Blockbusters* (New York: Routledge, 2003), pp. 101–113; Scott Bukatman, *Matters of Gravity: Special Effects and Supermen in the 20th Century* (Durham, NC and London: Duke University Press, 2003).
7 Peter Krämer, '"Want to take a ride?": Reflections on the Blockbuster Experience in *Contact* (1997)' in Stringer, *Movie Blockbusters*, pp. 128–140.
8 Acland, *American Blockbuster*, p. 8; emphasis mine.
9 Sheldon Hall, 'Pass the Ammunition: A Short Etymology of "Blockbuster"' in Andrew B.R. Elliott (ed.), *The Return of the Epic Film* (Edinburgh: Edinburgh University Press, 2015), p. 147.
10 Organized in descending size of budget from highest to lowest; alphabetized where equal. Budget and box office numbers have been rounded to the nearest million dollars. Data courtesy of *The Numbers* (https://www.the-numbers.com/market/1999/top-grossing-movies, accessed 26 May 2021).
11 While other 'R'-rated films outperformed *Eyes Wide Shut* financially – significant earners not featured above include *The Sixth Sense* (M. Night Shyamalan, 1999), *The Blair Witch Project* (Daniel Myrick and Eduardo Sánchez, 1999), *The Green Mile* (Frank Darabont, 1999) and *American Beauty* (Sam Mendes, 1999) – Kubrick's film cost more than all bar six of the crop of 'mature' studio films released over the course of the year. As the table illustrates, with the exception of two very costly endeavours, *The 13th Warrior* and *End of Days*, all other 'R'-rated films included fall into a small window – costing between $65 million and $75 million – and it is worth noting that several further 'R'-rated studio films, *Any Given Sunday* (Oliver Stone, 1999), *The General's Daughter* (Simon West, 1999) and *The Green Mile*, would have featured in a slightly longer version of Table 8.1, with budgets of $60 million each.
12 Jaime Estrada Torres, 'Letter to Nigel Galt', 20 August 1999, SK/17/6/7, Stanley Kubrick Archive, Archives and Special Collections Centre, University of the Arts, London (hereafter 'SKA').
13 Linda Ruth Williams, *The Erotic Thriller in Contemporary Cinema* (Edinburgh: Edinburgh University Press, 2005), p. 397.

14 There is no better account of the film's production than Robert P. Kolker and Nathan Abrams' extensive study *Eyes Wide Shut: Stanley Kubrick and the Making of his Final Film* (New York: Oxford University Press, 2019).
15 Bryan Appleyard, 'Blink and You've Missed Him', *The Sunday Times*, 3 August 1997, SKA.
16 Quoted in Shauna Snow, *LA Times*, 10 September 1998, p. 50, SK/17/6/7, SKA.
17 Geoff King, *Quality Hollywood: Markers of Distinction in Contemporary Studio Films* (London and New York: I.B. Tauris, 2016).
18 King, *Quality Hollywood*, 261.
19 Hannah McGill, 'Eyes of the Beholder: *Eyes Wide Shut* at 20', *Sight & Sound* 29.12 (2019), p. 24.
20 McGill, 'Eyes of the Beholder', p. 26.
21 Michel Chion, *Kubrick's Cinema Odyssey*, trans. Claudia Gorbman (London: BFI, 2001), pp. 112–143, 164–173.
22 James Naremore, *On Kubrick* (London: BFI, 2007), p. vii.
23 King, *Quality Hollywood*, p. 261.
24 James Fenwick, *Stanley Kubrick Produces* (New Brunswick, NJ: Rutgers University Press, 2020), p. 3.
25 Peter Krämer, *2001: A Space Odyssey* (*BFI Film Classics*) (London: Palgrave Macmillan, 2010), p. 40.
26 If the legacy of *2001: A Space Odyssey* paints a picture of it being, on studio terms, a work of near avant-gardist levels of innovation ('the absolute film' for Chion, see n. 21), then it is worth noting that it was a financial success, only being beaten at the American box office by *Funny Girl* (William Wyler) in 1968. Alongside *Spartacus* (the highest earning American film of 1960), *2001: A Space Odyssey* may comfortably be regarded as Kubrick's biggest commercial hit.
27 Fenwick, *Stanley Kubrick Produces*, p. 181.
28 On this point, in the most recent iteration of *Sight & Sound*'s greatest films polls (December 2022), Kubrick featured prominently on the final lists compiled by both critics and directors, with *2001: A Space Odyssey* achieving exceptionally high rankings at 6th on the former list (alongside *Barry Lyndon* at =45th and *The Shining* at =88th) and 1st on the latter list (alongside *Barry Lyndon* at =12th and *Dr. Strangelove* at =46th).
29 King, *Quality Hollywood*, p. 260.
30 On this point, it is worth noting once again that Fenwick's extensive analysis of Kubrick's producer status (*Stanley Kubrick Produces*, 2020) has done tremendous work to unpick his mythic status within film discourse.
31 Quoted in Kolker and Abrams, *Eyes Wide Shut*, p. 67.
32 This is certainly true if one considers how Jack Nicholson's star status was considerably larger in 1980 than, say, Malcolm McDowell's was in 1971 or Ryan O'Neal's in 1975, who both entertained more niche roles in the

industry than Nicholson, a critical and commercial darling more in keeping with Cruise a generation later.

33 Warner Press Briefings, SK/17/5/6, SKA.

34 Angie Errigo, '*Eyes Wide Shut* Review', *Empire* (October 1999), p. 13.

35 Quoted in Kolker and Abrams, *Eyes Wide Shut*, p. 129.

36 Michael Shnayerson, 'Portrait of an Actress', *Vanity Fair* (October 1997), pp. 314–321, 366–368.

37 Bernard Weinraub, 'Kubrick's *Eyes Wide Shut* Still Open', *New York Times*, 28 April 1998, https://www.nytimes.com/1998/04/28/movies/kubrick-s-eyes-wide-shut-still-open.html. Accessed 20 May 2021.

38 This tone is maintained in the article, which promises the film is 'starring the Cruises, naked, in love and at war' before posing the million-dollar question: 'Do they? Don't they? The Cruises aren't telling.' See Cathy Booth, 'Three of a Kind', *Time Magazine*, 12 July 1999, pp. 72–73.

39 The *Time Magazine* article makes direct reference to this fact, noting that 'the film's climactic orgy scene had threatened to earn it a restrictive NC-17 rating': Booth, 'Three of a Kind', p. 73.

40 Stanley Kubrick, Frederic Raphael and Arthur Schnitzler, *Eyes Wide Shut: Screenplay and Dream Story* (London: Penguin 1999).

41 Richard Dyer, *Heavenly Bodies: Film Stars and Society*, 2nd edn (London and New York: Routledge, 2004 [1986]), p. 24.

42 Quoted in Adam Smith, 'The Eyes Have It', *Empire* (October 1999), pp. 96–97.

43 Jon Lewis, *Hollywood v. Hard Core: How the Struggle Over Censorship Saved the Modern Film Industry* (New York and London: New York University Press, 2000), pp. 1–2.

44 *Eyes Wide Shut* Reviews, SK/17/6/7, SKA.

45 Stephen Hunter, 'Kubrick's Sleepy *Eyes Wide Shut*', *The Washington Post*, 16 July 1999.

46 Kolker and Abrams, *Eyes Wide Shut*, p. 129.

47 Kolker and Abrams, *Eyes Wide Shut*, p. 129.

48 Bill Ireton, 'Inter-office memo: *Eyes Wide Shut* Opening Report', 1 August 1999, SK/17/6/6, SKA.

49 *Eyes Wide Shut* Marketing Plans, SK/17/5/6, SKA.

50 Amy J. Ransom, 'Opening *Eyes Wide Shut*: Genre, Reception, and Kubrick's Last Film', *Journal of Film and Video* 62.4 (2010), p. 31.

51 Kolker and Abrams, *Eyes Wide Shut*, pp. 133–141.

52 Kolker and Abrams, *Eyes Wide Shut*, p. 10. See also Lee Siegel, '*Eyes Wide Shut*: What the Critics Failed to See in Kubrick's Last Film', *Harper's Magazine*, October 1999, SK/17/6/7, SKA.

53 See, for example, its consistent re-evaluation among popular film critics: among others, *Slant Magazine* named it the second-best film of the 1990s, behind *The Thin Red Line* (Terrence Malick, 1998): *Slant Magazine*, 5 November 2012, https://www.slantmagazine.com/film/

the-100-best-films-of-the-1990s/10/. Accessed 31 May 2021. *Rolling Stone*, meanwhile, placed it 23rd: *Rolling Stone*, 12 July 2017, https://www.rollingstone.com/movies/movie-lists/the-100-greatest-movies-of-the-nineties-195513/eyes-wide-shut-1999-3-196304/. Accessed 31 May 2021. The BFI placed it 19th: BFI, 28 May 2020, https://www.bfi.org.uk/lists/90-great-films-1990s. Accessed 31 May 2021.

54 Barry Salt, 'The Shape of 1999: The Stylistics of American Movies at the end of the Century' in Warren Buckland (ed.), *Film Theory and Contemporary Hollywood Movies* (New York: Routledge, 2009), p. 124.

55 King, *Quality Hollywood*, p. 49.

56 Thomas Allen Nelson, *Kubrick: Inside a Film Artist's Maze* (Bloomington, IN: Indiana University Press, 2000), p. 268.

57 King, *Quality Hollywood*, p. 65.

58 See, for example, Claire Perkins, *American Smart Cinema* (Edinburgh: University of Edinburgh Press, 2011); Geoff King, Claire Molloy and Yannis Tzioumakis (eds), *American Independent Cinema: Indie, Indiewood and Beyond* (London and New York: Routledge, 2012); Yannis Tzioumakis, *American Independent Cinema*, 2nd edn (Edinburgh: Edinburgh University Press, 2017).

59 King, *Quality Hollywood*, p. 62.

60 See Marie Brenner, 'The Man Who Knew Too Much', *Vanity Fair* (May 1996), https://www.vanityfair.com/magazine/1996/05/wigand199605. Accessed 31 May 2021.

61 See Geoff King, *Positing Art Cinema: Film and Cultural Value* (London and New York: I.B. Tauris, 2018).

62 As one might expect, this list is far from exhaustive. I have discounted films that I think illustrate separate traditions, including historical epics (therefore *Gladiator* [Ridley Scott, 2000] and *The Last Samurai* [Edward Zwick, 2003], etc.), as well as sequels to earlier hits (therefore *Hannibal* [Ridley Scott, 2000] and *The Matrix* sequels [Lana and Lilly Wachowski, 2003], etc.).

63 King, *Quality Hollywood*, pp. 219–258.

64 Warner Home Video's 'Comprehensive Plan for "The Stanley Kubrick Collection"', 20 July 2001, SK/17/5/6, SKA, emphasis in the original.

9

A Cloaked and Masked Film: Some Things *Eyes Wide Shut* May (Really) Be About

Jeremi Szaniawski

> 'Aren't insanity and depravity the same in the eyes of God?'
>
> Herr Gibiser, the costume shop owner, in Arthur Schnitzler's *Traumnovelle – Rhapsody: a Dream Story*

Fuck? (or, what is *Eyes Wide Shut* about, *really*?)

While it is no doubt difficult to add anything to the discussion on *Eyes Wide Shut* – a film about which so much has been written, and in such striking variety – perhaps it is not useless to interrogate and probe the strange relationship audiences retain with this quizzical work to this day. Ever since its release, Stanley Kubrick's final work – one that, to use Alexander Walker's description, 'filmed what the mind could see, but eyes could not',[1] has charmed and puzzled its viewers, who are uncertain how to respond to the film's unique tone and atmosphere, or to its message. In colloquial Hollywood parlance, while the question 'what's the story about?' may have a fairly straightforward answer, the one question that really matters, 'what's the story *really* about?' will elicit a score of responses, and possibly contradictory ones to boot. Due to this either complex or muddled quality, like every other Kubrick film *Eyes Wide Shut* was met upon its July 1999 release with mixed reviews and mixed fortunes: a hit in places such as Japan or Argentina, it was a commercial flop in America and the UK. 'The dirtiest film of 1958' claimed a derisive Stephen Hunter.[2] To Michel Ciment, it was 'a great film about anxiety and the fear of sex, cut through with a vein of grotesquerie and black humor' that (like so many films by Kubrick), 'disappointed many viewers' expectations'.[3]

Overall, those on the left who detested it for its politics missed important points;[4] those who denounced it for its absurd unrealism (the lavish Central Park West apartment of the Harfords, a middle-class family;[5] the emptiness and bustlelessness of these Greenwich Village streets) or for Tom Cruise's baffling predicament and excessive response ('my wife *fantasizes* about *other men*?'), all had a point but missed the bigger picture. Those who claimed that Kubrick had grown disconnected from the world after too many decades in the British countryside were off the mark: *Eyes Wide Shut* is not a film by someone who has lost touch with reality. It is a film by someone whose rapport with reality always was different than that of the majority of people, and who portrayed a subject moving through a reality alienated from itself, yet with a deeply layered, aggregate quality. As Walker, a long-time friend of the director, put it, 'Kubrick produced and directed a film that creates a world within and yet apart from the one his characters inhabit'.[6]

Those who expressed negative feelings about Kubrick's alleged prudishness were probably right in feeling cheated at the sight of the tame orgy at the centre of the film. But mostly they were quite foolish to expect the expected from Kubrick (in short, that he deliver a straightforward sexy thriller – that 1990s trend initiated by the success of the vastly incoherent but amusing *Basic Instinct* (Paul Verhoeven, 1992)), and for having let Warner Bros.' marketing cheat them so cheaply in promising to deliver just such a film. As for those critics who denounced the film's banal characters and dialogues,[7] or its slow and belaboured nature, definitely they were onto something. Except that the slowness and 'laborious' nature of the film are entirely deliberate: a measured 'dreamlike logic' and 'disconnected languor', to quote Robert Kolker and Nathan Abrams,[8] governs the film's proceedings like grotesquely superb and slowed-down clockwork. Or, to quote Janet Maslin's review:

> Part of the film's sustained tension comes from the slow, ribbonlike way in which these episodes unfold, with fidget-prompting long takes and not much background music to provide relief; part of it comes from the viewer's complete uncertainty about what will happen next.[9]

It was a titillating and tantalizing mechanism that many considered unfinished, including major filmmakers such as David Lynch (a great admirer of Kubrick, who admired Lynch in turn) and David Cronenberg (a filmmaker more sceptical of his *oeuvre*). Critics were also divided over whether to emphasize or minimize the problems related to Kubrick's interrupted authorship of the film. Conversely, those who loved the film unconditionally, across the board, were probably too easily swayed by its testamentary dimension as well as by its glossy, lush, impressionist and symbolist, painting-like imagery. Certainly, a lot of the positive criticism written about the film shortly following Kubrick's death lacked no fawning for the great auteur – often remaining on the surface (the gorgeous cinematography, work with music and choreography, the careful execution of it all), even when addressing the Somerton orgy sequence which lay at the heart of the film. Take Walker again, for example, who said

> [a] Gothic country house in Upstate New York where well-heeled guests hidden behind Venetian masks copulate with naked women in every corner of the cavernous room. This sequence is visually striking, but nearer to Schnitzler's Vienna than Manhattan's out-of-towners. The *Forbes* 500 caught with their pants down always tends to look slightly ridiculous, though Kubrick choreographs the revels with all the sinister solemnity of an impending sacrifice and peoples the standard cowled celebrants of Gothic romance with some phantasmagoric creations out of Max Ernst's sado-sexual canvases.[10]

Take another example, from James Naremore:

> Everything has the feeling of a confused dream about ancient and modern cultures: the interiors look like a cross between Xanadu and the *Playboy* mansion; the invited guests resemble Catholic monks dressed as Venetian revelers; and the music, written and conducted by the British avant-garde composer Jocelyn Pook, sounds like a religious ritual filtered through postmodern performance art … to lend an aura of all-purpose demonic ritual to a slightly weird erotic pageant.[11]

Naremore is then quick to add that the orgy, like some dreams, is sinister and silly.

This is all apt and accurate no doubt, but what does describing the film, however aptly, really tell us about it? And are these critics not conceding defeat, throwing their arms up in the air, in front of an epistemically sealed object, an impenetrable dream of a film? The latter, like any dream, has its inner logic and seems to make sense when we dream it, only then to haplessly try to reconstruct it and make sense of it in our waking time.

Eyes Wide Shut and the question of desire (or, a cloaked and masked film)

Kubrick's swan song was purportedly about love and sexuality within marriage. And on the surface, *Eyes Wide Shut* most definitely deals with these things. One should add that these manifest topics are most definitely not to be taken literally or at face value. They are merely motifs that cloak and mask quite a different message and meaning. The film's polysemy and ambiguities beg for some form of methodological framework that would allow us to apprehend it in a less elusive, fragmentary or vague fashion. Clearly, the frustration with the film expressed in contemporaneous negative reviews, and the continued outpouring of interpretations surrounding it since (including as a cult film), reveal something about its somewhat manifest theme (at least at the level of the script), namely, desire.[12]

In building anticipation among its fan base at least ever since *2001: A Space Odyssey* (1968) Kubrick's films were always generating a form of desire on the part of the audience. And it is evident that his final film, released after his death, came with a heightened, added share of anticipation and desire. In this way, the film is self-referentially embedded in its own production and in its release processes. And the fact that it was not quite finished added to the titillation that also pulsated at its story's base. Unsurprisingly, then, the viewers themselves desire to find something behind the film's 'mask', only to be endlessly frustrated by the fact that what the film may reveal remains ineffable – like desire itself: once it is sated, it vanishes. This desire and the quest thereof are also what fuelled the returns to the film by fans and critics alike. And what may connect a lot of the responses to the film, besides a form of befuddlement or frustration, is their desire for the film to be something else (and, of course, for the viewers themselves to be someone else, transported vicariously by the power of cinema).

Desire for what, exactly, then? The near-total ambiguity and tonal indeterminacy of the film are rendered even stranger by how deliberate and precise it is. Unlike a recent *ersatz*, David Robert Mitchell's *Under the Silver Lake* (2018), which flirts with Kubrick by means of Cukor, Hitchcock and Lynch, addressing matters of fantasy and schizophrenia *ad nauseam*, *Eyes Wide Shut* does not fall – it may not even ever trip – in its dizzying, but also dizzyingly suspended waltz with death. It forms a circle

Figure 9.1 Kubrick family poster for Eyes Wide Shut.

in the middle of which lies an empty, intriguing space of unknowability. The film's production history was epic, but also epicly secretive, bringing attention to itself by giving away very little: a sliver of flesh, the body of the film otherwise covered in a thick, dark cloak which suggested and promised a lot, but uncovered little, even as bodies were laid bare. And to this day the film, like any epistemic object, has retained its share of mystery, a hole in its middle – the suspicion of there being no one underneath the mask.

The motif of the mask, accordingly, is widespread in the promotional material related to the film: although it was not featured in the poster used at the time of the film's release in 1999, it appears in a poster designed by Katharina and Christiane Kubrick and recurs widely in fanart and other national release material of the film.

The notion of the mask is also rehearsed constantly throughout the film, as a layer of deception or pretence: the Christmas trees, big and small, garlands and lights as masks of merriment and promises of rebirth in an otherwise wintry environment, or the Christmas party concealing Ziegler's and other guests' philandering and hidden vice. The survival of forgotten customs, traces, moulds, evergreens once meant to suggest death and the dead, are now impositions of consumerist fantasy – not so much empty signifiers (although they are that too) as screens, repositories, fetishes. Masks, then, become increasingly literal as the film progresses, from Mr Milich's costume shop to the orgy scene and its aftermath.

But the masks are also of flesh and blood: Ziegler's power resides in his ability to wear many masks. As for Bill Harford, and perhaps Alice as well, their earnestness, their 'masklessness', is also a token of their dreadful emptiness and alienation in this strange New York City. The latter is a mix, as Naremore suggests, of past and present, of nascent turn-of-the-century capitalism and its late instantiation on the cusp of the twenty-first century. It is not useless to point out here, as does Matt Melia, that *Eyes Wide Shut* was the last cult film of the twentieth century. One could add that also, in a paradoxical way, it was the last big studio film to be conducted with the freedom of an independent film of that same decade, at once very much of its time and out of joint with its era. Markers of ending, but also of lateness and untimeliness – terms to which I shall return – are important here. Already Schnitzler's *Traumnovelle* was a work that seemed to come too late (published in 1926); it felt as though it dated from turn-of-the-nineteenth-century imperial Vienna, as though a modernist work were parading under the guise of a pre-modernist text.[13] Likewise, to see Tom Cruise as a hapless, clueless character after his heroics from the *Mission: Impossible* franchise suggests the presence of a decoy, a parade of sorts, and the evident parodic dimension of *Eyes Wide Shut*.

There are other masks as well here, among the layers of textual palimpsest. Schnitzler's Jewishness has been removed or rendered cryptic, as Frederic Raphael, as well as Abrams and Kolker, have told us.[14] Sandor Savoszt is now Hungarian, and Bill and Alice are New York WASPs as if the Holocaust had wiped Jewishness and lewd Polish seducers from the stage. This strange New York City replaces the vulgar imagery of social corruption portrayed by Martin Scorsese,[15] or Brian De Palma's gangster and horror films, with a more bawdy but also more refined brand of decadence: 'an imaginative melding of the city of [Kubrick's] memory and of old Vienna that had become fat with wealth'.[16] Yet it also does not shy away from the pedestrian: '[t]here is something so typically Kubrickian and, as always with his films, uncanny about its mixture of technical virtuosity with the quotidian, even the banal, and its mysterious aura at the borderline between wake and sleep and dream, sexual longing and frustration, an action hero celebrity playing a humbled man'.[17] Likewise, the film functions very much like a late modernist work in a sea of unabashed post-modernity – and necessarily feels painfully untimely, parodic and out of place as a result. Kubrick's final elaborate prank would be on the audience trying to apprehend it with a straight face – or the mask thereof.

Figure 9.2 Unofficial poster announcing a screening of Eyes Wide Shut.

The film's 'cloak and mask' aesthetic (its mystery, its mysteriousness or its fetishistic titillation, but also its carnivalesque, mutedly farcical nature) and its cryptic message, aligned with that aesthetic, have been some of the key factors contributing to the development of conspiracy theory around the film (which also, concomitantly, sprouted around *The Shining*, of which *Eyes Wide Shut* features echoes, and which it doubles in many ways).[18] As Marty Jonas writes, 'films that show a polished, attractive, enigmatic surface, but with little if anything underneath – especially if by a noted director – invite diverse, odd, and far-flung interpretation'.[19] As we see in this unofficial poster of the film (produced for a screening at San Francisco's Castro Theater), Satanist imagery is associated with the orgy.

We know from Frederic Raphael that the screenwriter allegedly invented a fake secret society narrative and served it to Kubrick early in their collaboration on the script, answering the director's interest in the matter. The imagery of secret societies (and their occasional corollary, 'naked parties') has elsewhere excited the US imaginary: Yale, Harvard and Princeton all have on their campuses (sometimes windowless) buildings dedicated to these meetings, which actually are more or less inherited from the European masonic system (with a modicum of ritual and a lot of networking involved). There is the idea, here, of the elite needing its own rituals, however hollow, to at once revive a form of excitement and neutralize it due to their decorum. The titillating 'conspiracy' of secret society members trying to get a kick out of their reified existence is here combined with the imaginary of intrigue and secrecy at the masked ball (and an inversion of its carnivalesque function – the revelers at the masked ball do not want to be recognized by the naked models, but they also replay the social stage, without undermining it). Kubrick no doubt found inspiration for the film in a Surrealist masked ball for the elite, organized by Nadine and Guy de Rothschild in 1972, of which many pictures are circulating online.[20]

While the pictures from the party give off a rather sinister vibe, the real, 1972 revellers seem mostly bored and made somewhat uncomfortable by their elaborate costumes. Marisa Berenson was a guest at that ball. It may be that Kubrick heard about it from her during the shooting of *Barry Lyndon*. At any rate, it is quite clear that there are parallels to be drawn between the original 1972 party and the film (the location, the naked mannequins, etc.). *Eyes Wide Shut* procures a dreamlike, weird, detached version of the real-life party (which, again, if one judges from the faces of the guests, was a contrived, turgid affair). This is clearly palpable in the slowed-down, unnerving yet sedate, mechanical 'orgy' part of the Somerton party. Most revellers are engaged not so much in intercourse as in performing a strange choreography of sex (case in point: the two women in sixty-nine position, presumably play-acting oral sex, made otherwise impossible by their wearing full-face covers). This zone of indeterminacy between ritual and spontaneous action, between detached performativity and engaged intercourse, speaks to this secret society as something of a leftover, a claim to be a community of the elite only

Figure 9.3 The Rothschilds' 1972 masked ball.

through contriving and then restricting, if not thwarting, desire, and of course through wearing a mask.

The titillating imagery and imaginary of secret societies and corollary conspiracy, of a dark and sinister kind, is congenial with the film's

Figure 9.4 The Rothschilds' ball – are we having fun yet?

unsatisfactory, endlessly elusive and frustrating nature. As Fredric Jameson taught us, conspiratorial thinking is the first step towards cognitive mapping – an attempt to understand the very nature of history and the working of dialectics under capitalism and its many iterations, transformations and mechanisms.[21] These are too complex for a more traditionally attuned neurocortex to grasp, and re-embedded and reimagined as a nefarious scheme of some sort. *Eyes Wide Shut* seems to teeter on the brink of a conspiratorial world view while also ridiculing it and revealing it for what it is: the rich and powerful bored and trying to recreate a sense of decorum or ritual as a response to their own alienation. In this sense, Bill Harford's attempts to uncover a secret, like the many more elaborate or outright demented theories so prevalent in online venues nowadays,[22] have to do with the fantasy of power for the otherwise powerless: a desire to master a world view and explain what otherwise cannot be cognitively mapped. In this sense, conspiratorial thinking becomes wish-fulfilment, and its uncovering, some kind of orgasmic resolution which however is blocked out by the clashing of Harford with reality and the fact that breaking one's nose against a mirror, even to the point of shattering the mirror's surface, will only reveal the wall behind it. There are two dynamics at play here: the desire to control, to rationalize, to provide a clear, closed-ended answer; and the ongoing desire to always renew the conspiratorial narrative (hence the impossibility for the psychotic mind to ever find closure to the delirium). This tension in the film – between an attempt at mastery and control and the ever-elusive nature of processes that entirely escape control, if they exist at all – explains the parodic nature of *Eyes Wide Shut*. This is where it becomes crucial to look at the genesis of the film as a dark comedy that underlies and makes palpable the grotesque contradictions of the characters' aspirations and predicaments. It turns their otherwise pedestrian nature into fodder for an absurdist morality or cautionary tale of sorts: the answer to Dr Harford's (and the viewer's) wish is so banal and silly that it is outright comical to take it at face value.

Eyes Wide Shut – a 'New York Jewish sex comedy'?

A 'New York Jewish sex comedy' under the mask of the 'sexy' or 'erotic thriller': such is the clever conceit which inverts Woody Allen's own play with genre (*Manhattan Murder Mystery*, 1993), and a bankable concept for studio executives with their mouths watering at the box office grosses of the films of Paul Verhoeven and Adrian Lyne, which were all the rage *circa* 1994 – when Kubrick's film officially went into pre-production.[23] But this marriage of a strange absurdist comedy with the sexy thriller genre felt odd to the viewer, now as it did then. There was something too suave, too languorous, but mostly too haunted, too detached – even beyond Kubrick's trademark play and transcending of genre boundaries – about *Eyes Wide Shut*, for it to be considered a sexy thriller, or even a 'sexual drama'. This tonal ambiguity did not give away its secrets until much more recently, not least through the extensive work by Robert Kolker and Nathan Abrams.

Kubrick at first considered Woody Allen to play his Fridolin – as early as the 1970s.[24] Indeed what became *Eyes Wide Shut* might have preoccupied Kubrick ever since his days in Greenwich Village, when he was an already established photographer and budding filmmaker. Many iterations and attempts at adapting the Schnitzler story are expertly documented by Kolker and Abrams (including a stab at it by John Le Carré – who may have inadvertently given the finished film its title). In this light, what became the finished 1999 project then acquires a very different sheen. One can hear Woody Allen uttering the lines of the film – the subduedly comical repetition of short sentences by Cruise (although Raphael penned them years after Kubrick had abandoned the idea of casting Allen, thinking then about Steve Martin, but also, allegedly, Bruce Willis and Demi Moore, and Kim Basinger and Alec Baldwin, before settling for the rather unfunny couple of Nicole Kidman and Tom Cruise.)

Just try the following thought experiment: imagine the bedroom/stoned sequence between Allen and Kidman (or, say, Allen and Mia Farrow or Allen and Diane Keaton), particularly sentences such as 'This pot is making you aggressive' or 'There are exceptions'. Or the infamous parroting by Tom Cruise of lines uttered by other actors, now in the high-pitched, nervous manner of Allen, New York Jewish accent and all:

Domino: Come inside with me.
[WA as Fridolin/Bill Harford]: Come inside with you?

Domino: What do you want to do?
[WA]: What do you recommend?

Sally: HIV positive.
[WA]: HIV positive?

Ziegler: I had you followed.
[WA]: You had me followed?

Or simply imagine Allen in the scene in which the masked man at the party orders him to remove his clothes. Or – perhaps my favourite – when the doctor tries to console the smitten patient over her father's dead body: 'Well, Michigan is a beautiful state. I think you'll like it a lot.'

It's all about intonation, of course – as in the old Jewish Soviet joke about Stalin receiving a cable from Trotsky reading 'You were right. I was wrong. I should apologize.' All members of the Politburo read the cable with glee as Stalin rejoices, until Lazar Kaganovich – the last Jewish member of Stalin's elite (and also one of its most ruthless and witty members), lifts his finger and says to Stalin: 'Yosif Visarionovich, with all due respect, I think Lev Borisovich meant "*You* were *right*? *I* was *wrong*? *I* should apologize?"'

Instead of what would have promised to be a jubilant Jewish comedy (probably in the impertinent inflexions of Stanley Kubrick, Peter George and Terry Southern's script for *Dr. Strangelove* – rather than the sententious Frederic Raphael), Kubrick settled in the end for something else.[25] Had he done a Woody Allen comedy, it would have been a riot, no doubt, but perhaps also a failure, or, at least, not a very profound film – suffering, like *Strangelove* did in certain ways, of an excess of comedic straightforwardness, the kind of farce to which Kubrick never returned in his mature work. The film would not have lasted in the way Kubrick probably intended. Instead, the director sacrificed the unapologetic glee of an awkward sex comedy and left it to Allen – the master of the genre. We can pine for the film this could have been – but now that we have deep fake technology, all hope is not lost of seeing one day not only Jim Carrey doing Jack Nicholson in *The Shining*, but indeed Allen as Bill Harford. There is an infinite universe of possibilities out there which the maker of *Eyes Wide Shut* and its endless interpretative coils would not have disavowed.

But thinking of Woody Allen as the protagonist, and of comedy as the underlying, submerged, tonal baseline of the film, also folds it back into the realm of something more sinister, including by a proleptic leap to *circa* 2019. In so doing, we account, too, for the film's fascinating interplay with time: in the years since, Woody Allen's image as a clever comedian has been smothered by a series of scandals, emphasized by the #MeToo movement. But it is also worth reminding ourselves that Allen was among the circle of celebrity acquaintances of Jeffrey Epstein. Another 'turn of the screw' in apprehending *Eyes Wide Shut*, the proleptic echoes of the Epstein scandal to be found here are eerily apt; film scholar Michael Cramer underlines

> the bizarre dynamic through which Epstein acted as a pimp for the rich and famous in a quest to be part of the select 'club', yet who then got *kompromat* on them and became a kind of ringmaster of desire. It's this very bizarre way of absorbing other people's fantasies into one's own, or almost making them one's property (in that, he's far ahead of the folks in the film).[26]

Knowledge of the genealogy and history of the film sheds new light on it, explaining in part why *Eyes Wide Shut* felt so strange, excessive and subdued, smug and neurotic, smart and dumb at one and the same time: it was initially meant and conceived as a comedy based on a fairly serious and rather dark novella, but it only retained a very few manifest hints of that lineage. Tom Cruise is so humourless and dull, that seemingly no real comedy can ever be directly teased out from him, even as he finds himself in the most absurdly funny and sordid situations, and even as he embodies the ridicule of the overambitious little man. Still, for all its dark hints, the underlying, submerged comedy still makes the ghost smile, with the sardonic humour that was Kubrick's trademark (Walker described it as a 'wit with a streak of refined amusement in it, both taunting and self-protective' and Marit Allen referred to his 'malicious humour, without taking it especially seriously').[27]

Next to the sex comedy lineage, we find strong undertones of the gothic and the horrific in *Eyes Wide Shut* (genres which, as we know at least since Linda Williams, always carry in themselves something of the excess of slapstick, in the broader constellation of body genres). The film may elicit no jump scares, but it is filled with dread. It is rife with references to *The Shining* (the Steadicam and cross-dissolves, the encounter of two levels of reality – including the horror of brushing past the higher class, the nightmares, the doubles, the ball, the teddy bears, but also Ziegler's false affection and congeniality, under which lurks a dark secret, akin to Ullman's, Grady's or Lloyd the bartender's). It also features an almost literal quote of Mario Bava's 1964 'Drop of Water' episode from the *Black Sabbath*, echoed in the way Marie Richardson's face is lit and her hair done, the lighting of her dead father's bedroom, and the unrealistic shades of purple, crimson and blue which bathe the film. In all this, we see that *Eyes Wide Shut* is closer to comedy and horror than to sexy thriller or even straightforward social critique or drama. The angst and distrust for the elites and authority remain firmly rooted throughout, but so does the old filmmaker's tongue – in his cheek. This, combined with the more eerie ways in which the film engages with dread and desire, procures something definitely unnerving and trippy.

A Schnitzler adaptation by way of Franz Kafka (or vice versa?)

The way Kubrick proceeds by indirection (case in point: submerged humour in the guise of dread) is replicated also in the film's lineage, adapting a novel by one author, yet invoking another one. In implementing

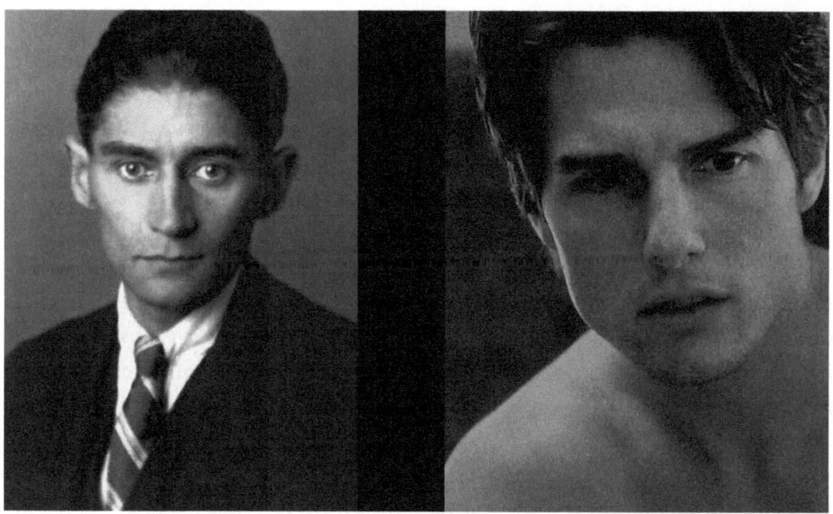

Figure 9.5 Bill Harford: Fridolin or Joseph K?

a father/superego figure, who also seems to hold the keys to an abominable id (I am talking of course of Ziegler, not Milich or the dead Lou Nathanson), Kubrick turns this picaresque with a touch of Dante away from Schnitzler's Viennese circles and rounds of unfulfilling promiscuity and missed opportunities, and towards Kafka's territory of unrealized connections. Such narratives of the loss of the illusion of control, and the clash of the subject with the real, are more Kafka (and Lacan) than Schnitzler–Freud, when all is said and done. In typical Kafka fashion, in *Eyes Wide Shut* the sexual impetus is thwarted each time and superego/paternal figures try to be reassuring yet are menacing. Ziegler tells the humiliated, castrated Dr Bill, in a paternalistic fashion, 'Life goes on until it doesn't. But you knew that already, didn't you?'

The plot of *Eyes Wide Shut* is by and large faithful to the Schnitzler novella, except for the scenes involving Ziegler – tellingly a fabrication of Raphael and Kubrick. The film's interplay of dream/fantasy and reality is masterfully rendered – including through a play with doublings of motifs and *Doppelgängers* dear to both Schnitzler and Kubrick. Yet it nonetheless strays significantly from the novella in spirit. As do the protagonists: Bill Harford, especially as impersonated by Tom Cruise, who meets prohibiting and tempting figures and never gets to consummate the sexual act, all the while being threatened by a strange, Lacanian gaze-like figure, is far closer to Joseph K from *The Trial* than he is to the Jewish doctor Fridolin.

The latter was an alter ego of Schnitzler – bold, proud, quick-witted, somewhat intrepid and prone to call people out for a duel, and spending not the first, but the second half of the novella trying to gain revenge for his wife's fantasized infidelity. Much diverging from the literary character, Cruise's angst-filled and ambiguous masculinity and endlessly unsatisfied pursuit of women is strongly redolent of Anthony Perkins' in Orson Welles' adaptation of Kafka's late novel.[28] Indeed, Bill Harford is not Schnitzlerian at all, at least not in the sense that Max Ophüls brought us Schnitzlerian characters: never so much naïve as on the brink of disenchantment and cynicism, a state Harford seems to be quite incapable of. He is, however, a distracted, wannabe philanderer as much as he is an anxious one, like Joseph K – a groper in the dark in need of superego figures (a priest in *The Trial*, Ziegler or a statuesque naked woman with Cate Blanchett's voice in *Eyes Wide Shut*) to warn him that he has wandered too far and that he is unaware of what awaits 'where the rainbow ends'.

Harford's fate may be less tragic than Joseph K's – he has little more substance or discernment. Against Cruise's Bill, and even though she occupies far less screen time, and spends it chiefly at home, Nicole Kidman's Alice is a far more interesting character (where Bill's asinine fantasies are images, flat like masks, Alice's are narratives, doubled like a script). Her psychic landscape contaminates the film, the viewer, and shakes her husband out of his Bill Harford, MD-*cum*-schmuck's lethargic state, only to plunge him – and us, the viewers – into the slow, dreamy voyage that is the film.

Eyes Wide Shut and the spatio-temporal uncanny

Surely one of the marvellous accomplishments of *Eyes Wide Shut* is the way it engages with time and space, a time that is dense (a function of Kubrick's unique and perfectionist work with repetition), and a space that is strange and uncanny, not least through the use of Steadicam and doubling effects (in this, it is again a close relative to *The Shining*). But we are dealing here also with a time of perambulation and rumination that is exquisitely addressed, creating an aesthetics of floating, aquatic, suspended, slowed-down time, and bringing welcome reprieve from the exhaustingly (and deliberately) pedestrian dialogue.[29] In this way, the film's closest next-of-kin in Kubrick's *corpus* is *2001: A Space Odyssey*, insofar as both works indeed procure a poetics that is visual, not verbal. Both films have ambiguous, open endings (is the Star Child going to save humanity or destroy it?). But whereas the ending of *2001* ranks among the most powerful and satisfying in the history of the medium, that of *Eyes Wide Shut* must remain underwhelming. One film is about resilience, rebirth and transformation, while the late work is about resignation and acceptance. Kubrick would likely have made more cuts to the film had he lived – but I doubt they would have involved changing the ending or cutting the wanderings of Bill Harford through the streets of New York or lavish interiors (although apparently, photographs picturing a happy Harford family in springtime have circulated online – it being unclear whether they were meant hypothetically to feature as a prologue or coda to the film). Nor would Kubrick have excised the moments of doubling and reckoning, those moments in the film playing with cinematic suture and self-reflexivity: 'je est un autre', when Bill finds himself at the gates of Somerton during the daytime, which he can no longer access, and one cannot help but think of Raphael's description of Kubrick's estate and its gates and cameras. It is as though Kubrick made a post-mortem commentary (no longer 'lucky to be alive', and yet somewhat with us forever), a bit like the ghosts in a later Nicole Kidman vehicle (*The Others* (Alejandro Amenábar, 2002)).

This is where the film, at last, starts revealing its cards: its deep loneliness is that of the dead. Perhaps, as Ian Christopher suggests about *The Shining* (that it may all be Wendy Torrance's fantasy, from her small Boulder apartment, trying to come to terms with Jack's death in a drunken car accident),[30] *Eyes Wide Shut* is all Alice's fantasy, sleeping next to a mask in bed: Bill has only been the ghost walking these strange streets, watching his wife dancing with another man, becoming helplessly jealous for not being able to get to her, then discovering his own death, his double, in bed next to his beautiful widow. There is here an oblique echo of the very beginning of the novella, perhaps, where Albertine and Fridolin go to a masked ball before making love passionately. And this obscure echo evokes also the longing, in any filmic adaptation, for the boundless possibilities of the written word over its more constricting cinematic representations: a longing that is awfully close to mourning but also to the uncanny quality of the forensic or post-mortem scrutiny and investigation.

Thomas Elsaesser writes at length about the importance of the 'post-mortem' narrative in late 1990s Hollywood cinema (using *American Beauty* and *The Sixth Sense* as his central examples). And in this, we can find an interpretative key to *Eyes Wide Shut*, an explanation perhaps for its strange tone and mood, but also its motifs of sexual mismatch and incommunicability, despite all the verbose dialogue. But this disconnect had to do with timing, with lateness, no doubt: Elsaesser also underlines the importance of *Nachtrachlichkeit* ('deferred action') when dealing with Kubrick.[31] It was, to Elsaesser, as though, necessarily, Kubrick's films always came too early and too late at one and the same time – a function of their prescience yet protracted production period, and resulting in their density and longevity as filmic texts; a function, too, of the fact that critics and scholars would only appreciate them fully at a much later time. A brilliant way to resist obsolescence, if there ever was one.[32]

As I stated in the opening, while on the surface the film is about mundane matters and banal and mediocre people, *Eyes Wide Shut* is almost never about what it purports or appears to be about. It proceeds almost exclusively by means of indirection, being a film about what goes on in the mind of the characters (and of cinema), about a beyondness, an interiority which it gives us to behold while concealing it. So, yes, *Eyes Wide Shut* is manifestly about marriage, infidelity, impotence, castration, damaged masculinity and feminine power, perhaps about secret societies, too – and also about the social comedy and performativity of it all, and the need for some form of secret or mystery to keep it all going. But it is never only about those things, if it is about them at all. It is also about the interconnectivity of things that seem dissociated or irreconcilable:

> it explores in complex and convincing ways the links between love and sex, between affective relationships and sexual fantasy, between sex as a male construct signifying anxiety, guilt and death and sex as a crucial ingredient in a healthy relationship, between sex as commodity and sex as emotion.[33]

On the other hand, as I also argued in the opening, *Eyes Wide Shut* is 'really' about many other things, and just summarizing what these (often contradictory) things are should not be the point. A magnificent work of art, a magnificent sleight of hand; but there seems to be a crack in the whole, a fundamental flaw. Could the film's message really only be about acceptance and resignation, as Michel Ciment suggests, that, in the end, individuals have to make peace with the world, go home and fuck their spouse – until death comes?

Fuck no (or, the hole in the bagel)

Like any such magnificently protracted sleight of hand, the spectacle must necessarily disappoint in the end. As with any desire, one of its important themes (or 'objects' or driving forces), there is always the danger of the delivery falling short of the promise. In this sense, the flaw of *Eyes Wide Shut* is outside it – in the hole in the bagel or the doughnut, in the dark recesses of the 'brain film', to use Gilles Deleuze's coinage.[34] It seems to reside with the viewer, not the film. The latter is no mere sleight of hand, luckily, for what mere sleight of the hand contains philosophical teachings? *Eyes Wide Shut* surely tells us that words can be deceiving and that no solid information can ever be obtained through language, despite a 'million years of evolution'. As for the memorable visuals and their orgy of purple, pink and dark blue, they remain a surface, which cannot allow us to access any form of truth. Discourse tells us nothing meaningful – it is just descriptive or prescriptive, even as advice and warnings will not be heeded; images teach us nothing – lessons will not be learned. In other words, seeing is believing, misbelieving, disbelieving, but seeing is not knowing. Thus, we are forever ignorant and alone and cannot establish real or meaningful connections. Perhaps we are indeed to try to apprehend the world with eyes wide shut rather than with eyes wide open, after all.

Stanley Kubrick's final film contained the lesson of his life and his death. It was obviously about the excitement and danger of breaking down routine. But more importantly, it is about the process of information entering the brain and of a thought forming there as a result. Geoffrey Kleinman wrote about the film that it 'makes you think about people, relationships, and the secrets we all keep',[35] and, I would argue, removing the rest of the quote, that 'it makes you think' – about an intrusion, with all the productive and fertile dimensions, contained therein – until it doesn't.

In short, trying to access the hole in the bagel that is the film – amusingly, a semi-fictitious *knishery* is featured behind Domino and Dr Bill in the middle of the film, straight out of the 1940s Lower East Side Kubrick surely knew and loved – will only lead to an interpretative rabbit hole.

> The fact is that all of Kubrick's films require more than one viewing. The more they are seen, the deeper they burrow into the unconscious, the more they become templates for our judging of other films or even seeing the world around us. They also become fodder for a variety of interpretations, from initial reviews, to scholarly readings, to conspiracy theories.[36]

Just as he had done masterfully with *The Shining*, Kubrick devised *Eyes Wide Shut* for the age of video – a film to watch over and over again, one never entirely yielding its secrets for lack of a determinate 'answer' to its epistemic and generic riddles (including that deliberately crassest of all, when Louis Skorecki asks, of the opening toilet scene ahead of the Christmas party, whether Alice is wiping 'her cunt or her ass').[37] What we can productively end on, however, while admitting to the ineffable, ever-elusive mechanism of the work of art in itself, is to situate the film in its context – to historicize but also to see how it was the continuation of an ongoing, lifelong preoccupation on Kubrick's part, which also projected into the future. Like the wrapping paper of some poisoned Christmas gift, *Eyes Wide Shut* is the last laugh in Kubrick's vast enterprise in the capitalist sublime, slicing through all of late capitalism, and ending, arguably, on the eve of its global and 'ethical' turn (located by Jacques Rancière around the 9/11 events and the US government's 'absolute justice' rhetoric, which has led to all the transformations in the Western world we have been witnessing at dizzying speed since). It took a scholar of the ilk of Fredric Jameson to immediately identify, at the heart of *The Shining*, Kubrick's pining for an America of clearly demarcated social classes, and that the horror of that film was at the dissolution of social class itself.[38] In *Eyes Wide Shut*, the neoliberal myth of social mobility is given its schizophrenic expression – that of the alienated late-capitalist subject's incoherent fantasy: one which can no longer find any community to take shelter in, and therefore cannot find any answer, unless perhaps in the necessarily frustrating solution. A desperate, self-reassuring proposal by Alice in the toy shop quizzically closes the film (is she suggesting that they have sex, or is she just uttering a befuddled curse-word in reply to her hapless, miserably castrated husband's question?).[39] With little else at our disposal, it is time for the post-freedom, post-democratic subject in the making to find, at long last, the desperate energy to laugh at the ridiculousness and irony of it all.

Notes

1 Alexander Walker, *Stanley Kubrick, Director* (London: Weidenfeld & Nicolson, 1999), pp. 344–345.
2 Stephen Hunter, 'Kubrick's Sleepy *Eyes Wide Shut*', *The Washington Post*, 16 July 1999.
3 Michel Ciment, *Kubrick: The Definitive Edition* (New York: Faber & Faber, 2001) p. 156.
4 The scathing rebuke written in the French newspaper *Libération* by Louis Skorecki upon the film's release on DVD is emblematic of the Left's distaste (to put it mildly) for Kubrick.

5 See, for instance, a Reddit post echoing this sentiment: https://www.reddit.com/r/StanleyKubrick/comments/a9tbt2/the_harford_nyc_apartment_is_way_too_expensive/. Accessed 21 April 2023.
6 Walker, *Stanley Kubrick, Director*, p. 359.
7 This list includes Manohla Dargis in *LA Weekly*, Ann Hornaday in the *Baltimore Sun*, J. Hoberman in *The Village Voice*, Andrew Sarris in *The Observer*, Stephen Hunter in *The Washington Post*, Louis Menand in *The New York Review of Books* and Paul Tatara on CNN.
8 Robert P. Kolker and Nathan Abrams, *Eyes Wide Shut: Stanley Kubrick and the Making of His Final Film* (New York: Oxford University Press, 2019), p. 10.
9 Janet Maslin, 'Review of *Eyes Wide Shut*', *The New York Times*, 16 July 1999.
10 Walker, *Stanley Kubrick, Director*, p. 358.
11 James Naremore, *On Kubrick: Revised Edition* (London: British Film Institute, 2023), p. 227.
12 'Our subject is desire', Frederic Raphael wrote in his diary in late 1994. Frederic Raphael, *Eyes Wide Open: A Memoir of Stanley Kubrick* (London: Orion, 1999), p. 59.
13 This is partly explained by the extremely long gestation of the work, which Schnitzler began in 1907 under the Austro-Hungarian Empire. Kubrick's film had an equally long gestation, ranging from 50 years (if we place the director's first encounter with the Schnitzler novella in his youth), to 30 years (the period Kubrick himself claimed to have worked on the novella) to at least the 6 years of the actual production. Both were late works, and Schnitzler and Kubrick died at similar ages (Schnitzler aged 69, Kubrick aged 70).
14 According to Kolker and Abrams, Kubrick wanted to tone down both Jewishness and sex from Raphael's script. See their *Eyes Wide Shut*, pp. 51–52. See also Raphael, *Eyes Wide Open*.
15 *Eyes Wide Shut* bears a resemblance to Martin Scorsese's *After Hours* (1985) – though that film is a post-modern pastiche through and through of the modernist theme of aimless meandering and exploration of time, articulated by Kubrick in far more spatial terms as befits our moment and its dominant ideology of a perpetual present.
16 Kolker and Abrams, *Eyes Wide Shut*, p. 19.
17 Kolker and Abrams, *Eyes Wide Shut*, p. vii.
18 Kolker and Abrams, *Eyes Wide Shut*, pp. 142–145.
19 Marty Jonas, 'Another Comment on *Eyes Wide Shut*', World Socialist Web Site, 30 August 1999. https://www.wsws.org/en/articles/1999/08/eyes-a30.html. Accessed 10 March 2021.
20 See, for example, Ed Cripps, 'Party Animals: The Rothschild Surrealist Ball', *The Rake*, https://therake.com/stories/icons/party-animals-the-rothschild-surrealist-ball/. Accessed January 2023. In what may be seen as a huge

coincidence, the exterior of Somerton, the palatial Long Island mansion that houses the orgy, was that of Mentmore Towers, a Georgian-style building built for the Rothschilds.

21 See Fredric Jameson, *The Geopolitical Aesthetic* (Bloomington: Indiana University Press, 1992).

22 See, for instance, 'Stanley Kubrick Said "Pedophiles Run The World" Claims Nicole Kidman', Disclose.tv, 26 June 2017, https://www.disclose.tv/stanley-kubrick-said-pedophiles-run-the-world-claims-nicole-kidman-314706. Accessed 22 March 2021.

23 John Dahl, Louis Malle, William Friedkin, Philip Noyce, John MacNaughton, Harold Becker, or even David Cronenberg, David Lynch, Barry Levinson (*Disclosure*) and Sidney Lumet (*Guilty as Sin*).

24 'At this point, Kubrick was considering filming *Traumnovelle* in black and white, as a low-budget arthouse film, perhaps in the manner of *Lolita*. The film would take place in Dublin, influenced by James Joyce's *Ulysses* and his short story "The Dead," or "mock New York" (using surrogate locations in Ireland and London), with Woody Allen in the lead, playing a middle-aged Jewish doctor. "It was always New York and present time," Harlan recalls. But Kubrick never spoke to Woody Allen, says Harlan. "I met Woody in New York and told him all this and he said that Stanley had never asked him. But I know that Stanley had him in mind and he was pretty sure that Woody would play the part, had this become a project – it's a great part and the two would have harmonised splendidly. Stanley loved Woody Allen's films – 'particularly the early funny ones'."' Kolker and Abrams, *Eyes Wide Shut*, pp. 31–32. See also Nathan Abrams, *Stanley Kubrick: New York Jewish Intellectual* (New Brunswick, NJ: Rutgers University Press, 2018).

25 Many years before Raphael took on the job, Southern was asked by Kubrick to work on an adaptation of Schnitzler's novella, and delivered some drafts of it.

26 Correspondence with Michael Cramer, 16 March 2021. He goes on: 'Woody [Allen] was good buddies with Epstein … He and Soon-Yi both. Then this got me reading things by his teen mistress from the '70s, who went on to be Epstein's personal secretary.' I thank Michael for this telling piece of information, as well as his illuminating feedback on my piece.

27 Walker, *Stanley Kubrick, Director*, p. 360; Marit Allen, quoted in Ciment, *Kubrick: The Definitive Edition*, p. 278.

28 Brigitte Peucker identifies echoes of Kafka in *The Shining* and *Eyes Wide Shut*. See her '*Kubrick* and *Kafka*: The Corporeal Uncanny', *Modernism/modernity* 8.4 (2001), pp. 663–674.

29 On this note, Fabian Broeker's 'Dream Walking' video surely reveals that the film is very much about interiority, as it removes most dialogue and just shows the many scenes of Tom Cruise just walking into a space.

30 Ian Christopher, *The Games Room* (London: De Valion, 2020).

31 Thomas Elsaesser, 'Stanley Kubrick's Prototypes: The Author as World-Maker', in Jeremi Szaniawski (ed.), *After Kubrick: a Filmmaker's Legacy* (New York, London: Bloomsbury Academic, 2020), pp. 29–50.
32 To this, as do Kolker and Abrams, we may add Edward Said's notion of 'late style', in which the artist 'is no longer under pressure to do other than what he or she wants or needs to do, to create out of the artist's mature subjectivity, stripped of hubris and pomposity, unashamed either of its fallibility or of the modest assurance it has gained as a result of age and exile'. Kolker and Abrams, *Eyes Wide Shut*, p. 10.
33 Celestino Deleyto, '1999 – A Closet Odyssey', *Atlantis* 28.1 (2006), p. 41.
34 See Gilles Deleuze, *Cinéma 2 – L'Image-Temps* (Paris: Minuit, 1986). We could also relate this to the 'dream's navel' as does Freud – see Kolker and Abrams, *Eyes Wide Shut*, p. 164.
35 Geoffrey Kleinman, 'Review of *Eyes Wide Shut*', DVD Talk, 23 February 2000.
36 Kolker and Abrams, *Eyes Wide Shut*, p. 133.
37 Louis Skorecki, 'Review of *Eyes Wide Shut*', *Libération*, 16 January 2003. In the same text, Skorecki reduced Kubrick to a lecherous old man obsessed with the intersection of commerce and technology ('*Eyes Wide Shut* is a demo for home cinema store clerks').
38 See Fredric Jameson, 'Historicism in *The Shining*', in Jameson, *Signatures of the Visible* (London, New York: Routledge, 1990), pp. 82–98.
39 Seductive though this interpretation may be, one of the many drafts of the script, dated December 1997, seems to contradict it somewhat:

Bill: 'No dream is just a dream.'
Alice: 'No wife is just a wife ... Fuck me, will you, please?'

10

Eyes Wide Shut: A Cult Film?

Matt Melia

The term 'cult' is nebulous and hard to pin down. Its meaning ebbs and flows with the industrial and cultural shifts of cinema, its audiences and its modes of reception. Xavier Mendik and Ernest Mathijs offer the following definition:

A cult film is defined through a variety of combinations that include four major elements:

1. *Anatomy*: the film itself: content, style, format and generic modes.
2. *Consumption*: the ways in which it is received – audience reactions, fan celebrations and critical receptions.
3. *Political economy*: the financial and physical conditions of the presence of the film – its ownerships, intentions, promotions, channels of presentation, and the spaces and times of its exhibition.
4. *Cultural status*: the way in which a cult film fits a time or region – how it comments on its surroundings, by complying, exploiting, critiquing, or offending.

They list the following as key criteria: *innovation* ('curious overlap (though far from tonal) between regular canons of cinema and cult cinema'); *badness* (films 'considered aesthetically, morally bad; inept; "poor cinematic achievement"'); *transgression* ('the *transgression of barriers: taste, censorship; good/bad*'); *genre* ('cult films are often made within the constraints and possibilities of genres. They push generic conventions'); *intertextuality* ('*how* a film invites comparison, connections and linkages with other films and other parts of culture are crucial in determining a film as cult'); *loose ends* ('film as a puzzle') and *nostalgia*.[1]

In Chapter 8 of this book, Eddie Falvey proposes Stanley Kubrick's final film, *Eyes Wide Shut* (1999), be considered a 'quality' studio production. This chapter, however, considers it as a cult film – and even possibly the last truly 'cult' film of the twentieth century. A cursory glance at the film as measured against Mathijs and Mendik's criteria demonstrates that it indeed ticks some, if not all, of their boxes in its complex relationship with the mainstream. After a lengthy production, it was not met rapturously by either critics or audiences but, as Robert P. Kolker and Nathan Abrams remind us, '[t]he initial public reaction to *Eyes Wide Shut* was by no means unanimously bad'.[2] It contains transgressive sexual imagery (Linda Ruth Williams maintains its status as an erotic thriller),[3] and it certainly offers a set of narrative puzzles for the viewer. But is its cult identity more complex than this? This chapter expands on the film's cult identity and considers the film against the backdrop of a shift in cinema that occurred at the turn of the millennium.

Mainstream (post)-cult cinema in the 1990s

The 1990s was a transitional decade for 'cult' cinema in which the notion itself began to be reunderstood in terms of self-reflexive, post-modern, nostalgia films that were consciously conceived as 'cult', as opposed to cult texts which developed more organically. This trend continued well into the 2000s when redefinitions of cult cinema were aided and abetted not only by industrial changes but also by the rise of social media and the internet. Mendik and Mathijs's thesis, published halfway through the first decade of the twenty-first century, responds to both the traditions of and new definitions of cult film.

One of the watershed moments in this shift came in the early 2000s with Richard Kelly's *Donnie Darko* (2001). It exhibited all the hallmarks of a 'traditional' cult movie: it had a relatively low budget, was a critical success albeit a failure at the box office,[4] and its reputation was gained by word of mouth. It offered the viewer a set of narrative puzzles that were immersed in a sense of nostalgia for the late 1980s and its pop culture. It was marketed as a cult film and a subsequent DVD 'Director's Cut' of the film further deepened the film's rabbit hole, consolidating its identity as a cult film. Furthermore, given that the film is set in the age of the VHS cassette, it found success and audiences in the era of the DVD market. In more recent years, hits like the Netflix series *Stranger Things* (2016–), and the more recent adaptation of the Stephen King horror novel *It* (Andy Muschietti, 2017), have, as critics have regularly suggested, paved the way for a new wave of 1980s and 1990s cult nostalgia. Both owe a debt to *Donnie Darko* in their post-modern and ironic sense of pastiche and cultural reminiscence.

A full critical study of the status of the term 'cult' in the 1990s has yet to be undertaken. Thus the transitions and changes in how the term has been reunderstood and theorized have gone largely unremarked-upon. The understanding of cult in terms of post-modern irony and nostalgia was established across the decade through films like *Wes Craven's New Nightmare* (Wes Craven, 1994), *Scream* (Wes Craven, 1996), *Clerks* (Kevin Smith, 1994) and, of course, *Pulp Fiction* (Quentin Tarantino, 1994). These were mainstream films dressed in the perceived style of cult cinema and marketed as such. The critic of the cult and cinematic arcane, Jonathan Rosenbaum, defines this as what he terms 'Post-Cult', noting how 'cult' was appropriated as a marketing tool. Rosenbaum writes:

> One of the problems inherent in using the term 'cult' within a contemporary context relating to film, either as a noun or as an adjective, is that it refers to various social structures that no longer exist, at least not in the ways that they once did. When indiscriminate moviegoing (as opposed to going to see particular films) was a routine everyday activity, it was theoretically possible for cults to form around exceptional items – 'sleepers,' as they were then called by film exhibitors – that were spontaneously adopted and anointed by audiences rather than generated by advertising. But once advertising started to anticipate and supersede such a selection process, the whole concept of the cult film became dubious at the same time it became more prominent, a marketing term rather than a self-generating social process.[5]

This shift in understanding invites us to ask what makes a cult film? Can a cult film be successful and mainstream; deliberately constructed to be consumed as a cult text or franchise; or is the achievement of cult status an organic process and does the deliberate construction of a text as cult (through marketing for instance) undermine its 'cultness'? Rosenbaum offers an essential differentiation: true 'cult' films, he suggests, are 'anointed' as such by audiences rather than by studios, production companies or even directors. 'Cult' had its own infrastructure and culture too: fleapit, grindhouse and repertory cinemas such as the Scala Cinema in London, for example, with its loyal misfit audience. The Scala was a haven for the fringe and non-mainstream, and it screened midnight movies, arthouse, exploitation and genre cinema – as well as secret screenings of Kubrick's *A Clockwork Orange* (1971) for which programmer Jane Giles was prosecuted.[6]

As the decade wore on and the millennium edged ever closer, mainstream cinema also became increasingly dystopic and apocalyptic. In the years since, notable films released into the mainstream have attained semi-cult status, appealing to the impending end-of-the-century sense of existential dread.[7] *The Matrix* (Lily and Lana Wachowski, 1999), for instance, remains a prominent example of an increasingly paranoid, pre-millennial cinema that offered the viewer multiple pathways of interpretation. This is something one might even suggest can be traced back to Kubrick with the ambiguity of his *2001: A Space Odyssey* (1968) and the 'Interpretative Maze'[8] of *The Shining*. Nathan Abrams' article 'Kubrick and the Paranoid Style: Antisemitism, Conspiracy Theories and *The Shining*' also places the maze at the centre of an understanding of a set of conspiracy theories.[9]

If Quentin Tarantino's kitsch, cult nostalgia-fests were situated at one end of the cult–mainstream spectrum – produced and distributed by pioneering (and not unproblematic), era-defining, independent film distributor Miramax – then a director like David Fincher occupied the other. If *Se7en* (1995) and *Fight Club* (1999) exhibited a wearied nihilism as the century rolled to a close, then the ultra-low-budget box office smash hit *The Blair Witch Project* (Myrick and Sanchez, 1999) – the film that launched a thousand found-footage films into the 2000s – displayed a sense of end-of-the-century existential lostness – a theme that underpins *Eyes Wide Shut*. Both films feature characters who find themselves adrift and lost within a disorienting landscape and space – the three filmmakers adrift in the haunted Birkitsville Woods in *Blair Witch* and Dr Bill's picaresque night-time perambulations around Greenwich Village.

In his book of the same name, Jon Lewis refers to the American cinema of the 1990s as 'The End of Cinema as We Know It'. He notes in his introduction that the trajectory of 1990s American cinema can be measured against the backdrop of the celebrations of the centenary of the medium in 1995. However, he goes on to state that

> [f]rom the mid-decade on, the celebration of film's past gave way to the inevitable countdown to the millennium. Films staging the end of the world proved to be exciting, profitable and fun … The millennium on and off screen promised a sort of cosmic spring cleaning. Cinema loomed as a possible casualty.[10]

Both *The Blair Witch Project* and *Fight Club* (released in October and November of 1999 respectively) came out in the slipstream of *Eyes Wide Shut* (released in September of that year). These are both films whose cult identity is challenged by their mainstream success (and vice versa). *The Blair Witch Project* was made on a minuscule budget and grossed over $248.6 million at the box office, hardly the definition of a cult film, one might argue. The film's pioneering use of viral marketing, the creation of a 'genuine' website detailing the legend and folklore at the heart of the film, and the listing of its (very much alive) actors as deceased on IMDb, was designed to both lead viewers into the belief it was 'real' (not unlike Orson Welles's 1938 *War of the Worlds* 'hoax') and in doing so make use of the emergent world wide web to market the film; and create a mythos that audiences could buy into. As Pete Turner notes:

> *The Blair Witch Project* was one of the first films to fully explore the potential of the internet as a marketing tool. The internet was fast becoming a medium of discovery meaning that fans of the film had to explore and find their way around the web to find out more about the Blair Witch mythology and this augmented the sense of authenticity surrounding the film at the time of its release.[11]

It is interesting, then, that in the immediate wake of its release, media outlets and the mainstream press were labelling it a 'cult'. *Newsweek*, for instance, printed the following headline, 'The *Blair Witch* Cult: Two young filmmakers have set the summer – and the box office on fire with a creepy tale audiences love or hate. The making, and marketing, of a stealth smash.'[12] If Eduardo Sanchez and Daniel Myrick had intended to create a small cult film, they failed in their aims, ending up with a surprise mainstream box-office smash on their hands. Turner also notes that it went toe to toe with *Star Wars: The Phantom Menace* (George Lucas, 1999), making nearly 10,000 times its budget. And with its use of the digital camcorder, the film paved the way for the digital cinema revolution in the first decade of the new millennium.[13] *The Blair Witch Project* is a film that has all the production hallmarks and appearances of a cult film, was marketed as such, but became a mainstream phenomenon. It is an indication also that by the end of the decade definitions of the term 'cult' had become more indistinct (no doubt also exacerbated by the increasing demise of analogue VHS culture) and were being applied to any small independent film that enjoyed a modicum of mainstream success.

Fight Club had the 'cult' label applied to it retrospectively, mainly owing to its post-release success. It was a flop on its theatrical release but enjoyed greater success on DVD and VHS – cultivating a male-centric cult around itself, one which (as Peter C. Baker in *The New Yorker* noted in 2019) was consolidated by the emergence of the internet and internet chat boards. Its legacy, however, has increasingly been compromised by misogynistic male fan communities who today would be labelled 'INCELS' (as discussed by McAvoy and Ritzenhoff in Chapter 4 of this volume):

> The first sign that *Fight Club* might inspire men to do anything other than quote *Fight Club* on their Facebook walls came in the mid-two-thousands, with the rise of the 'seduction community.' These were groups of men searching together – sometimes in live seminars, but increasingly via online Listservs – for an objectively reliable set of techniques that would maximize their chances of getting women in bed.[14]

Fight Club, adapted from the cult novel by Chuck Palahniuk, might have been conceived as mainstream, but its pulp exploitation aesthetic, its commercial failure and its subsequent appropriation by certain audience groups conferred upon it a cult identity that did not emerge until midway through the next decade. However, as Baker also points out, '[t]he movie [*Fight Club*] has become part of the contemporary mass-cultural canon', further problematizing its pulpy pseudo-exploitation film cult identity.

Eyes Wide Shut had similar literary roots, adapted from Arthur Schnitzler's 1926 novella *Traumnovelle* by screenwriter Frederic Raphael, who transposed its early-twentieth-century Viennese setting to contemporary New York. Interestingly, the playwright and director David Hare suggests that Schnitzler himself 'has attained almost cult status thanks partly to the way he was revered by later generations of writers for both stage and screen. His works have inspired Tom Stoppard's *Dalliance* and *Undiscovered Country*, David Hare's *The Blue Room* and Stanley Kubrick's final film *Eyes Wide Shut*.'[15]

Stanley Kubrick, *Eyes Wide Shut* and cult cinema

Kubrick's *Eyes Wide Shut,* then, is a mixture of all these things. It is auteur-driven, mainstream, underpinned thematically by pre-millennial male anxiety and lostness, yet its journey to cult acceptance was more organic, relying less on the deliberately pulpy pleasures and cartoon excesses of films like *Fight Club.*[16] It was made for $65 million (less than *Fight Club*, but many times more than *The Blair Witch Project*) by a bona fide, canonized auteur of Western cinema; it features two of the world's biggest film stars (who were married at the time) – Tom Cruise and Nicole Kidman (and another American auteur, Sydney Pollack, in the antagonist role); and it has largely evaded the mainstream acceptance of either of the other films (despite the star power behind it).

It is only in recent years that the film's place within the milieu of 1990s American cinema and even within the canon of Kubrick's work has been cemented, having remained for some time as something of an outlier alongside Kubrick's planned science fiction film, an adaptation of Brian Aldiss's short story 'Super-Toys Last All Summer Long', completed by Steven Spielberg as *A.I. Artificial Intelligence* in 2001.[17] Kolker and Abrams interrogate *Eyes Wide Shut*'s cultural positioning:

> In the case of critical essays, there is deep, analytic, speculation. The graph of responses follows a steady line: the initial journalist reviews were mixed, sometimes downright negative or uncomprehending. Within a relatively few years, as the power and complexity of the film sink in, academic critics get to work. The cultists come somewhere in between, creating their own interpretive universe based on an ancient conspiracy theory or obsessive viewing and reviewing of the film. Then the film enters the cultural surround. This is the arc that can be traced across the reception of *Eyes Wide Shut.*[18]

For Kolker and Abrams, the film's cult identity, in part, lies in its reception by conspiracy-mad film fans (the same fans who presumably propagate the myth that Kubrick faked the Moon landings through readings of *2001: A Space Odyssey* and *The Shining*). Wider critical writing on Kubrick as a 'cult' director is relatively limited. James Fenwick notes that the study of Kubrick as a cult director is still a relatively unmined field of inquiry. Only two scholars have made direct inroads.[19] Jeremi Szaniawski is among the few others to engage with this area of Kubrick scholarship, noting Kubrick's interplay with and hybridity of genre. He remarks that Kubrick's films 'often fit the bill of another meta-genre (and commercial category), namely cult films with their mix of transgression, initial incomprehension of the critics and general public' and the 'quasi-religious admiration of fans'. He observes that Kubrick's 'most celebrated period (the late 1960s to the early 1980s)' coincides with the 'golden age of cult movie culture'.[20]

Eyes Wide Shut falls outside this timeframe and milieu, yet it carries the hallmarks of various aspects of genre cinema. It was marketed as an erotic thriller – its poster marketing campaign dangled the tempting proposition of seeing a potential erotic tryst between Cruise and Kidman (made all the more enticing and illicit as a result of their off-screen married status). It certainly chimed with a 1990s predilection for the erotic thriller genre with films like *Basic Instinct* (Paul Verhoeven, 1992), *Body of Evidence* (Uli Edel, 1993), *Disclosure* (Barry Levinson, 1994) and even *Showgirls* (Verhoeven, 1995) – a film whose 'so bad it's good' cult status was cemented in the years after its release. It is now considered to be the epitome of the 1990s 'cult film', as discussed by I.Q. Hunter.[21] *Eyes Wide Shut*'s poster campaign promised a tantalizing whiff of the illicit and transgressive. That the film did not live up to its erotic promise was something that was felt by several critics at the time. Rod Dreher of the *New York Post*, for example, wrote how it was 'shocking only in its banality, impotence, and utter lack of heat ... it is a sex-themed movie made by someone who hadn't left the house in 30 years'.[22]

Eyes Wide Shut, then, presents an interesting case for an example of late 1990s 'organic' cult cinema, as opposed to 'Post-Cult' cinema. It was a film by an ageing director (Kubrick reached his 70th birthday during the making), whose previous film, *Full Metal Jacket*, had been released almost 13 years previously, in 1987. It was still in post-production when Kubrick died in March 1999, giving it the distinction of being the director's final film. The sense of finality that surrounded it is consolidated by the fact that it was also released four months before the end of the century. This sense of finality, that Kubrick left one last intricate puzzle to be solved, has emboldened and strengthened its cult reputation in the years since its release. Further to this, as Kolker and Abrams remind us,

> *Eyes Wide Shut* is among the most demanding of Kubrick's films. Its tempo is unhurried and deliberate. Its acting slow and measured, sometimes even incantatory. And the film, as a whole, requires the viewer to respond to its unusual rhythms, to see it more than once in order to fully absorb its complexities. These are not the demands made by the great majority of conventional films, and the result was a return on investment less – especially on its initial release – than Kubrick or Warner Bros. expected or hoped for.[23]

The film offered a challenging experience to the average filmgoer at a time when, as Turner notes, 'cinema was very much about spectacle at the end of the century and audiences lapped up explosive, visual effects-laden blockbusters in their millions'.[24] The critic Jonathan Foreman, in reviewing the film, wrote

> It combines all the flaws that marred some of his earlier work – including a glacial pace, emotional coldness and the sudden eruption of scenes that seem to belong in a different movie. But what makes the film actively bad is its combination of sheer silliness with a grotesque lack of authenticity.[25]

Eyes Wide Shut and 'trash'

Eyes Wide Shut, at least at first glance, eschews any cult or 'trash' aesthetics. Todd McCarthy noted the 'Humanism' of the film, writing in *Variety*, while Jack Kroll in *Newsweek* wrote of the film's opening image: 'Kidman ... snakehipping out of a black dress, to stand there nude in possibly the most beautiful human image ever to open a movie'.[26] While he also salaciously called this sequence a 'Viagra trap', his statement calls to mind the transcendental image of the female nude across art history. The statuesque depiction of Alice (Kidman) in the film's opening draws on classical antiquity, the female imagery of Modigliani, the Pre-Raphaelites, Gustav Klimt (the references to whose work locate the film in relation to the context, time and place of Schnitzler's novel) and even Hieronymus Bosch.[27]

The film is semiotically rich and complex. Readings of its aesthetics, style and design have contributed to all manner of textual interpretation and decoding, much in the same way as the *mise-en-scène* of *The Shining* has been approached by both critical scholars and fans as well as the more conspiracy-minded as part of an 'interpretative maze' or puzzle to be solved. Ian Christopher's 2021 novel *The Games Room: A Novel Interpretation of Stanley Kubrick's Film The Shining*,[28] for instance, situates an incisive and exhaustive body of research at the Stanley Kubrick Archive within a prose framework in an attempt to finally unpack and find its way to the heart of *The Shining*'s puzzling textual maze. *Eyes Wide Shut* seemingly presents a similarly enigmatic narrative filled with visual clues, 'easter eggs' and narrative puzzles which the viewer is invited to solve.

While the film may outwardly evidence the prestige aesthetics of a studio production when the action moves to the ritual and orgy sequence (once Bill Harford has conned his way into the country house using the password 'Fidelio'), the sexually transgressive imagery finds correspondence in a variety of art-cult films (by the likes of Walerian Borowczyk. for instance) and high camp 'trash', connecting it back (whether intentionally or unintentionally) to a milieu of 1970s transgressive and erotic Eurotrash or cult fiction. In an online article discussing the film, Zach Clark not only draws on the work of Pasolini but comments that:

> *Eyes Wide Shut* is a movie about spectacle, it's about performance, it's about costumes (it is literally about costumes), it's about the neon blue light of the moon. Two decades earlier, they would've given this script to Russ Meyer and he also would have turned it

> into a complex, contradictory horror smut melodrama, which is what *Eyes Wide Shut* is.[29]

Furthermore, as has been noted by Kolker and Abrams, the influence of Roger Corman's seminal art-cult-horror film *The Masque of the Red Death* (1964) may be detected in the rich red tones of the *mise-en-scène* for the 'Fidelio' sequence. This is also a film where the 1% gather to behave orgiastically and with abandon. The sinister 'Red Cloak' (Leon Vitali) in *Eyes Wide Shut* recalls not only the Red Death in Corman's film but also the central antagonist – the Satanic Prince Prospero (Vincent Price). Kubrick incorporates noirish, gothic and Sadeian overtones – not least in the depiction of the depraved libertine costumier Mr Milich (Rade Serbedzjia) and his seductive teenage daughter (Leelee Sobieski), whose innocence, the second time we meet her, has been well and truly corrupted. Like Sade's *Justine* (1791) she has made the journey from virtue to vice. *Justine* was an *ur*-text for the transgressive, quasi-pornographic milieux of global and European cult cinema from the late 1960s, notably Spanish director Jess Franco's *Marquis de Sade: Justine* (1969) starring Klaus Kinski, Jack Palance and Romina Power, which Kubrick most likely saw. This inclusion of a Justine-esque figure in *Eyes Wide Shut* further emboldens the film's claim to cult identity and to latterly engage or reference this era of filmmaking.

The final cut? Post-production and critical approaches to *Eyes Wide Shut* as a cult film

Contributing further to the film's cult identity is its production background. Kubrick was not alive to oversee the final stages of post-production; the many conflicting opinions of collaborators, critics and fans as to whether the film released by Warner Bros. was the film that Kubrick intended have contributed to the enigma surrounding the film (and its organic emergence as a late-twentieth-century cult text). Kolker and Abrams suggest that 'postproduction should be the calm after the storm' but that

> Leon Vitali … described the postproduction of *Eyes Wide Shut* as 'mayhem'. Kubrick had over a million feet of film, and he was editing digitally for the first time on an Avid suite. He developed a system by means of which he could display a number of takes at the same time and, out of the multitude, choose the one that worked the best. As part of that process, he kept a diary or log

> called 'cutting' notes in which he kept track of each shot and checked off the best ones. Despite the shorthand and occasionally cryptic remarks on these notes, they are the closest we come to the creative process of editing which Kubrick often said was the most important part of turning the jigsaw puzzle of shots into a narrative of finished work.[30]

In the introduction to his novelized investigation into *The Shining*, Ian Christopher offers archival evidence that Kubrick stated he constructed that film as a puzzle.[31] In some ways, perhaps *Eyes Wide Shut* was both intentionally *and also unintentionally* an attempt to create a filmic puzzle. I contend that the puzzle here operates on a much deeper level than in the previous film, however. Appropriating Kolker and Abrams' words above, one could argue that Kubrick's editing likewise presents a puzzle for the viewer wanting to come up with a definitive understanding of the film.

Furthermore, Kubrick died after showing his 'final cut' of the film to Warner Bros., Cruise and Kidman at a private screening in New York. The film went into the very final stages of post-production without Kubrick but with Jan Harlan, Christiane Kubrick and Leon Vitali overseeing the process, adding a further layer of confusion. With all these moving parts, any sense of fixed meaning or interpretation becomes more and more distant and difficult to pin down. It is for this reason that *Eyes Wide Shut* is one of the more enigmatic of Kubrick's films, the release version pieced together and constructed through the contributions of other creative minds, notably editors Nigel Galt and Melanie Viner-Cuneo, Jan Harlan and Christiane Kubrick (as discussed in Manca Perko's Chapter 3 in this volume).[32]

Cult criticism

Twenty-first-century criticism has seen a (re)assessment of *Eyes Wide Shut* in terms of its cult identity, and as part of a renewal of wider critical interest in Kubrick as a cult director whose work encourages a certain level of 'fan engagement'. In Jeremi Szaniawski's recent collection on Kubrick's legacy, *After Kubrick*, Rick Warner identified a series of directors whose work may be considered to a greater or lesser extent as 'fan fiction', a particular mode of cult engagement – including Christopher Nolan, the Coen Brothers, David Lynch and Jonathan Glazer, whose work knowingly references Kubrick's.[33] Joy McEntee has recently noted the influence of Kubrick in the work of Jordan Peele (notably in his *Get Out* [2017]) – a discussion that forms part of a burgeoning critical discussion on Kubrick and race.[34] Most 'cult' studies of Kubrick's films tend to be geared towards *The Shining*, or maybe *A Clockwork Orange* and *2001: A Space Odyssey*. Kate Egan, for example, explores 'the centrality to Kubrick's cult reputation of a touchstone resource for Kubrick fans: Vivian Kubrick's 1980 documentary *Making the Shining*'.[35] Here is the rub: *The Shining* is a culturally beloved horror film. It exists outwith the canon of Kubrick's work in the wider sphere of cinematic critical cultural, cult and popular interest. It is not just a touchstone in Kubrick's work, but a canonical touchstone in popular horror cinema itself. *Eyes Wide Shut* is certainly not a culturally beloved film and certainly not one beloved of the critics – British film critic Mark Kermode has regularly retitled it '*Eyes Wide Shit*' on his Radio 5 Live show *Kermode and Mayo's Film Review*, for instance (and I have noted above some of the mixed critical responses to the film at the time). Until fairly recently it was not even beloved within the field of Kubrick scholarship. It occupies a peripheral position and while its intricacies and puzzles are as interesting as those of *The Shining*, there is comparatively much less popular interest in it as a film. It occupies a niche space of interest within the Kubrick *oeuvre*.

Yet, despite its divisive critical legacy, *Eyes Wide Shut*, as Kolker and Abrams note, 'did, in the end, make money' despite its initially poor reception in the United States in particular. 'The film cost $65 million to make and earned a worldwide gross of $162 million – ultimately making it one of the biggest money-makers of all of Kubrick's films.'[36] So, what were the reasons for its opening lack of popularity and the resurgence of interest in the film? Kolker and Abrams explain, '[t]he commonplace about Kubrick's films is that they do not fare well at first sight. Try as he might to create films of commercial value only a few were "hits" in the conventional sense.'[37] Kubrick's death certainly focused interest on the film at the time (if not in the film itself). By turning to fan discourse on the Alt.Movies.Kubrick (AMK) web forum, James Fenwick observed

> The notion of post-object fandom, whereby fans transition from active to dormant fandom upon cessation of their central fan object. 'Post-object fandom' has been applied to television series and films … – Kubrick was such a dominant figure, a brand and perhaps the ultimate director in defining the idea of the auteur that he eclipsed even his own filmic texts. He owned the texts due to the weight his name carried and was the central object for Kubrick fans. The transition to post-object fandom for Kubrick fans was complicated by the director's death, occurring prior to the release,

> and maybe even – according to some – the completion of *Eyes Wide Shut*.[38]

In dealing with the issue of 'post-object fandom', Fenwick suggests that the completion of *Eyes Wide Shut* after Kubrick's death has created a complicated relationship between the Kubrick fan and the text. He reminds us that the film's supposed incompleteness and the (perceived) interference of Warner Bros. were also elements that contributed to consolidating the film's conspiratorial (cult-like) cult fandom:

> AMK users began to interact with each other on this issue and to protest the film's distributor, Warner Bros., who they believed was tampering with Kubrick's final vision. Such a reaction can be seen as a way of negotiating the transition to post-object fandom, linked with the loss of control that some fans may have felt due to the absence of Kubrick's authority and control over the film's release ... A number of fans on AMK were confused as to why the film did not meet their expectations, whilst others had constructed a 'halo' effect around Kubrick, building on the cult of personality and refusing to see him as anything other than a genius and all of his films as masterpieces.[39]

The film's textual complexities and the complexities and politics of its completion and release all contribute to its enigma. In *Cult Film as a Guide to Life*, I.Q. Hunter devotes an entire chapter, 'Wasting Time in The Stanley Hotel', to an analysis of Kubrick's films as cult properties, juxtaposing renewed critical evaluation with fan-led textual interpretation. Devoting much of his analysis to the documentary film *Room 237* (Rodney Ascher, 2012), fandom and the prevalence of fan-led conspiracy theories in *The Shining*, he notes how, for instance, despite its many obvious flaws, *Room 237* has become a central beacon in twenty-first-century Kubrick fandom. He also offers a comparative analysis of *Eyes Wide Shut*, claiming,

> [a]lthough *Eyes Wide Shut* has attracted much 'conventional', peer-reviewed analysis, it too has fallen prey to immersive criticism that verges on cinephile paranoia. Or, more accurately, it has been inserted into existing conspiracy theories of which the analysts are true cultists, especially theories fixated with a secret elite group, the Illuminati and that confused, often anti-Semitic zone where the Far Right and Far Left meet and swap places.[40]

For Hunter, *Eyes Wide Shut* is a metatextual exercise, a cult film about a cult. His reading of *Eyes Wide Shut* as a cult text is filtered through a discussion of conspiracy-led fandom and textual overreading and interpretation: something which has dogged Kubrick's work for decades, at least since *2001: A Space Odyssey* and the faked Moon landing theory. Hunter cites Lauren Vachaud's reading of *Eyes Wide Shut* as an example:[41] Vachaud proposes that Alice Harford is a procurer of sex slaves for the elite – a reading which of course has attained a contemporary resonance since 2019 with the revelations surrounding Ghislaine Maxwell, Jeffrey Epstein and Prince Andrew. Rich Cohen also uses *Eyes Wide Shut* to prefigure an analysis of the Epstein affair. He writes:

> In short, *Eyes Wide Shut* is not fiction. It's documentary. It's a great artist, at the end of a brilliant career, uncovering hidden evil. What is the function of art? Is it to show us something diverting, beautiful, new? Or is it to tell us what we've always known but never admitted to ourselves? The Epstein affair is a microcosm of our era, a miniature that stands for the whole. It's not just a cabal of cultists that devours young women, as seen in the movie, but the culture itself, which worships an ancient Canaanite god that can be appeased only with the lives of children. *Eyes Wide Shut* is an eschatological guide to that era, a book of Revelation that prophesized terrible events.[42]

At the end of the film, in the toy shop, Vachaud claims (via a reading of staging and *mise-en-scène*) that the Harfords' daughter Helena (Madison Eginton) is abducted by members of the cult. Furthermore, Vachaud also presents *Eyes Wide Shut* as an allegory of Vivian Kubrick's membership of the Church of Scientology (with which, at the time the film went into production, Tom Cruise was himself becoming embroiled – presenting another allegorical interpretation). Hunter glosses:

> Videos online and available to purchase subject *Eyes Wide Shut* to detailed explications in the spirit of 9/11 'truthers', which veer from quoting 'sanctioned' criticism like academic articles to wilder readings based on prior commitment to the existence of the Illuminati in real life. This fine interpretative madness is, once again, a product of finding significance in any random element of the film – for example, set decoration (stars, pentangles) with Illuminati significance – and integrating it into a totalizing external theory that depends on counter-knowledge about the Illuminati's

> goddess worship or the hidden persuaders of MK Ultra mind control techniques.[43]

Such fandom, we might argue, has less to do with the fandom of Kubrick and more to do with a paranoid obsession with, or fandom of, conspiracy theories in and of themselves. Nevertheless, such readings also confer upon *Eyes Wide Shut* a sense of millennial and post-millennial anxiety and dread: its focus on secret elite cabals of power would be refocused in the wake of 9/11, emboldening the film's cult reputation. One far-fetched theory is that Kubrick's obsession with recurring images of monoliths and pillars across his work foreshadowed and foresaw the 9/11 terrorist attacks on the Twin Towers. That Kubrick died suspiciously shortly after the production of the film had ended lent further fuel to the fire.

I.Q. Hunter likens *Eyes Wide Shut* to conspiratorial horror movies such as *Rosemary's Baby* (Roman Polanski, 1968) but also more broadly to the conspiracy thriller genre of the 1970s, such as *The Parallax View* (Alan J. Pakula, 1974). He also notes that the film's representation of the relationship between power and sexuality presents a fantasy. It

> ambivalently draws on these fantasies [and] suggests that images of sexual decadence are themselves expressions of a widespread fantasy relationship with power (as in *Society* (1989), *The Ninth Gate* (1999), *Hostel* (2005) and *Fifty Shades of Grey* (2015)), in which the ultra-rich are not only supremely powerful, but, rather more excitingly, sexually depraved. No wonder the film, usefully bringing together these conspiratorial references, has energized cult interpretation of the wildest kind. The truth is out there, and *Eyes Wide Shut* is an insider's skeleton key to a monomaniacal wider framework, as the readings potentially link everything to anything – Illuminati Watcher's marvellously swivel-eyed article ropes in *The Wizard of Oz*, Lady Gaga, the Windsors, Scientology and homosexual hazing rituals at Yale.[44]

In (seemingly) inviting the viewer to explore the semiotic rabbit hole of conspiratorial interpretation, viewers are encouraged to take a psychogeographical walk around the landscape and environments of the film, engaging with its landmarks, images and things found *en route* – not unlike Bill Harford as he navigates the night-time streets of New York. It is not only Bill who embodies a sense of end-of-the-century lostness; the viewer is invited to become 'lost' and only in doing so can they uncover the 'true' meaning of the film. And of course, psychogeographical practices were essential to the film's production – the location scouting that occurred as the film was being shot on top of Manuel Harlan's pre-production photographic wanderings around London's Commercial Road (resulting in the iconic and archived panoramic images of the area), detailing doorways, shop fronts, fixtures and fittings – found objects incorporated into the film's staging.[45]

Conclusion: is *Eyes Wide Shut* the last truly cult film of the twentieth century?

So how do we align *Eyes Wide Shut* with shifting critical discourses and paradigms of cult cinema at the turn of the millennium? This is a more complicated task than we might first think. Certainly, the 2008 Cult Film Symposium published in *Cineaste* offers several conflicting critical responses to the question what is a cult film?[46] One might argue that *Eyes Wide Shut* follows a trend of transgressive *mainstream* cinema in the 1990s around which cult attention has developed organically for a variety of reasons. It also provoked conspiracy theorists and fan reactions to its potential incompleteness and the politics of its authorship and completion. We may also refer to the negative critical response to the film and its relative failure at the box office, which brings it into line with Hunter's definition of cult as 'disasters on first release'. Furthermore, the film reflects a sense of dreamlike lostness and anxiety at the turn of the millennium. This sense of lostness (also present in those ambivalently cult films released the same year – *The Blair Witch Project* and *Fight Club*) is reflected in what Scott Tobias observes as the film's own out-of-place-ness. He writes:

> Stanley Kubrick's *Eyes Wide Shut* is a movie out of time – or to put it another way, it's timeless. It was released in the middle of 1999's summer-movie season, preceded by *Wild Wild West* and *American Pie*, and followed the next week by an abysmal remake of *The Haunting*. In retrospect, it seems absurd that Kubrick's enigmatic final film could be a part of blockbuster season, even though it starred Tom Cruise and Nicole Kidman, who at the time were Hollywood's biggest power couple. But it's a good example of what happens when films of genuine ambition and artistry are caught up in the swells of studio mass marketing and hype.[47]

Eyes Wide Shut fits within the paradigm of auteurist mainstream films that have found a second life as a cult object. David Church noted in 2008 that '[t]he term "cult" seems to have become more culturally diffuse over the past two decades, earning not only a place as a popular marketing term, but also blurring with "mainstream" entertainment (as with Hollywood's "cult blockbusters," such as the *Lord of the Rings* and *Star Wars* series'.[48]

If *Eyes Wide Shut* exists at the tail end of the millennium, then it is interesting to note how cult manifested itself in the wake of the millennium. Richard Kelly's enigmatic *Donnie Darko* may lay claim to being the first cult film of the twenty-first century, but it is a markedly different film to *Eyes Wide Shut* which exhibits, at the end of the twentieth century, a range of criteria for a film that organically develops as a cult object. It does so during a period in which a new 'Post-Cult' paradigm is developing. *Donnie Darko* continues this new, post-modern paradigm of nostalgic, ironic and deliberately cultish mainstream films, establishing it in the next decade and century. Furthermore, Richard Kelly *does* respond to both Kubrick's death and the esoteric and cult appeal of *Eyes Wide Shut*, while also locating the director in a matrix of influence with *Fight Club's* director David Fincher.[49] As well as noting the film's conspiracy-obsessed fandom, he considers the film's legacy – drawing a comparison between its representation of marriage and the inference and representation of blood sacrifice in the film and Fincher's *Gone Girl* (2014), and noting:

> Both *Gone Girl* and *Eyes Wide Shut* are deeply twisted, satirical and borderline maniacal erotic thrillers that seem to be made by a snickering auteur – well aware that the institution of marriage itself is being bathed in a hot dose of Tyler Durden's corrosive lye soap from *Fight Club*. Both films show broken marriages that can only be repaired by ritualistic, meticulously calculated blood sacrifices.[50]

This chapter has aimed to offer a broader discussion of how *Eyes Wide Shut* emerged organically as a cult text and how its position at the end of the twentieth century stands as a chapter break in how the term 'cult' is understood. Maybe, if we consider Kelly's reading, we may also suggest that *Eyes Wide Shut* embodies the shifting definitions of cult cinema and cult cinema's own unstable identity at the end of the millennium.

Notes

1 Ernest Mathijs and Xavier Mendik, *The Cult Film Reader* (Maidenhead: Open University Press, 2008), p. 1.
2 Robert P. Kolker and Nathan Abrams, *Eyes Wide Shut: Stanley Kubrick and His Final Film* (New York: Oxford University Press, 2019), p. 133.
3 Linda Ruth Williams, *The Erotic Thriller in Contemporary Cinema* (Edinburgh: Edinburgh University Press, 2005), p. 397.
4 'Shown on just 58 screens, *Donnie Darko* opened at just $110,494, which led to a grand total of $517,375 by the end of its theatrical run in April 2002. Many credit the film's depiction of a commercial plane crashing into Donnie's house near the beginning and its release just a month after 9/11 as the ultimate cause of its initial failure': J. Wiese, 'The Time Christopher Nolan Saved *Donnie Darko* from Being a Direct to TV Movie', *Cinemablend*, https://www.cinemablend.com/news/2475273/that-time-christopher-nolan-saved-donnie-darko-from-being-a-direct-to-tv-movie. Accessed 13 September 2021.
5 Jonathan Rosenbaum, 'Joe Dante, Anonymous King of the Post-Cult Cinema Community', https://jonathanrosenbaum.net/2018/06/joe-dante-anonymous-king-of-the-post-cult-cinema-community-tk/. Accessed 13 September 2021.
6 By the time *Eyes Wide Shut* was released Kubrick had died and The Scala had been closed for six years although it is interesting to speculate whether it would have been screened there.
7 Epitomized by the then ever-looming threat of the supposed 'Millennium Bug', which ultimately failed to materialize.
8 Vincent Jaunas, 'Inside the Interpretative Maze of *The Shining* (1980): The Search for Meaning in Crisis', *Essais* [online], Hors-série 4 (2018), http://journals.openedition.org/essais/622. Accessed 2 December 2021.
9 Nathan Abrams, 'Kubrick and the Paranoid Style: Antisemitism, Conspiracy Theories and *The Shining*', in Jeremi Szaniawski (ed.), '*The Shining* at 40', *Senses of Cinema* [Online] https://www.sensesofcinema.com/2020/the-shining-at-40/kubrick-paranoid-style-antisemitism-conspiracy-theories/. Accessed 2 December 2021.
10 Jon L. Lewis, *The End of Cinema as We Know It* (New York: New York University Press, 2001), pp. 1–2.
11 Pete Turner, The *Blair Witch Project* (Leighton Buzzard: Auteur, 2014), p. 79.
12 *Newsweek*, 16 August 1999, p. 44.
13 Turner, *Blair Witch*, pp. 7–8.
14 P.C. Baker, 'The Men Who Still Love *Fight Club*', *The New Yorker*, 4 November 2019. https://www.newyorker.com/culture/cultural-comment/the-men-who-still-love-fight-club#:~:text=The%20first%20sign%20that%20

%E2%80%9CFight,via%20online%20Listservs%E2%80%94for%20an. Accessed 30 September 2021.

15 David Hare, 'Schnitzler's Hidden Manuscript Explored', University of Cambridge https://www.cam.ac.uk/research/news/schnitzler%E2%80%99s-hidden-manuscripts-explored. Accessed 30 September 2021.

16 *Fight Club*'s cult appeal was not only predicated on a consciously pulp pseudo-exploitation aesthetic, but also on a soundtrack which included tracks by cult and independent bands like LCD Soundsystem, Eels and Pixies. This could be argued to diminish its 'organic' cult status.

17 A film which remained unmade within his own lifetime but a version of which was brought to the screen by Steven Spielberg in 2001, two years after Kubrick's death.

18 Kolker and Abrams, *Eyes Wide Shut*, pp. 133–134.

19 James Fenwick, '"Let this be Kubrick's final word. Do you hear us Warner Bros.?": Fan Reception to the Death of Stanley Kubrick and his Final Film, *Eyes Wide Shut*', *The Journal of Fandom Studies* 6.1 (2018), pp. 21–32. Fenwick cites David Church and Kate Egan whose own (interlinked) inquiries are built around a 'Mythic cult of personality' – Kubrick the auteur and the cult fandom emerging out of Kubrick's own reclusive persona.

20 Jeremi Szaniawski, 'Kubrick and Genre', in Nathan Abrams and I.Q. Hunter (eds), *The Bloomsbury Companion to Stanley Kubrick* (New York: Bloomsbury, 2021), p. 299.

21 I.Q. Hunter, 'Beaver Las Vegas! A Fan's Defense of *Showgirls*', *Logos* 5 (2014), pp. 79–96.

22 In Graham Fuller, 'Is *Eyes Wide Shut* a Genius's Final Erotic Masterpiece? Over to the US Critics ...' *The Guardian*, 18 July 1999 https://www.theguardian.com/film/1999/jul/18/3. Accessed 29 September 2021.

23 Kolker and Abrams, *Eyes Wide Shut*, p. 133.

24 Turner, *Blair Witch*, p. 7.

25 Cited in Fuller, 'Is *Eyes Wide Shut*'.

26 Cited in Fuller, 'Is *Eyes Wide Shut*'.

27 Dijana Metlić looks at Kubrick's film through the filter of Bosch's masterpiece and proposes that Kubrick used the painting, with its depictions of sensual and forbidden human pleasures, as a template for his film, demonstrating 'how both Bosch and Kubrick construct a didactic, moralising world picture, and how they use their unique artistic expressions to amuse viewers and instruct them how to overcome their personal weaknesses through tolerance and love'. See her 'Stanley Kubrick and Hieronymus Bosch: In the *Garden of Earthly Delights*', *Essais* 4 (2018), p. 633.

28 Ian Christopher, *The Games Room: A Novel Interpretation of Stanley Kubrick's Film The Shining*, 2nd edn (Kingston: De Valion, 2021).

29 Zach Clark, 'Expiring Soon: *Eyes Wide Shut*, Whatever Movie You Need it to Be', *Talkhouse*, 20 September 2016 https://www.talkhouse.com/expiring-soon-eyes-wide-shut-whatever-movie-need/. Accessed 4 December 2021.

30 Kolker and Abrams, *Eyes Wide Shut*, p. 113.
31 Christopher, *The Games Room*, p. 1.
32 Kolker and Abrams, *Eyes Wide Shut*, pp. 114–116.
33 Rick Warner, 'Kubrickian Dread: Echoes of *2001* and *The Shining* in Works by Jonathan Glazer, Paul Thomas Anderson, and David Lynch', in Jeremi Szaniawski (ed.), *After Kubrick: A Filmmaker's Legacy* (London, New York: Bloomsbury Academic, 2020), pp. 125–145.
34 Joy McEntee, 'The Tethered Shadow: Jordan Peele and Stanley Kubrick', *Film Criticism* 46.1 (2022). https://journals.publishing.umich.edu/fc/article/id/2715/. Accessed 15 January 2023.
35 Kate Egan, 'Precious Footage of the Auteur at Work: Framing, Accessing, Using, and Cultifying Vivian Kubrick's *Making The Shining*', *New Review of Film and Television Studies* 13.1 (2015), pp. 63–82.
36 Kolker and Abrams, *Eyes Wide Shut*, p. 133.
37 Kolker and Abrams, *Eyes Wide Shut*, p. 133.
38 Fenwick, 'Let this be Kubrick's Final Word …', p. 21.
39 Fenwick, 'Let this be Kubrick's Final Word …', p. 22.
40 I.Q. Hunter, *Cult Film as a Guide to Life Fandom, Adaptation, and Identity* (New York: Bloomsbury Academic, 2016), p. 48.
41 Lauren Vachaud, 'Le secret de la pyramide', *Positif* (January 2013), p. 623.
42 Rich Cohen, 'Behind the Mask of Corruption', *Paris Review*, 6 April 2020 https://www.theparisreview.org/blog/2020/04/06/behind-the-mask-of-corruption/. Accessed 30 September 2021.
43 I.Q. Hunter, *Cult Film as a Guide to Life*, p. 48.
44 I.Q. Hunter, *Cult Film as a Guide to Life*, p. 49.
45 See Kolker and Abrams, *Eyes Wide Shut*, p. 77. There is more work to do on Kubrick, the city and psychogeography and in particularly psychogeographic approaches to location research across his films.
46 'Cult Film: A Critical Symposium', *Cineaste* 34.1 (2008), https://www.cineaste.com/winter2008/cult-film-a-critical-symposium. Accessed 2 December 2021.
47 Scott Tobias, 'The New Cult Canon: *Eyes Wide Shut*', The AV Club (2009) https://www.avclub.com/the-new-cult-canon-eyes-wide-shut-1798215769. Accessed 15 January 2023.
48 David Church in 'Cult Film: A Critical Symposium'.
49 R. Kelly, '*Gone Girl* and *Eyes Wide Shut*: A Study of Psychopathy in the Heteronormative Patriarchal Occult', Tumblr, https://ronaldtaverner.tumblr.com/. Accessed 30 September 2021.
50 A. Billington, 'Director Richard Kelly Breaks Down Fincher's *Gone Girl*', Firstshowing.Net (2014) https://www.firstshowing.net/2014/read-this-director-richard-kelly-breaks-down-finchers-gone-girl/. Accessed 30 September 2021.

Afterword

Robert P. Kolker

> *It is a film by someone whose rapport to reality always was different than that of the majority of people, and who portrayed a subject moving through a reality alienated from itself ...*
>
> Jeremi Szaniawski

I remember the first time. *Eyes Wide Shut* had just been released in the United States and I was on vacation in Naples, Florida. (Kubrick would not have approved; he didn't believe in the waste of time called vacations.) It was in a local cinema, long past its prime, its projector lamps dim and in need of replacement. It was the kind of venue Kubrick would have disallowed had he been alive and, as was typical, in control of the exhibition of this film. I went in with the enormous expectation of seeing a new Kubrick film after all these years. I came out utterly dispirited. The pacing seemed dismally slow. The acting wooden. The orgy was laughable. What was that last word of Alice's about? What was *his* last word about? What was he thinking? I was depressed.

But this was not the first time. Apart from *Paths of Glory*, *Dr. Strangelove* and *Barry Lyndon*, Kubrick films that moved me on first viewing, all the others took time and constant reviewing, writing and teaching. I was not alone with this experience. His films took time to settle in, to be understood and *felt*. This is why Kubrick took such time and care with the transfers of his films to home media. He knew that they would grow in esteem and comprehension, that they would become part of the cultural unconscious and he wanted them prepared for that. I knew that I needed to get to work reclaiming the film. The demon had to be repulsed. And that did not come in a flash. I taught the film many times, each lecture or discussion pushing my (and, I hope, my students') understanding of what was going on in this difficult film. And writing. Thinking through the writing process – as Kubrick well knew – gets slowly to the core of comprehension, it is a labour of discovery. In the fourth edition of *A Cinema of Loneliness*, I wrote:

> It is not an inviting work; its characters are self-absorbed; their motions and counter motions, actions and reactions take place as in the slow motion of a dream. It is a work that, in Edward Said's words [in his book *On Late Style*], is stripped of hubris and pomposity, a work of mature subjectivity that holds in a pitiless gaze a man for whom the world is too much and completely insufficient.[1]

I was slowly getting to the point, or points, because there are many. *Eyes Wide Shut* is stripped-down Kubrick, subtle, purposeful, devious, uncanny, its emotional weight held in reserve until the next time we hear Shostakovich's *Jazz Suite*, when a sudden recall of the film flows out of our unconscious with aching melancholy and moves into a full realization of its latent power.

That power emerges from the very slowness of the acting, editing and camera work that had put me off in the first place. The emotional and indeed intellectual charge of *Eyes Wide Shut* comes deliberately and with resistance to a quick reaction. Perhaps, to push the metaphor, the film creates a continuing current rather than a charge. Sparks don't fly but burn slowly; what Kubrick called the 'non-submersible units', most especially the orgy, are all but too outrageous, too much like Roger Corman's *Masque of the Red Death*, to take seriously. We need the billiards table scene (which on initial viewings I thought much in need of editing, but now understand to be the final *danse macabre* of the film), with Ziegler's warnings and threats, to reflect back on what at first looked like farce but that now might be the scene of murder. We needed Jeffrey Epstein to recognize the profound corruption the orgy represented. 'They weren't just ordinary people there. If I told you their names … I don't think you'd sleep so well.' Prince Andrew? Bill Clinton? Donald Trump? Dr Bill doesn't get to sleep so well even without knowing their names.

My imagination didn't sleep so well either. I needed to get closer to this enigma of a film. I wanted to write a 'making of', not only of the film but of Kubrick's creative processes as well. I wanted to use the newly established archives for information. It took a bit of doing to convince Oxford University Press, my publishers since *A Cinema of Loneliness*, to take this on and when they did, I realized I could not do it alone. I live in Charlottesville, Virginia and get to London only infrequently. Besides, I am not a great researcher; I haven't the patience or fluency in the process of searching for, discovering and linking together archival material.

Nathan Abrams and I had been corresponding about Kubrick for a while and finally met at a Kubrick conference in Leicester in 2016. Nathan has all the research talents (and patience) that I lack and is excellent at putting his discoveries together in lucid prose. We decided to collaborate, with all the potential pitfalls that might entail. We divided the labour. Nathan asked me to research the scripts of *Eyes Wide Shut* at the archives, as well as the books Kubrick read in preparation for the film and peripheral material, like the catalogues of underwear purchased from a supplier in Long Island. The process was extraordinary and revealing. The struggles he had with Frederic Raphael are clear from the notes Kubrick scribbled on the various drafts, from the fax from 'Freddie', voicing his frustration over the process. ('Freddie', of course, wrote his own anti-Kubrick memoir of the process he found impossible.) There were the books the director read, from critical studies of Schnitzler to Karen Horney's *The Neurotic Personality of our Time* to a collection of the odd and bizarre with a chapter on 'Sex, Sin, and Sacrament' that seemed of particular interest to Kubrick.

Kubrick rarely had a completed script before shooting began, and *Eyes Wide Shut* was no exception. Of all the drafts we examined, none had the coda in the toy store that ends the film. We had to make a leap to fill the gap and concluded that the scene was added at the last minute, perhaps during the long shoot itself. In fact, most of the script was rewritten by Kubrick, just as he did his beloved *Traumnovelle* itself. Located not in turn-of-the-twentieth-century Vienna, but in a contemporary, imagined New York, it is played through the sensibility of a well-to-do doctor whose seemingly endless supply of cash and anxiety alienates him from himself and his own grounding in the corrupt world he moves through like a sleepwalker.

As Nathan and I worked through the creation of the film and its characters, we came to understand how Kubrick created his characters' tenuous standing in his imaginary world. The chaotic business of pre-production, with its search for underwear, the perfect female body (according to Kubrick) and occult sexuality, the long, meandering shoot – meandering for everyone but Kubrick, who knew exactly what he wanted throughout, even if it changed moment to moment – the mostly finished work of post-production; all yielded a film so steeped in the history of cinema, so gripped by its own artifice, so airtight yet permeable that our only conclusion was an acknowledgement of everyone's question: 'what is *Eyes Wide Shut* about?' Or, more accurately, 'where does *Eyes Wide Shut* stand in the Kubrick canon?' since his films, so different one from the other, still follow a coherent train of thought. The paradox of researching and writing our 'making of' was not, I think, atypical for biographers. The more we learned about the details of the production, the more we had to imagine ourselves inside Kubrick's head. The lists, scripts, the editing decision lists gave us most of the externals we needed. The internals, the meanings of the film had to come from intelligent reading of the film itself.

We know that Kubrick had wanted to make *Eyes Wide Shut* for at least fifty years and kept returning to it whenever he was at odds for a new project, only to discard it, because his wife Christiane didn't want him to touch it, because he didn't know whether it should be comedy or melodrama, because he couldn't realize a final act … because, because, because. It stands to reason that, when he finally did make the film, it might have been already stale in his mind, or he might still have had reservations. This may account for the long shoot, the careful movement of Kubrick's imagination and subsequently the characters he creates. Hence the calmness and restraint of old age, the need, after all these years, to take it slow, to not make any mistakes. The readiness is all. In the end, our conclusion seemed inevitable. *Eyes Wide Shut* is every film Kubrick wanted to make, minus the bravura and spectacle on which the earlier films thrived. Like *Lolita*, it burrows into the dissolution of the middle-class family; it even contains a Lolita character in the person of Milich's daughter and an upper-class version of Quilty in Ziegler. *Lolita* is about a reckless love that fails miserably. Dr Bill is differently reckless from Humbert: he seeks the stability of an unmoored ego, cut loose by the not-so-shocking statement that Alice had fantasized about another man. Like Humbert, he ends by weeping before his wife: Humbert over his sense of loss; Dr Bill over his guilty conscience and wish for contrition.

Traumnovelle infiltrates *Barry Lyndon*. Both are about blasted domesticity, as is *The Shining*, which, as Jeremi Szaniawski suggests in Chapter 9 of this volume, is the inverted double of *Eyes Wide Shut*. In *The Shining* domesticity loudly implodes; in *Eyes Wide Shut* it quietly explodes. In both films, the male character seeks sexual contact with a diseased woman, the old laughing lady in the former, the prostitute with HIV in the latter. Jack Torrance is a drunken abuser, who goes insane because domesticity is too much for him. Dr Bill is driven crazy by the anxiety of sexual inadequacy and gender panic. Jack wanders forever the corridors of the Overlook, Dr Bill the studio streets of lower Manhattan. Both are on odysseys inside their heads, their imaginations sprouting fever dreams of paranoia in Jack's case, of a crisis of masculinity in Bill's. Jack dies; Bill is saved from bodily harm by a woman whose life he had previously saved and who now gives hers for him. Or so he is led to believe. Bill is not redeemed, only the women who keep tripping him up during his odyssey.

Even as the pieces fell into place, still none of our research could answer the ultimate question of meaning. It still lingered. What was *Eyes Wide Shut* about? All the contributors to this volume have asked this question in one way or another. Meaning transcends the sum of its parts, of course. Kubrick's interest in the occult mysticism of sexual intercourse, for example, does not tell us much about the orgy, in which mysticism becomes camp mixed with the horror of the rich preying on women. Understanding how he sutured together various locations to create an imagined, unitary space for the orgy does not tell us about the orgy's absurd profundity. No quantity of script revisions reveals the slow, dreamlike tempo of the dialogue. In the making of a biography, whether of a film or a person, there must be, as I said, that leap from facts to the finished work. Within that leap is, for want of a better word, the magic of the imaginative event, the ineffability of intuitions that makes the work we have before us, while behind us is all the information we can gather about what went into its creation.

Including that lingering question for which we did not have the conclusive information we needed. Is the *Eyes Wide Shut* we have the film Kubrick wanted us to see? Is *Eyes Wide Shut* finished? The simplest answer we could supply was 'yes, of course'. Would Kubrick have tinkered more with the editing? Possibly. Does it matter? No, because all we have is the *Eyes Wide Shut* that he left when he died and whose finishing touches were carried out by Leon Vitali and the family. To the best of our knowledge, they followed his instructions; he no doubt knew about the digital tinkering with the orgy scene that Warners demanded; his editing and suggestions for elements like the 'erotic glimpses' – Alice disrobing in the film's opening shot, for example – were set down in advance and needed to be placed. The only thing over which he did not have complete control was publicity, and that is what killed the film commercially, at least, in the USA. Expecting eroticism, audiences were given a complex meditation on sexuality and domesticity. Instead of an 'erotic thriller', they were given a slow introspection of dreamwork gone astray.

Film reviews did little to help audience comprehension. There was much negativity, though with a few outliers, like Janet Maslin in *The New York Times* and Roger Ebert. Both understood the rhythms and intensity of the film. Michiko Kakutani, also in the *Times,* recognized that 'Kubrick's movies are a virtual archive of sophisticated techniques, designed to dazzle the intellect and delight the eye while distancing the emotions'. But she condemns *Eyes Wide Shut* for not going beyond these traits to a more intimate view of domesticity.[2] What, we could only imagine, would a more intimate view involve? Todd McCarthy in *Variety* was more charitable: 'And so the career of a great filmmaker comes to a close with a work that, while not his most startling or innovative or subversive, nonetheless sees him striking out in exciting and sometimes new directions with his stylistic confidence and boldness intact.'[3]

Movie reviewers, seeing a film only once, tend to miss subtleties and resonances. They are likely to emerge perplexed from a film like this, as I did from my first viewing, and the easiest way to come to terms with perplexity is to criticize the film. Because of this, they often fail at their job and substitute wisecracks for insight. Lee Siegel, writing in *The Atlantic* shortly after the film's release, called the reviewers to task:

> Not a single critic, not even those few who claimed to like *Eyes Wide Shut*, made any attempt to understand the film on its own artistic terms. Instead, the critics denounced the film for not living up to the claims its publicists had made for it, reduced it to a question of its director's personality, measured it by how much information it conveyed about the familiar world around us. And I realized that something that had been stirring around in the depths of the culture had risen to the surface. [What he found stirring to the surface was the dullness that had settled in from the constant drumbeat of loud brainless movies.] At a time when we are surrounded by movies about killing, and movies about murdering, and movies about slaughtering; by cheap caricatured reflections of human life; by dishonest and money-driven and career-driven drivel at every turn – at a time like this, you'd think someone would have given a genuine work of honest art its due.[4]

Kubrick had the courage to make, in the late 1990s, an 'art' film that demanded the kind of attention we are not used to giving, the kind of attention that might come close to that paid by the director himself. Siegel provided the key to an understanding of the film. Interestingly enough, it was the conspiracy theorists who provided some of the 'subversive' undercurrent that *Variety* had missed. Clearing away their obsession with the 'Illuminati' and their not-so-latent anti-semitism, we can see, however dimly, a perception of the film's attack on the very rich and their joyless eroticism. We can see the dangerous games they play with women's lives, their careless manipulation of anyone without the power they hold. One conspiracy theorist asks 'we know he was talking about satanic human sacrifice, but what else was he saying? Well, who was behind it? Kidman asks "who were those two girls?" Well we know one as a Windsor and the other related to Rockefeller somehow.' Somehow indeed.

In the end, I came to understand how fragile *Eyes Wide Shut* is. Kubrick was in fragile physical condition when he made it, but that is only part of the issue. *Eyes Wide Shut* holds together so much, is so unlike any contemporary film, yet so steeped in the history of film – from Max Ophüls to Roger Corman to Luis Buñuel – that it requires not only intelligence but a willingness to give it care and attention. This may be a big ask for a film so tender, lucid, dreamlike, tough-minded, unyielding, cool, passionate and obdurate. For me, it is a film that now elicits a great and loving sadness, that its maker is dead, that the world it creates is a beautiful rendering of lives squandered, endangered and lost; that it puts a period to a small body of films the likes of which we won't see again.

Notes

1 Robert P. Kolker, *A Cinema of Loneliness*, 4th edn (New York: Oxford University Press, 2011), p. 179.
2 Michiko Kakutani, 'A Connoisseur of Cool Tries to Raise the Temperature', *The New York Times*, 18 July 1999.
3 Todd McCarthy, '*Eyes Wide Shut* – Kubrick Casts a Riveting Spell', *Variety*, 12 July 1999.
4 Lee Siegel, '*Eyes Wide Shut*: What the Critics Failed to See in Kubrick's Last Film', *Harper's* Magazine 299.1793 (October 1999), pp. 76–83.

their cards's manipulation of anyone without the power they hold. One conspiracy theorist asks: we know he was talking about satanic human sacrifice, but what else was he saying? Well, who was behind it? Kidman asks 'Who were those two girls?' Well we know one is a Windsor and the other related to Rockefeller somehow. Somehow indeed.

In the end, I came to understand how fragile *Eyes Wide Shut* is. Kubrick was in fragile physical condition when he made it, but that is only part of the story. [illegible]

[illegible]

Contributors

Nathan Abrams is a professor in film at Bangor University (since 2006) and lead director of the Centre for Film, Television and Screen Studies. He lectures, writes and broadcasts widely (in English and Welsh) on British and American popular culture, history film and intellectual culture. He co-founded *Jewish Film and New Media: An International Journal* and co-edits the Stanley Kubrick series for Liverpool University Press. His most recent books are *New Wave, New Hollywood: Reassessment, Recovery, and Legacy* (with Gregory Frame; London: Bloomsbury Academic, 2021), *The Bloomsbury Companion to Stanley Kubrick* with I.Q. Hunter, London: Bloomsbury Academic, 2021), *Eyes Wide Shut: Stanley Kubrick and the Making of His Final Film* (with Robert Kolker, New York: Oxford University Press, 2019), *Stanley Kubrick: New York Jewish Intellectual* (New Brunswick, Camden and Newark, NJ and London: Rutgers University Press, 2018), *Hidden in Plain Sight: Jews and Jewishness in British Film, Television, and Popular Culture* (Northwestern University Press, 2016), and *The New Jew in Film: Exploring Jewishness and Judaism in Contemporary Cinema* (New Brunswick: IB Tauris; Rutgers University Press, 2012). He is currently working on a biography of Stanley Kubrick with Robert P. Kolker.

Georgina Orgill is the Stanley Kubrick archivist at the University of the Arts London, where she is responsible for managing and preserving the Stanley Kubrick Archive and for promoting and facilitating its use in research. She is a qualified archivist with an MA in Archives and Records Management and a BA (Hons) in English from University College London. She co-convened the 2019 conference *Behind Eyes Wide Shut* and the 2018 conference *A Clockwork Symposium* and has contributed to documentaries on Stanley Kubrick and the Stanley Kubrick Archive (for example, BBC Radio 4's *2001: The Ultimate Trip*: https://www.bbc.co.uk/programmes/b09y6wg3). She also worked with the Design Museum to identify and loan suitable material for their 2019 exhibition 'Stanley Kubrick'. She contributed to *The Bloomsbury Companion to Stanley*

Kubrick (ed. Nathan Abrams and I.Q. Hunter, London: Bloomsbury Academic, 2021), is currently co-editing a volume on *A Clockwork Orange*, and has also written on archival cataloguing and access for the teaching and learning journal *SPARK* (2019).

Marie Josephine Bennett is a PhD candidate in the Faculty of Arts at the University of Winchester. Her research focuses on critical readings of queer performance in several mainstream post-Production Code Hollywood film musicals released between 1970 and 1985. Publications include: 'Shamadeus? Reconstructing Mozart: The Continuing Impact of *Amadeus* and Myths on Mozart Reception' in Celia Lam, Jackie Raphael and Millicent Weber (eds), *Disassembling the Celebrity Figure: Credibility and the Incredible* (Brill Rodopi, 2018) and 'Mercury's Message to Go On With the Show' in Marie Josephine Bennett and David Gracon (eds) *Music and Death: Interdisciplinary Readings and Perspectives* (Emerald Publishing, 2020).

Eddie Falvey completed his AHRC-funded PhD project on the early films of New York at the University of Exeter. Since finishing his PhD, Eddie has been a lecturer in contextual studies at Plymouth College of Art. He has recently started working on developing his thesis into a monograph for the University of Amsterdam Press. Moreover, Falvey is the author of an upcoming volume *Re-Animator* (Auteur), co-editor of a forthcoming edited collection on contemporary horror (University of Wales Press) and has chapters and articles on adaptation in the films of Spike Jonze, queer fandoms and adult animation.

Robert P. Kolker, Professor Emeritus, University of Maryland, taught cinema studies for almost fifty years. He is the author of *A Cinema of Loneliness and The Extraordinary Image: Orson Welles, Alfred Hitchcock, Stanley Kubrick and the Reimagining of Cinema*; editor of *2001: A Space Odyssey: New Essays* and *The Oxford Handbook of Film and Media Studies*; and co-author of *Eyes Wide Shut: Stanley Kubrick and the Making of his Final Film*.

Ohad Landesman is a lecturer in film studies at the Steve Tisch School of Film and Television at Tel Aviv University. He holds a PhD from the Department of Cinema Studies at New York University, and his writing has appeared in several academic journals such as *Studies in Documentary Film*, *Animation: An Interdisciplinary Journal*, *Projections: The Journal for*

Movies and Mind and *Visual Anthropology Review*. He is currently working on a monograph focused on documentary visits to Israel in the 1960s and 1970s.

Catriona McAvoy is based in London and works as a post-producer at Hijack Post. Her Master's degree from the University of the Arts began her interest in archive research and academic writing. She co-edited the volume *Selling Sex on Screen: From Weimar Cinema to Zombie Porn* (with Karen A. Ritzenhoff, Lanham, MD: Rowman & Littlefield, 2015) and has contributed chapters to *Stanley Kubrick: New Perspectives* (ed. Tatjana Ljujić, Peter Krämer and Richard Daniels, London: Black Dog Publishing, 2015), *Studies in the Horror Film: Stanley Kubrick's The Shining* (ed. Daniel Olson, Lakewood, CO: Centipede Press, 2015) and *The Apocalypse in Film* (ed. Karen A. Ritzenhoff and Angela Krewani, Lanham, MD: Rowman & Littlefield, 2016). McAvoy also has an article in the 'Kubrick and Adaptation' (2015) special issue of the journal *Adaptation* and has presented papers at several international conferences on archive theory and the work of the film directors Stanley Kubrick, Steve McQueen and Lars von Trier.

Joy McEntee is a senior lecturer in the Department of English and Creative Writing at the University of Adelaide. Apart from the cinema of Stanley Kubrick, her research focuses on adaptation studies and masculinities in American Cold War film. Her work has been published in *Camera Obscura*, *Screening the Past*, *Adaptation*, *Literature/Film Quarterly* and *The Journal of Adaptation in Film and Performance*.

Matthew Melia is a senior lecturer in the School of Arts, Culture and Communication at Kingston University in London He was awarded his PhD from Kingston in 'Architecture and Cruelty in the Writings of Antonin Artaud, Samuel Beckett and Jean Genet' in 2007. He is currently revising his PhD for possible publication. His ongoing research into the work of Stanley Kubrick and Ken Russell focuses on such areas as the unwritten production histories of *A Clockwork Orange*, and the unmade and unreleased films of Ken Russell.

Manca Perko teaches film production and documentary at the University of East Anglia (Norwich, UK), and is a filmmaker. She researches Stanley Kubrick's collaborations: his filmmaking practice, creative autonomy and authorship, and the history of Yugoslav cinematography. As a member of the Education Committee of the International Federation of Cinematographers (IMAGO), she actively promotes the importance of building a bridge between film practice and film studies.

Karen A. Ritzenhoff is a professor in the Department of Communication at Central Connecticut State University where she teaches classes on film and television studies, gender studies and visual communication. She is co-chair of the Women, Gender and Sexuality Studies Program. Ritzenhoff has co-edited numerous books, including *Screening the Dark Side of Love* (with Karen Randall, Springer, 2012); *Border Visions: Diaspora and Identity in Film* (with Jakub Kazecki and Cynthia J. Miller, Scarecrow Press, 2013); *Selling Sex on Screen: From Weimar Cinema to Zombie Porn* (with Catriona McAvoy, Lanham, MD: Rowman & Littlefield, 2015); *The Apocalypse in Film* (with Angela Krewani, Lanham, MD: Rowman & Littlefield, 2016); *The Handmaid's Tale: Teaching Dystopia, Feminism, and Resistance Across Disciplines and Borders* (with Janis Goldie, Lanham, MD: Rowman & Littlefield, 2019) and *New Perspectives on the War Film* (with Clémentine Tholas and Janis Goldie, Palgrave Macmillan, 2019). She is currently working on a co-edited volume on *Black Panther: Afro-Futurism, Gender, Identity and the Re-Making of Blackness* as well as a co-edited book on *Mediated Terror in the 21st Century.* Ritzenhoff is co-chair of the Special Interest Group on War and Media Studies at the Society for Cinema and Media Studies where she also served as co-chair of the Women's Caucus.

Yolande Snaith is an award-winning choreographer and performer whose work navigates the merge between different creative and performative practices. She has worked collaboratively in the worlds of dance, theatre and film for over 35 years, and her accumulative experience both informs and guides her performance practice, choreographic systems, methodologies and conceptual and aesthetic languages. Bridging spaces between embodied practices of movement, sound, spoken word and visual elements, her work seeks to create a palpable and holistic synthesis of artistic language and form. Yolande's former critically acclaimed UK-based company, Yolande Snaith Theatredance, toured internationally to over 15 countries from 1985 to 2004. Yolande has received commissions from dance, theatre, opera, film and television companies, and in 1997 she choreographed Stanley Kubrick's final film *Eyes Wide Shut*. In 2002 Yolande joined the theatre and dance faculty at UC San Diego, where she teaches extensively in the areas of choreography and improvisation. In 2005, she established IMAGOmoves, an umbrella company for collaborative dance theatre projects based in San Diego. Since relocating to the USA, Yolande has fostered collaborations with renowned dance and theatre practitioners, composers and designers on numerous international projects, including theatre directors Gabor Tompa and Robert Castro; composer/sound designers Shahrokh Yadegari and Kristopher Apple; scenic/projection designers Ian Wallace and Victoria Pertovich; lighting designers Thomas Ontiveros and Wen-Ling Liao; dance-maker Katie Duck; visual/performance artist Eleanor Antin; theatre company The Hungarian State Theatre of Cluj; filmmakers Mark Freeman and Loren Robertson; music ensemble The Bach Collegium San Diego and musical directors Pierre Joubert and Rodolfo Richter. Yolande has also created several full-length solo works in recent years including *Once I Dreamed I Was a Dinosaur Swimming Backwards* (2016) and *Of Body And Ghost* (2019). Yolande's full biography and an extensive archive of her work can be found on www.yolandesnaith.com.

Jeremi Szaniawski is an assistant professor of film studies and comparative literature, and the Amesbury professor of Polish language and culture at UMass Amherst. He is the editor, among other volumes, of *After Kubrick: A Filmmaker's Legacy* (Bloomsbury, 2020).

Filippo Ulivieri is a writer and lecturer. Italy's leading expert on Stanley Kubrick, he is the author of *Stanley Kubrick and Me: Thirty Years at His Side* (Arcade Publishing, 2016), the memoir of Kubrick's personal assistant Emilio D'Alessandro. He has adapted the book for the screen as *S Is For Stanley* (Alex Infascelli, 2015), winner of the David di Donatello award for Best Documentary Feature. His research on *2001: A Space Odyssey*, *A Clockwork Orange*, Kubrick's unrealised films and the myths surrounding his public image have been presented in several international conferences and published in Italian and English. His most recent book is *2001 between Kubrick and Clarke: The Genesis, Making and Authorship of a Masterpiece* (Ulivieri, 2019).

Index